The Brainwashing of
The American Investor

The Brainwashing of
The American Investor, Rev. ed.
The book that Wall Street does not want you to read!

Steven R. Selengut

PUBLISHING

P.O. Box 849, Cedar Falls, Iowa 50613
www.w-apublishing.com

*In the publication of this book, every effort has been made to offer the most
current, correct and clearly expressed information possible. Nonetheless,
inadvertent errors can occur, and rules and regulations governing personal
finance and investing often change. The advice and strategies contained herein
may not be suitable for your situation, and there is a risk of loss trading stocks,
commodity futures, options and foreign exchange products. Neither the publisher
nor author shall be liable for any loss of profit or any other commercial damages,
including but not limited to special, incidental, consequential, or other damages,
that is incurred as a consequence of the use and application, directly or indirectly,
of any information presented in this book. If legal, tax advice, or other expert
assistance is required; the services of a professional should be sought.*

Library of Congress Control Number: 2007936059
ISBN: 978-1-934354-03-2
ISBN-10: 1-934354-03-1

Printed in the United States of America

10 9 8 7 6 5 4 3 2 1

FSC

Mixed Sources
Product group from well-managed
forests and other controlled sources

Cert no. SW-COC-002283
www.fsc.org
© 1996 Forest Stewardship Council

*This book is dedicated to my wife Sandie, to the rest of my family,
and to my friends. Thank y'all for putting up with my years of obsessive-compulsive
behavior. This book was written for the benefit of the heirs of those who read it.*

Contents

List of Tables

Preface

This revised edition of *The Brainwashing of the American Investor* is still a hands-on action book, designed to provide a safer and more realistic approach to the stock market and investing. It outlines a conservative trading strategy that has been used to manage diversified client portfolios for nearly thirty years and will provide you with all the information needed to implement your personal plan. It is a unique approach—definitely not mainstream Wall Street propaganda. In fact, I'll take every opportunity to explain precisely how my methodology differs from the approach that Wall Street would want you to use.

The investment process exists in a constantly changing environment, and even the most time tested of strategies needs to be fine-tuned periodically. My working capital model is no exception, and some slight adjustments have been made in recent years that simplify the decision-making process considerably. Additionally, new developments (i.e., products) on Wall Street require close examination, and there is a new section on applying this strategy to the area of income investing.

In addition to the procedural changes, this edition includes more instructional excerpts from real-life investment management experiences and a chapter that should make you more knowledgeable about income securities than any salesperson who might get through your filters. A glossary and index have been added to help readers get back to the discussion of the most important concepts, and some further clarification has been given to concepts that gave first edition readers the most difficulty.

Too often in the field of investing, formulas are provided, tricks for success are proposed, and gimmicks are sold as though they are foolproof guarantees. If they were true, we would all be millionaires! The trading approach presented here is different from anything you have encountered before. This approach is logical, conservative, and understandable, but it doesn't mean that it can be implemented without a clear understanding of some basic principles of investing and management. The (oft requested) hand-held tri-fold short cut to key concepts, tricks, and gimmicks is just never going to happen. The more effort you put into the understanding, the more reward you will get from the implementation. Readers are expected to think about, study, and process what they are reading.

Once you have digested the content, you will realize that this is more than just a book about disciplined investment portfolio management... it's a whole new investment management discipline.

Introduction
The Premise

P ower! With the possible exception of Washington, D.C., Wall Street exerts more power and influence per square mile than any other place in the world. Although the federal government (through the SEC, FTC, FCC, and several other entities) tries to regulate and control the beast, it cannot possibly succeed. Why? The Street has grown so powerful that its incredible influence on Washington has become a special interest group of mammoth proportions. Additionally, it is so quick to change the appearance of its many enterprises, that the feeble efforts of legislators and regulators are always too little too late! The beast rules, and there is no doubt about it!

Someone once made the point that power corrupts, and that absolute power corrupts, absolutely. In order to protect the investing-speculating public from being manipulated and abused by this smiling, red-suspendered, beast in pinstripes, we probably need volumes of better regulations and an encyclopedia of less self-serving rules of behavior. But, as unlikely as it is that meaningful change will happen any time soon, we need to educate the investing public about how they should interact with those who are conspiring to separate them from their money. It is this conspiracy that really makes Wall Street tick.

Slaughter on 10th Avenue.com

Once upon a time, a new kid with great potential came to town. It was speculated that he had communications skills and powers that were light years ahead of all present technology and that all one had to do was sign up, log on, and invest money to become a millionaire. Thousands of techies, recognizing the potential of the new kid, wrote tens of thousands of business plans, raised billions of dollars in seed money, spent small country GNPs on marketing, and ran to their downtown underwriting friends to sell their dot-coms to the public.

Now in the land of huge salaries, pinstripes, and suspenders that is known with some respect (if not awe) as Wall Street, there are financial institutions that are charged with many responsibilities, not the least of which is to protect the weak, the ignorant, the uninformed, and the uninitiated from investments, investment plans, ideas, and products that are unsuitable. These institutions go to enormous lengths to gather information about their customers so that their financial advisors know exactly the types of investments a person should or should not be making. Thus, they just never let their clients make an investment mistake! Right?

WRONG! They collect the information to protect themselves from lawsuits, knowing full well that the very structure of the industry (from the separation of underwriting and retail, right down the line to broker commission schedules) has absolutely nothing to do with what is in the best interests of the client.

Arm in arm with their expert associates in the financial media, the institutions launched their dot-com invasion on an unsuspecting public. Wisdom from the oracle of Wall Street: buy everything with dot-com, technology, or tele-anything in its name or product mix. Beg (your broker to get you some of that new issue at any price), borrow (all the money you can on margin in all of your accounts), steal (from your children's educational funds), and sell all of those boring high-quality securities with their old-fashioned products and concepts (food, shelter, clothing, etc.), including your treasury securities, municipal and corporate bonds. The future is now. Don't get left behind—this is the new financial plan—an investing utopia where prices only go up and everybody wins! Damn the torpedoes, full speed ahead!

Far away, in the land of Washington, a wizened economics guru cautioned Wall Street and its armies of smooth talking, opinion-for-hire analysts, that their irrational exuberance was out of control and that eventually reality would happen. But no one heeded his sage warning or those of other professional investors as they continued to caution the public that the speculative fire in the NASDAQ Market was certain to be extinguished, painfully for all involved.

But the institutional hydra continued to pump out more product to whet the insatiable appetites of professional financial advisors and their incredibly greedy squeezes (clients). They knowingly continued to pave the road to disaster with their promotions, predictions, and irresponsible marketing of just-about-anything-you-can-conceive-of.com, knowing that they were playing to an unlimited audience of avaricious speculators. A Herculean rock was needed to stop the immortal beast! None would be found.

The record is unclear, but filtering down through generations of expert opinion and testimony is rumor of a high-level meeting that took place between many of the elite institutional CEOs late one evening, just after their millennium hoax had played itself out. Sitting around an impressive mahogany conference table amidst magnums of champagne, tins of caviar, and other pretentious symbols of their great status and power, they developed a wealth enhancement scheme whose brilliance is lauded throughout Leavenworth to this very day! No one really knows who is responsible, but financial institution CEOs have no shortage of MBAs from whom they can freely borrow ideas to call their own. Here is how this one might have played out as the chiefs engineered the latest move from greed to fear:

> *The Chairperson speaks: As you all know, our institutional money machine is transaction driven. It doesn't matter what the client does, or with whom, so long as he does something. So let's start to move some of our own trading account dollars back into securities with some real value. We'll take our profits in the technology sector slowly so that nobody notices right away. Then, we'll start to talk about those old-fashioned asset allocation ideas, and start to promote our quality and value stock mutual funds that have been such dogs for two years.*
>
> *Now one of our high-priced law firms has suggested that we could have some very serious class action suits if NASDAQ crashes, so we have to create an illusion of innocence. It has to appear as though our clients were properly advised to put all their money into (those ridiculously speculative) NASDAQ securities.*

The problem has to be something totally out of our hands, so we're going to create the perception of an economic downturn. First, we'll play up a few surprise dot-com failures. (No one seems to care that 95 percent of all restaurant start-ups fail, but then we've never tried hard enough to take them public. Maybe next year...) Next, we'll lay off some high priced analysts and create some negative figures in a few technology areas. Ever since we banded together to exploit this news hungry media, self fulfilling prophecies like this one are a piece of cake to get rolling!

It won't take long for the media sharks to dive into the water and create a panic of about the same proportion as the one we created with that ingenious computer loop back in '87. We'll double dip big time on this one. Money will be flying all over the place as the fools (Wall Street jargon meaning clients) sell everything we just convinced them to buy, and begin buying the new stuff we just purchased for our own accounts. I bet we can even get the fed to start lowering interest rates! Then we'll be able to sell fixed income securities again. Hmmm, I never could understand why people like bonds better at lower yields than at higher ones. I don't know about you guys, but I've always appreciated those invisible 3-percent markups a lot more than commissions. This is just too easy. I can see the headlines: May Day! May Day! NASDAQ Flight 1999 has Crashed and Burned; Body Count High and Few Survivors.

I guess that's about it for the overall plan. Now, whose turn is it to have an analyst that predicted this crash? This is a biggie so let's go with someone who's pretty well established; none of us needs another million-dollar salary to support. Right? Make sure you get all of your people to push the same story about the economy. Then, if my interview on CNBC goes the way it should, we should be in the clear again. Brilliant! We'll discuss the duration of this new rally in the quality and value sector at our next meeting. That one's in Rio, isn't it?

Brainwashing the American Investor

Wall Street firms spend billions of dollars annually to make people transact—to move their money from one financial product to another and change direction. One firm's recent advertising campaign headline is: "Move Your Money." Most people who are qualified to be investors are painfully unqualified to make investment decisions. Most of the brokers and financial planners from whom they buy investment products are equally unqualified, if not intellectually, at least motivationally.

People are encouraged to be speculative by the media, by the brokerage firms, and by their peer groups. If you were to take a poll, you would find that the majority of people wouldn't be able to distinguish between investing and speculating. They aren't trained to think in those terms. Risk, what's that? There are hundreds of thousands of people out there who couldn't begin to tell you anything about the structure of a mutual fund. It's your responsibility to either know what you're doing or to hire someone who does. Why do you think Wall Street wants you to think that you know what you are doing? So that you will transact, and move your money!

You are expected to believe that Wall Street has your best interests at heart, and that they are not at all responsible when one of their recommendations goes bad. They may lead you down the speculative path to destruction but you are ultimately responsible. Wall Street sells hard to a get-rich-quick mentality. If you get caught up in that approach, you can count on failure in the long run. You'll find yourself crying about your bad luck or the dismal economy. But it's totally your own fault for trying to do part time what Wall Street professionals fail to do full time.

Wall Street sells its products as cost effectively as it can through its least experienced, hungriest employees. It is likely that these are the people you will be in contact with unless you do something about it. Why would you take advice from anyone who has no investments of his or her own? If the idea fails, was it yours, his, or one of those "we thinkisms" that Wall Street know-nothings promote so ardently? It's your money at risk and it's your fault. It's your fault for listening to wet-behind-the-ears trainees and self-proclaimed experts with little or no hands-on experience, other than canvassing the telephone book for suckers. It's your fault for accepting simple sales propaganda as research material just because it comes from a high-salaried executive at a prestigious Wall Street firm. AND, if you do it the new-fashioned way, it's your own fault for fantasizing that minimal or zero commissions and on-line trading capabilities make you a savvy investor.

Stop crying and learn from your mistakes. Yes, you blew it all by yourself through your own greed or fear. Try to keep in mind that Wall Street is the single most powerful sales entity in the world and it will always make a fool of you if you allow it to. Every firm is the same, every one, period! No one out there has even the slightest respect for your intelligence, and why should they? You gleefully allow yourself to be manipulated all the time. Do you have a strategy? Does your financial advisor? Just what is the difference between financial planners and financial advisors, investment advisors and investment managers? Most people have no clue as to investment strategy, but establishing a viable operating plan is a huge step in assuring that an investment program will work. Employee financial advisors and commission-driven financial planners can neither afford to have a strategy of their own nor can they be expected to make you operate within yours! Why? Because it requires an ability to say, "No, Mr. Client, I won't do that for you, it's not going to help you meet your objectives," or something to that effect. You absolutely do not want a yes man as a financial advisor!

Just as a test, ask your guy to do something that you know is wrong for you and see what happens. Better yet, tell him you're going to receive a $500,000 windfall and see, not only what is recommended but, more importantly, what questions are asked before the recommendations are made. Annuities and mutual funds will be on the list of products to purchase. If your financial person is a stock broker, you'll hear about wrap accounts and index funds/ETFs (the new dot.coms). Accountants and attorneys may add a private deal or two to the mix.

Find yourself a method of identifying reality. Find statistics you can look to that mean something and that are not controlled or manipulated by Wall Street. For example: why, after one hundred years without an over-the-counter (NASDAQ) stock in the Dow Jones Industrial Average, were two added in 2000? Are the indices designed to report the performance of the stock market or that of the economy? Why do stronger price performers constantly replace weaker ones in the DJIA and S&P average? Because the averages and indices are in competition with one another... it doesn't matter what they actually mean! And just what is performance anyway? (see chapter 7).

The Dow Jones Industrial Average was originally designed to be an indicator of the direction of the overall economy. Over the years it was only restructured to reflect major changes in the nature of the economy, such as adding a company to represent the rapidly growing services sector, etc. As an economy moves from agrarian, to industrial, to service, such changes are appropriate. Companies that either went out of business or changed industries through divestiture or acquisition were replaced with ones that were more in tune with the present combination. BUT, they were always well known New York Stock Exchange Companies, and the objective of the exercise was to provide a useful indicator of the direction of the economy…just another tool. The S&P 500 average had similar roots until recently.

Now we simply have a horse race between the averages (a trifecta for those who venture into the NASDAQ market). What can we do to make the Dow more reflective of what's going on in the stock market? How can we keep these averages climbing? These are totally new questions, and the answers have totally changed the meaning and usefulness of these once well-respected numbers. They are just a few more instruments in the Wall Street orchestra, where the power conductor determines how the beat goes on during the next season.

Further complicating this whole scenario (the amount of money it must have taken to sneak this one by the regulators boggles the mind!) are the new and improved index funds. Do you have a huge embarrassment in your firm's trading account? Just get it placed in one of the averages and, abracadabra, the stock becomes the best performer on The Street for the week! A thousand puppet-like account managers must run out and buy the correct weighting of the stock for their portfolios, regardless of the investment merits of the company! Now tell me, does this sound anything like investing to you? The index funds were a huge mistake that will be painful to correct. And the even more popular, yet unmanaged, index ETFs could easily become the next major Wall Street disaster.

Wall Street is always selling something, and they always try to follow the path of least resistance. The person you are relying upon is probably someone's employee, or a representative of some entity that controls his product mix. It is not likely that he is allowed to be too independent a thinker. You can also bet that he or she will do (buy, sell, borrow, short) absolutely anything you ask. Keep looking until you find someone who has the backbone to say, "NO!"

Shooting From the Hip
By Wall Street broker, "Deep Pockets"

Deep Pockets is a real live person and a top producer at a major brokerage firm. His claim to fame is that he has been successful as a broker while maintaining his integrity. He does what his clients ask him to do, but not without stating his opinion. So, you say, what's the big deal? You'll learn. This is the first of a series of contributions from Deep Pockets:

What a snowstorm! I awoke to eighteen inches of fresh snow that January morning (the blizzard of '77). As a resident of northwest New Jersey who loved to ski and to snowmobile, it would have been a welcome sight on any other day, but not this day. I had an interview with a major Wall Street wire house (brokerage firm). A father of one with a schoolteacher wife and graduation from business school only a few months away, I needed a job! The radio had announced the closing of the New York Stock Exchange for the day, but maybe someone in the personnel department of this Wall Street giant was waiting to interview me.

I took a chance and drove to the train station, the start of an incredible journey. Not the one to New York City that day, but the one to a thirty-year career on Wall Street that has seen it all, taken some bruises, and taught some valuable lessons.

The first day back from training class was filled with optimism. A new career, passing the Series 7 Exam, and a $1,000 a month training salary… life just couldn't get much better. In my wildest dreams I couldn't have imagined what was lying just ahead. We were called "account executives," the first of many titles to follow and replacing "customers' man." Each week we had a sales meeting where we learned the name of the new stock of the week. Wall Street had few products back then. There were stocks and there were bonds, and perhaps a fixed income unit trust. Forget mutual funds! People were still reeling from their losses in the big bear market of the early seventies.

Each week we cold-called name after name in the phone book—thousands of calls. I reviewed all of the key points about the stock of the week, but there were few, and I mean very few buyers. People didn't want to hear the word equities and, having been burned in the wake of one of the greatest secular bull markets in history, people hated stockbrokers. Once again the buy-at-any-price mentality burned the masses. Buy and sell disciplines had been thrown out the window as P/E (price divided by earnings) ratios went from single digits to one hundred and two hundred times earnings. As valuations adjusted from their unreasonable levels, the correction of the early seventies brought great pain to investors. People couldn't get enough at two hundred times earnings, yet no one wanted the same issues when they were cheap. The stock of the week never seemed to work out too well either. They moved up a point or two (at a time when that was a big move) that week, only to move back down as they became a source of funds for the next stock of the week. So it went month after month. Few of the trainees survived.

Eventually the correction was over and people warmed up to equities once again. It started with gaming stocks (Atlantic City) and spread to the oils, through the banks, on to the blue chips, then into technology and on to the net. The markets have boomed and busted through the eighties, the nineties, and into the new millennium. The wire houses have managed people's money until it has disappeared—one scam after another: partnerships that sold everything from oil and gas to horse semen, mutual fund after mutual fund (now more than 10,000), all designed to make you (the investor) rich, loaded and no-load, chock full of fees, each taking its turn in the limelight and then becoming just another fund.

New launches were always timed to the current hot sector, always buying in at the top and always marketed based on the past, or most recent performance. And so it goes, the cheap funds (sectors out of favor) get sold and the most expensive funds (hot sectors) get bought. The cycle goes on and on: buy high, sell low, over and over again! The markets (powered by our great economy) over time move higher and higher. The brokers move from firm to firm (for the front money), and the investors try to get even. A few investors have a plan and the discipline to follow it. The masses fall into the cycle. The smart ones hire someone who knows what they are doing, someone who brings reason to the investment process and keeps emotion out.

I started doing business with an investment manager some twenty years ago. I have watched his investment process bring accounts to new high levels through all of the market cycles just described. There are a few items that set his investment style apart from the Wall Street crowd:

Buy low, sell high! What a great idea. No, he didn't invent it, but he put it into practice on a disciplined basis. He buys stocks when they are cheap, letting someone else be the hero who has paid the all-time-high price for a given company.

Stock analysts make recommendations for many reasons. All too few of those reasons are designed to provide you with timely investment advice. Think about this: more than 90 percent of all Wall Street recommendations are on the buy side. Less than 5 percent are on the sell side. Why? Sometimes a firm has a lucrative investment banking (underwriting) relationship with a company and a strong rating is a reward for doing business with the firm. Can a wire house (and those in the syndicate) bring a billion dollar deal to investors and then rate the stock a sell? I don't think so. When other analysts on The Street collectively see only good things for a stock, it takes a lot of guts to go against the tide and offer a negative rating individually. If you're wrong your career may be over. Why all of these recommendations anyway? Commissions. Typically a lower rating follows bad news and a large drop in the price of the stock. Too late!

Whatever Wall Street is pushing, under analysis, will turn out to be better for them than it is for you. They just don't try to make less money. It's your money and your responsibility to find out what's going on. Is it really a bad/good economy and/or a correcting/rallying stock market? Get real, people! It is probably not what they say it is. Forget the averages, they've been manipulated too long and are no longer valid. Avoid the snake oil salesmen with their red suspenders and glossy presentations. Establish a personal plan. Adopt a strategy that doesn't require future prediction. Find some statistics that really matter. Enter the fray with valid expectations.

The brainwashing of investors is certainly nothing new, nor is it something that is going to go away any time soon. And the purpose of this book is not to complain or to cry about it either. In fact, I absolutely love it! The purpose of this book is to teach you how to use the process to your advantage—how to keep one step ahead of the manipulative Wall Street menagerie and use them as surely as they try to use you. You can make money in the markets with a minimum of risk through the proper use of simple tools and information (but, absolutely not the ones you hear being advertised). Managing your assets is the same as any other form of management. You must establish reasonable goals and objectives. If you don't plan, organize, control, and direct what is going on; if you don't establish rules, guidelines, strategies, and procedures you will fail.

In the chapters that follow, you will learn one of two things. You will learn either how to manage your assets safely and productively toward the achievement of clearly stated objectives, or

Introduction: The Premise   13

you will come to the important conclusion that you need to find someone to manage your assets for you. Not everyone is equipped emotionally or intellectually to be a successful investor (too smart is not necessarily a good thing here). Analyzing the incredible amount of information out there can become paralytic. You will also learn a whole lot about the investment minefield we call Wall Street, and that education starts now!

The Learning Curve: Not Just a Box of Chocolates

You are about to embark on a learning experience just as revealing as the one Deep Pockets began more than thirty years ago. Open your mind! New ideas are coming at you that could permanently change the way you look at things financial. You will begin to question what Wall Street experts put out there for you to believe. You will start to question the index numbers, averages, and analytical garbage that pollute the airwaves. You will become free of the drugs Wall Street uses to manipulate your every financial move.

The following is a selection of thoughts, concepts, and considerations you may not agree with now or even thoroughly understand. A few chapters from now, you will.

- In thirty years of investing, I've been unable to find a correlation between a calendar year and any meaningful investment, economic, business, market, or interest rate cycle.
- We won't hesitate to caution you now that paper profits increase nothing but hat size. Control your greed with some profit taking.
- One of the advantages of dealing with individual stocks is that you can selectively take profits on winners and reinvest the proceeds either in undervalued issues, or income producers. Thus, you are never out of the market and, more importantly, never caught without cash when a correction (inevitably) happens. By the way, corrections only become visible when it's too late to prepare for them.
- Ultimately, the income generated by your assets is more important than their current market value. Realized income pays the bills!
- Stop analyzing, charting, predicting, reading, reviewing, classifying, and crying. It's time for action.

- The best way to reduce your taxes is with your vote. It is never smart to lose a dollar (on a fundamentally sound investment) to pay 30 cents less in taxes.
- Trading absolutely always produces more growth in capital, more growth in income, and more inflation insurance than any other strategy.
- Portfolio management is the effort to achieve personal goals and objectives using a stable strategy. Speculation, on the other hand, is a lotteryesque approach that seeks a shortcut to the objective while introducing excessive risk into the process. Ninety-nine percent of all speculators think of themselves as investors.
- Averages and indices are investment tools designed to provide a sense of direction, but certainly not of a particular portfolio. There is no clear relationship between any of these tools and the actual performance of any properly diversified portfolio.
- Profit taking is a management or business decision. It is not an attempt at timing or an effort to predict the future. Profit taking throttles greed and protects wealth. The problem with most investment strategies is that they are based on the premise that the future direction of the market is predictable. It isn't.
- To benefit from a correction, you must take action during the rally. Trading eliminates dangerous positions in overpriced securities and replaces them with safer ones in undervalued issues. Try to think of it as correction insurance.
- Working capital is expected to rise every year, even if the market crashes and interest rates rise. It's a totally new and different kind of analytical tool.
- Aggressive trading of quality issues is a winning strategy, period. Aggressive selection of high-risk securities without a sell discipline is not.
- Most market gurus will advise you too late to unload last year's favorites and, unfortunately, they don't have the courage to recommend new names until significant moves to the upside have been made.
- Anything that goes up in price for an extended period of time becomes vulnerable, particularly when the rise has been fast. For the mutual fund investor, the similarity to a chain letter is very real. Someone is going to be left holding a bag full of securities purchased at the highest prices in the history of mankind.

• Investors look for opportunities which fall within particular pre-defined guidelines. Speculators look for good bets based on biased research they receive from paid analysts, and commissioned sales persons. The point is that plain vanilla management guidelines can get you through the whole investment exercise with less expense, less frustration, and more success than all the Wall Street wisdom combined.

Ladies and gentlemen, start your engines!

Chapter 1
Wall Street 101

For most investors, the DJIA provides all the information they want to consider. It is worshiped mindlessly and treated as though it has mystical predictive and analytic powers far beyond the scope of any other market number. New York Stock Exchange (NYSE) issue breadth figures clearly show that the Dow has been neither prescient nor accurate with regard to broad market movements for nearly ten years. Additionally, fewer than half of the thirty Dow companies boast an S&P "A" rating, and 25 percent are ranked below investment grade.

Is the 120-year-old DJIA impotent? Probably not entirely, but it's based upon a seriously flawed buy and hold investment strategy and universally thought of as a market barometer instead of as an economic indicator, as originally intended. This is not just semantics. It's Wall Street's rendition of *The Emperor's New Clothes*. Clearly, there is no way that any average can measure the progress of the thousands of individual securities (and mutual funds masquerading as individual securities) that together comprise the market. And is there just one market, when REITs, index ETFs, equity CEFs, income CEFs, and even some preferred stocks are all mixed together? Investors are dealing with multiple markets of many types. Markets that don't follow the same rules or respond to the same changes in the same ways. The Dow is dead, long live reality.

Feeling statistically naked? Don't fret, Nell, there are real market statistics and lists that are easy to understand, easy to put your cursor on, and useful in keeping you up to date on what's going on in the multiple markets of today's investment world. We'll be looking at issue breadth, new fifty-two week highs and lows, and market statistics for the real deal on daily, monthly, and annual activity. And we'll be looking at them for a different reason entirely. The time has come to stop beating yourself up quarter-by-quarter, year after year, producing the unhappy scenario that makes financial institution CEOs salivate. It's time to abandon performance comparisons with unrelated-to-my-portfolio numbers and to look at statistics that allow you to understand what to expect from your portfolio in varying stock market and interest rate expectation scenarios! You will find it much easier than that sounded and you will be smiling more.

I know you are tempted to shout, "blasphemy" at the top of your lungs, but the DJIA was developed in a pre-Internet world (actually, pre-automobile) where only the very small wealthy class cared about the stock market. It is likely that not one person reading this book has an investment portfolio that closely resembles today's DJIA. But, it is just as likely that nearly all of you will use the Dow to evaluate portfolio performance. I've never understood this phenomenon, and I know that change takes time...but really, the Dow has had its day, and following it blindly has cost far too much of your nest egg for you to continue the fantasy.

Rope Drop!

Most of us come out of high school, even college, with absolutely no knowledge of securities, investing, retirement planning, etc. Investments 101 is rarely listed in any non-business curriculum, and, even if it were, how much of a draw would it be for people so unlikely to have funds available for investment? Most people go out into the business world barely able to balance their own checkbooks!

If you're lucky, Mom and Dad took the time to explain some of the basics to you (if they really understood them themselves). They may even have developed a personal or IRA portfolio for you over the years to get you started more comfortably. Still, it's likely that your first experience with investing was with a stockbroker, insurance agent, banker, employee benefits person, or some form of financial planner. With the possible exception of the employee benefits person, all of these individuals feed their families with the commissions or other financial incentives they receive for placing your money in various forms of investment products.

Investment Products

Could you sense the disdain in my keystrokes as I typed the words "investment products"? The reason for this is that I belong to the old fashioned school of investing that considers portfolio design, development, and management a very personal exercise. How can a packaged product be right for thousands, even millions of people? How does one even know what he owns, specifically? Believe it or not, investment products are relatively new on the investment scene.

In the 1970s there were very few mutual funds of any kind, and public participation money market funds didn't exist. Today there are more mutual funds than there are common stocks listed on the New York Stock Exchange! It's just incredible how these products have become so popular, and it's more incredible still how Wall Street has made the investing public love them so well. Most people would tell you that they are safer than the stock market, not even realizing that most of their mutual funds are common stock portfolios.

So clever is Wall Street, particularly when it comes to their seduction of the media and the coercion of their employees, that one often hears statements from either source that, to a professional investor, sound like the screech of metal on a grammar school chalk board. So news thirsty is the media that they will publish any and all analyst predictions just to sell papers, gain market share, and woo listeners from other stations. The newscaster, commentator, or analyst will explain things matter-of-factly in terms that he fully expects everyone not only to understand, but also to accept, as the proper way of doing things in the investment world. For example, a few years ago radio commentators were analyzing the impact of a court ruling that would allow a well-known company to remain intact. Well, it was speculated, you can expect a spike in the stock price because portfolio managers will load up on the stock so that their quarterly reports show how smart they were to have held such a large position. How smart indeed! How stupid do they think the mutual fund-buying public really is? You don't need to hear the answer, but the point is that media experts didn't go on to offer any cautionary remarks about the validity of those quarterly reports or the morality of the practice.

Is the mutual-fund-performance statistics con game an institution in and of itself? Do you really want to be there?

Similarly, a few weeks earlier, a commentator was explaining how fund managers are compensated, evaluated by their bosses, and rated by analysts. The performance of the funds they manage is compared with the performance of other funds managed by other managers in the same or different investment houses. Superficially this could even sound fair. But what is advertised as most important (i.e., the interests of the client) is missing. If performance is poor, it's OK because everyone else was pretty bad too! The only way they could all be bad at the same time, as they generally are, is if they all invest in the same securities and take the same amounts of risk. What does that tell you? Is this the result of what the investor wants or what the speculators insist upon? Probably neither—it's what the culture demands.

Still, some investment products are an easy-to-understand, acceptable method of investing for people who are just getting their portfolios started. We'll dig into this later. The larger the asset base, however, the less need for this type of investing, with few exceptions. As the asset base gets larger, so does the commission prize for product salespersons, and this is the first place where your investment program is likely to be ambushed.

The insurance and annuity industry is in first place when it comes to concealing the risks of the stock market within products that were originally designed to preserve estates and to provide retirement income. It took many years for company lobbyists to pressure state insurance departments to allow them to attach mutual funds to insurance and annuity contracts. Most owners of these contracts have no idea of the dangers involved. Mutual funds, contrary to current opinion, were once considered so risky that they were not acceptable securities for satisfying margin-borrowing requirements, and that was when those requirements were pretty lax anyway. The vast majority of stocks traded on the NASDAQ are still not acceptable.

The protection provided by life insurance is an essential element of most personal financial plans. I'm not even opposed to the idea that whole life insurance is important to force younger people to save. But, I seriously question the morality of including stock market investments in a policy or contract that has been marketed for centuries as a guaranteed benefit provider. It was totally irresponsible of insurance industry regulators to allow the marketing of variable benefit products! Why not let the insurance industry take over the Social Security/Medicare mess. Now there's something they are actually good at...guaranteeing low levels of monthly income, forever. It is nothing short of shocking to think that the Bush Administration was considering privatizing a portion of Social Security Trust Funds to individuals! Has Wall Street hypnotized Congress as well? There may be a better word...Why would Wall Street approve of the plan? Think about it...

Similarly, deferred annuity contracts are excellent for less affluent people to use to develop a cash pool that can either be annuitized (converted into a guaranteed lifetime series of monthly payments, a la Social Security...hmmm) or liquidated to become part of a larger retirement portfolio. But, annuities were never intended for people of means because they are self-liquidating entities designed specifically for the protection of people with limited assets (i.e., those who have less than enough capital to generate the income needed for retirement). Variable annuities make such protection impossible, replacing safety with more risk than reward, and at great expense. Neither the buying public nor insurance company sales people are sophisticated enough to appreciate the risks involved.

Consumers Buy Products, Investors Buy Securities
As a stock market investor, you should not be interested in the vast majority of investment products anyway. Never purchase a package unless you know what's inside. Then, compare the benefits with the costs and restrictions on your liquidity. There is no doubt that individual security portfolios do better in the long run (compared even with outdated averages) than mutual funds, no matter how creative the fund managers' model record keeping happens to be. But, investment management needs to be done more frequently than evenings and weekends, and you have to decide how serious you are about running your own portfolio. Delegating the management to a personally unknown mutual fund manager is a pretty scary idea!

Finally, don't think for a minute that mutual funds are cheaper than individually managed portfolios. If Wall Street made little or no money from them, why would they push them so hard? Think about it and read the commentary in chapter 8.

Wall Street Corporate Culture

Raise your right hand if you've ever had a boss. Keep that hand in the air if you've worked in a large company in a supervisory or managerial position. If your hand is up, you know about corporate culture, a euphemism for describing the amount of independent expression that is allowed within an organizational structure. Can you speak your mind? Does your boss really want your input? How much interest do your superiors have in your advancement? How do your peer level managers spend their day? Remember the Peter Principle of organizations: people in organizations tend to rise to their levels of incompetence? Truer words were never spoken, and, consequently, more time is spent trying to impress the boss than is spent doing the work of the organization. Doing lunch or after-work activities with the right people is the way to get ahead in large organizations. Independence, honesty, integrity, long hours, and hard work are just not enough.

Wall Street is no different. The most important thing to the drones, the analysts, the money managers, the investment committee members, and even your personal wealth manager is career growth and earnings potential. When a BMW Salesman gets restless, off he goes to Mercedes. Funny how the BMW Growth Fund he was managing/analyzing/selling is no longer better than the Mercedes Value Fund being pushed by his new employer. And what will be best next month...perhaps the Hummer World Index Fund? The job is to advance the career. The method used is the same in large organizations of all varieties and in all industries: kissin' up moves the career along. That's what it's all about.

So it is rare that you will experience independent thought and advice from your contacts in big companies. They often sell what their superiors want them to sell and they tell what they are told to tell. Your interests are secondary, at best. Never lose sight of this! Go one step further. When a Wall Street analyst does original research at my-new-mousetrap.com, do you really think that he's going to receive an honest appraisal of the company's prospects? If one of your employees told the press how bad your products are selling, what would you do?

The balance of this section is devoted to basic investment concepts that must be understood. Don't breeze through it. In fact, come back often.

Money in Motion

Wealth is power. Few would dispute this tenet but fewer still understand how the wealthy are able to remain so (i.e., wealthy and powerful) while having a significant presence in many different investment arenas. Simply, they keep their money moving between a seemingly endless supply of investment opportunities. When they lose (and everybody loses occasionally), their losses are not devastating. The principles that allow the rich to seem so smart are easily assimilated into any size investment portfolio (even one that doesn't include movie studios and professional sports franchises). These principles are quality, diversification, and income generation, three simple investment concepts that help to minimize both risk and greed. Wealthy people understand risk; they became (and stayed) wealthy by managing it!

Wealth is knowledge. Getting rich in the stock market is not as easy as many on Wall Street would like you to believe (but not so difficult that you need a staff of thousands to identify investment opportunities). If all those salespeople and gurus were so good at investing, why are they still selling and soothsaying? This book contains the knowledge of the market, human nature, and wealth accumulation that has come from nearly forty years of experience. You will have to wade through the knowledge to have any hope of executing the strategy.

I used to advertise on a financial talk show that aired on a New York radio station. I was initially impressed with the host of the program because I was interviewed to determine if my product was within the realm of sound investment advice and practice. I was accepted and assured that I would be the only investment manager recommended to the audience.

As the show's popularity grew, more and more speculative ventures, exotic funds, boutique products, and commodity programs began to advertise on the show, and the host started to do paid investment seminars with all of us. Interviews were no longer necessary. Appearance fees had replaced them. Eventually, the integrity of the show succumbed to the pressure of the bucks that were to be made by endorsing every conceivable product out there. The relationship could not be sustained because the show had become a Wall Street sideshow with no direction and no message. As self-righteous as the media is about their role in preserving our constitutional rights of free speech and expression, you better believe that the almighty dollar is worshipped just as fervently!

Every profession has its teachers, critics, sales people, and practitioners. Monday morning quarterbacking has become as much an art form in the investment world as it has always been in the world of sports. Hindsight rules! But, just as you wouldn't hire a respected sportscaster to manage your NFL franchise, neither should you rely on a product salesperson, a professor, or a radio talk show host or news analyst to manage your investment portfolio. There is book learning; there is concept, theory, and analysis; and there is practice. Who's going to perform your heart surgery, the head of Columbia Presbyterian Hospital's cardiac surgery unit or the professor of advanced anatomy and physiology at Columbia University?

There is theory and there is practice. It has been said that what most investors know about investing could fit upon the head of a pin! This holds true for the majority of financial advisors as well. Answer this question before you act on anyone's advice: how much sense does it make to take investment advice from any person who has not become wealthy through the hands-on experience of investing? How many brokers do you think have a portfolio of their own with a value of $50,000, $100,000, or a million dollars? What percentages of brokers even make it into their fifth year? Here are two others to which you really should find the answer: How many years of experience does the average mutual fund manager have? How many mutual funds have a ten-year track record (in their original design)?

You may not be able to find an advisor who is an investments-only millionaire, but you must find one who is at least an experienced investor. There are hundreds of investment managers out there, and thousands of advisors. Some are actually willing to operate a separately designed portfolio for each of their clients. Be selective. Understand the motivations and embrace the strategy being used. Apply plenty of time and patience. Ask questions directly of your manager.

Don't smile if you recognize yourself here! Have you followed the advice of trainee advisors or, worse yet, bought something hot from a cold caller? Have you ever owned a zero coupon bond, or held it to maturity; owned a variable annuity; used DRIP programs; lost a big short-term gain because of commission or tax issues. This book should expand the head of your investment-knowledge pin by opening your eyes to the realities of the investment world. Knowledge is power. Experience is knowledge in practice!

Buy and Hold vs. Trading

The conservative buy and hold investment strategy developed when three major (and ancient) force fields converged sometime early in the last century. Equity investing was a noble pursuit reserved for the rich and famous. They provided the financing for, and participated in the growth of, the bubbling new American economy. Trading was left to the companies they owned. Historical records proved unequivocally that an investment portfolio, unmanaged in this way would grow along with the overall economy in the long run (which at the time was believed to be upwards of ten years). As a bonus, the markets would remain stable. In most circles, stability is still thought of as a good thing, but not for a trading strategy, and the definition of long term has changed considerably.

Bolstering the commitment to this uniquely unbusinesslike strategy (businesses buy and sell, or die) were two lesser but growing forces:(a) a desire to avoid the Robin Hood-like confiscation tactics of the federal government, and (b) a reluctance to pay a fee for periodically changing positions in one's portfolio.

But the growth of the economy accelerated so quickly and so broadly that equity ownership became the right of the masses. It would be difficult to find an employed person today who does not have an (in)vested interest in the success of big business in America. The early captains of industry recognized that they could no longer control the equity markets so easily, so in a major change of direction, they took over and now control the primary distribution channels of the securities markets! You got it; they are the Wall Street institutions, masters of the universe!

In a world without tax codes and commissions, few would argue that a trading approach to stock market investing makes more sense than the ancient buy and hold. Ironically though, the illusion of wealth produced by large tax-deferred portfolios is a gotcha that few appreciate until much too late. Investors could change this but just don't seem interested. The buy and hold approach was developed in an era where the DJIA didn't move more than a few hundred points per year, a 100,000-share day was huge volume, mutual funds weren't even a twinkle in a young man's eye, and frankly, Scarlett, no one really gave a damn!

Buy and hold is an investment dinosaur, although it makes a modicum of sense in very small start-up portfolios comprised of closed end mutual funds (CEFs, not ETFs, where trading opportunities occur less frequently than in larger portfolios with multiple positions). If you were to choose a dozen A-rated companies and examine their charts, you would quickly appreciate just how easy profitable trading can be in the very stocks that buy and hold advocates would consider core, long-term holdings. Few people take the time to figure this out. Most tend to fall head over heals in love with a stock whose price goes up, up, and up. They will even buy more at ever-higher prices until their position (from a diversification standpoint) becomes far too large. Wall Street loves you! Most of you, just as surely, will watch the stock price go back down, down, and down. My accountant says that I don't need any more income this year so I'll just kiss off this bonanza and pay less in taxes. Sound familiar?

Why sell? they say with wonder at your stupidity in their eyes? My _____ (fill in the blank with the last stock you rode all the way up and all the way back down) will never go down in price, The Street says it's going to $167 per share before it splits, and what about the tax consequences? Historically, very few stocks fail to correct occasionally. It's much more productive to trade regularly within a group of fundamentally sound companies that can reasonably be expected to survive into the foreseeable future. We'll get into the selection process in chapter 3.

In today's investment world, we can defer taxation on earnings, salary even, until retirement. We can avoid high commission rates, and probably the best service from experienced people by using a variety of discount brokerages. This writer would argue that commissions should be of little concern anyway, but no one seems to want to hear about that. Have you ever wondered why Charles

Schwab is always grinning? This genius (and I sincerely mean genius) created a huge industry with a fix for a non-problem. Wall Street is exceptionally adept in giving you what you want whether it's good for you or not. Street walkers are particularly good at profiting from human frailties and addictions, kind of like drug dealers. You want to bet on the future, you got it! You think there's money to be made in horse semen, we'll get it for you! Speculating in the stock market is just as real an addiction as slot machines and cocaine. Just say no.

The fact that we can do something more cheaply does not mean that we will be able to do it better. Variable costs are not as important to control as fixed costs. Consult any management textbook. If my cost for something is X and I sell it for a 10 percent gain, my gross dollar profit is actually higher if the X is larger! And a 10 percent profit after commissions is, after all, a 10 percent profit. In a perfect world, all commissions would be equal and we could focus on more important matters!

Isn't it ironic that the very same people, who will do whatever it takes to slice the last pennies off of a commission, will blindly pay the huge markup included in a new issue or dollars more per share by using market orders?

Wouldn't it be nice if the financial world were less hysterical and easier to understand? Financial planners, accountants, and lawyers are (partially) necessary because: (1) the educational system stops at how to make money, not how to invest it; (2) the tax code is incomprehensible and punishes investors and corporations as if they were the criminal element in society; (3) major speculators are not barred from suing companies when they lose money. On top of all the hype, ignorance, and confusion, we have a paranoid-schizophrenic government whose solution for creating a comfortable retirement in America is taxing Social Security and private pension plans. How dumb is that? The point is that the economic quality of your investment thinking is compromised by concerns about tax impacts, lawsuits, and asset confiscation. Getting your fellow investors united behind some sane approach to tax reform is one thing you could do to increase the long-run return on all of your investments. Think about how zero taxation of all investment income would benefit society; think about how repeal of the corporate income tax would benefit investors and increase employment; think about how trading high quality stocks and income producing securities will make you a lot more money, with or without commissions and taxes. Now you're talkin'!

If pay taxes you must, you will be able to use more of your retirement nest egg if the taxes have been paid during the asset accumulation stage.

Heed the voice of experience. I once had a client who had inherited a million-dollar estate that had been poorly managed by a bank trust department for generations. It was badly managed, not for lack of growth in value, but for lack of foresight. Somehow, my client received the stock portfolio at his grandfather's cost basis. Wow! Not quite as bad as a gift of a Great Dane puppy, but there are similarities. It's great to have assets, so long as you can afford the upkeep! Imagine 12,000 shares of $60 Exxon with a $.15 cost basis. He had similar low-basis holdings in other solid (and once solid) companies. Things change over such a long period of time, and it appears as though the managers were instructed to buy and hold. The allocation of the positions was way out of proportion, especially the 70 percent or more that remained in Exxon! The taxable gain on the portfolio would have been about $900,000.

So what's the problem? Simply this. The man had a reasonable income, but no other assets. There were things he wanted to do to diversify his new portfolio and to improve his lifestyle, but he couldn't deal with the idea of paying the taxes, even at long-term capital gain rates. Without changes, he wouldn't be able to significantly increase his income. In developing wealth, don't lose sight of one important long-term objective: a comfortable retirement, paid for by the income from your investment portfolio. Try to position yourself on the way there, instead of waiting for the last minute. $1,000,000 worth of Microsoft (in 2001) generated how much retirement income?

Microsoft has always had a cult-like following of shareholders who thought themselves invulnerable to losses. The stock has been flat now for years, at about 50 percent of what it sold for in 1999. Does anyone remember what happened to Occidental Petroleum when Armand Hammer died? How do you think investors would have reacted had it been Bill Gates instead of Payne Stewart in that runaway jet? Chew on that one! What would you have done? Be honest. Now put a paper clip on this page and come back to answer this question again after I'm done with you. Profit taking rules!

Sometimes the Tail Wags the Dog

Why do people bother investing at all? If you buy securities you have to pay someone a commission. If you're fortunate enough to make some profits (note that you have no profits until you realize them), you have to give some away in the form of taxes.

Let's consider another scenario. When you buy your morning coffee and newspaper, do you resent the money the store owner is making? Or, would you try to negotiate with the newspaper company to whittle down their profit per paper? And what about the middleman who sold the store owner the coffee beans, paper cups, lids, sugar, Sweet 'n Low, and cream? Aren't these extra costs the same as commissions? Should the government make retailers disclose their markups?

What about those taxes! Why not storm into your boss's office and demand a cut in salary so you can move into a lower tax bracket? Ridiculous? No more ridiculous than your accountant's advice that you should lose money on some investments to offset profits you've made elsewhere. Sure, it's the right thing to do when a company has become worthless, not just unpopular. But your accountant is probably not qualified to determine which securities should be sold, or when; and why is this strategy only implemented at the end of the year? Three questions come to mind. Would he suggest the sale of all or part of a mutual fund, particularly if he sold it to you? Would he mind if you only paid half of his bill to help him reduce his own tax bite? Is he suggesting another security that you should buy?

The voice of experience (again, sorry): tune your way-back machine to the early '80s when oil prices skyrocketed (to almost $40 a barrel!), interest rates went into the high double digits, and prices of oil company shares went through the roof. One phone call cost a client of mine thousands of dollars when he insisted that I defer taking profits on his oil company shares until the following year. Prices plunged before year-end, erasing nearly all of his gains.

Never lose sight of the dog. Income and profits are the Holy Grail of investing. Nothing else really matters. Stick with the plan and take profits when your targets are reached. Sit, Brutus. Good dog!

Contrarian Trading

Contrarian trading is different from contrarian thinking, which is based on the premise that we should do the opposite of whatever the popular trend seems to be, with no other rules or parameters involved in the decision making. This is not really a viable investment strategy because it has neither management nor investment principles at its foundation. The opposite of speculating in one thing could be speculating in another. Contrarian trading, on the other hand, takes place within a very well-defined set of rules and procedures. It is a strictly disciplined and totally managed approach that doesn't allow much divergence from classic textbook investment principles. Sticking to the basic principles of investing is often, in and of itself, contrarian!

This approach has no time or position size constraints like day trading may have, and it applies management and investment considerations to such Wall Street realities as: group and sector dynamics, overreactions to both good news and bad, and portfolio window dressing.

The November Syndrome

Every fall, a good year in the market or not (who makes this determination anyway, the institutions, the media?), I explain to my clients why year end is always a special time in the stock market. Investors are encouraged to lose capital in order to pay less in taxes. A related misconception is that it is better to wait until next year to take profits (refer to the lesson above). Here is a message you will absolutely not receive from your Wall Street financial advisor:

Unless a security has lost its fundamental quality, and unless you have some form of guarantee that your profits will still be there in January, I intend to realize each and every profit as soon as the sell target has been reached, irrespective of the tax implications.

By the way, only banks, insurance companies, and the federal government can issue securities that are guaranteed as to principal or interest. If you ever hear it with regard to future market value performance of any security, plan, fund, program, etc., call 911!

Another year-end phenomenon, which plays out to a lesser degree at the end of each calendar quarter, is institutional window dressing, a euphemism for consumer fraud. This is a process that will be examined in more detail later, but you need to understand its impact. Remember always that Wall Street institutions have little or no respect for your intelligence. They will not publish quarterly or annual reports that either show holdings in unpopular securities and sectors, or are missing the names of hot stocks.

You may not even see these reports until they are several quarters out of date. However, major client employee benefits committees meet with their investment company money managers regularly, and there is just no way the fund managers are going to jeopardize their careers by appearing stupid. They will always, and without conscience or question, sell low and buy high to give the appearance of brilliance. Hey! Get angry! It's your money they're playing with!

Window dressing strategies generally add to the weakness of securities that have been weak throughout the year (buy more of these) and to the strength of those that have been more popular (take profits on these.) If you were to selectively buy high-quality names from the list of New York Stock Exchange twelve-month lows in November, it is likely that you will be able to sell these very same issues profitably within a few months. I Guarantee it! The last phrase was a test. Your left eyebrow should have moved up and you should have been looking around for your cell phone when you heard the "G" word.

The basic point is that the stock market functions outside the realm of the tax code, the calendar, the basic principles of investing, and even the law. Don't take unnecessary losses that just deplete capital. You must never accept this practice as either appropriate or necessary behavior. If you have an emotional problem with paying taxes on your gains, send me the money. I'll be happy to pay more taxes.

Make decisions based on sound investment principles and in a time continuum that has no artificial constraints. And, most importantly, recognize that Wall Street will not. The November syndrome creates tremendous misinformation as well as incredible opportunity. A few months later, the financial media will discover a mysterious January effect that suddenly moves many of last year's losers higher...as the wizards of Wall Street sell their overpriced look-smart securities to pay more for the ones that they just sold!

On the personal account level, some professionals recommend this practice as a tax-bite reliever... thirty days can be an awfully long time. Interesting place Wall Street is!

A Store Filled with Symbols

Let's take a trip to the local hardware store (HD or LOW). We see shelves filled with merchandise: paint (SHW), plywood (WY), light-bulbs (PHG), appliances (WHR, GE), tools (SWK, BDK), tractors (DE), lawnmowers (TTC), and more. Thousands of products produced by hundreds of manufacturers. How did they get there? Who were they purchased from? How much did they cost? What's the point of having so many products on the shelves? Is the objective to increase the value of the inventory? How much will you have to pay to buy something?

They may have been purchased directly from the manufacturers, but many were certainly delivered through layers of middlemen (brokers) who added a little profit for themselves to the final cost of the merchandise (commissions). Many of the products may have been purchased during weakness in commodity or raw material prices to take advantage of lower prices. What a concept, this buy low that we all do routinely in every other market except in the security markets!

And the goods got to the merchant's shelves for one purpose and one purpose alone! They are to be sold for a profit as quickly and as effortlessly as possible. And yes, if we can get the consumer to come into our shop for pick-up, we'll keep delivery costs down and spend less on customer service. But how do we fix a price to charge for those kitchen cabinets, chain saws, carpets, hinges, nails, clothespins, and bags of fertilizer? What is a reasonable profit objective?

Would any real-world enterprise buy and hold? Of course not, they trade. Commodity-based firms deplete inventory. Retailers buy the highest quality product they can, even competing brands. They establish a reasonable markup above their cost basis. And then, when you come into the store, they actually sell the thing to you for the price they had stamped on the merchandise well beforehand. What a concept: trading. What were the very first global business-men called? Buy and holders, or was it traders? Did Columbus come to the Americas to obtain and to hoard spices? Trading runs the

TABLE 1: A tale of two strategies

Your General Store (Reasonable Objectives)

ITEM	COST BASIS	MARK UP	SELLING PRICE	TURNOVER GOAL	TOTAL GAIN	RETURN	SUCCESS PERCENT
Lamp Shades	$10	10%	$11	24 x Yr	$24	240%	95%
Chain Saws	$100	10%	$110	6 x Yr	$60	60%	95%
Televisions	$400	10%	$440	4 x Yr	$160	40%	95%

Your Stock Portfolio (on Street Drugs)

ITEM	COST BASIS	MARK UP	SELLING PRICE	TURNOVER GOAL	TOTAL GAIN	RETURN	SUCCESS PERCENT
Lampshades, Inc.	$10	210%	$31	Once, after 12 months	$21	210%	30%
Saws.com	$100	150%	$250	Once	$150	150%	40%
TV's 'R' Us	$400	75%	$700	Once	$300	75%	50%

Your Stock Portfolio (off Drugs)

ITEM	COST BASIS	MARK UP	SELLING PRICE	TURNOVER GOAL	TOTAL GAIN	RETURN	SUCCESS PERCENT
100 LOW	$4,000	10%	$4,400	2 x Yr	$800	20%	90%
100 CLX	$3,500	10%	$3,850	2 x Yr	$700	20%	90%
100 BMY	$6,000	10%	$6,600	2 x Yr	$1,200	20%	90%

There's no reason not to manage your stock portfolio in the same manner you would run your general store!

world because trading works. America would never have been discovered in a buy and hold world. And, by the way, consumers don't question the amount of the commission when they make the purchase. Hmmm...

Investing must be handled in the same manner as the management of a retail enterprise. Love profits, not increasing inventory value. Worship turnover. Sell as many burgers as you can. Let's see: is it easier to sell a hundred items at a 10-percent profit or ten items at a 100-percent profit? Every security, either equity or income, has to be for sale. The key is to set a reasonable target price, or markup. It's easy to get all caught up in Wall Street-analyst hype and hold on until that $80 stock actually gets there. But, it's easier to set a more attainable target that can be reached quickly, and count on rapid inventory turnover to produce big profits. Go back to the charts and observe the price ranges of even the most staid old companies. I'd be surprised if you didn't find dozens that could have been traded for 10-percent gains (after full service commissions) multiple times per year, and during all market scenarios. Eureka!

> *If we start the year with twenty-five different quality products (equities) on our shelves, and we can sell 75 percent of them at a reasonable profit throughout the year, we'll be able to stay in business. If, however, we can turn over our inventory several times each year, we can make a lot of money!*
>
> *— R. McDonald*

I Once Had a Client...

I once had a client who insisted that I avoid buying two or more competing companies. This was many years ago when there were a whole lot more oil companies than there are today, and a guy named Pickens was going to do all he could to change that. Most of my clients had positions in two or three of the oils, and we celebrated repeatedly as one after the other was taken over. The other client did well with his Exxon, but nothing big ever happened.

The lesson here is that the market moves in groups of many different shapes and sizes, particularly when it comes to the popularity or disapproval of specific industries. It pays big time to own several different positions within the same industry while staying within the boundaries of proper diversification and quality standards. I sent my son a framed picture of Mr. Pickens to put over his fireplace. My message to him was: Every now and then you should thank this man for paying your way through college!

Types of groups include more than just industrial classifications. Wall Street will popularize such things as big-, mid-, and small-cap, or emphasize value or growth as the place to be right now. It makes a whole lot more investment sense to watch groups with names like drugs, retailers, and oils, than to watch the buzz word group of the day. Hmmm! A small cap stock might just be last year's big cap company that failed to meet analyst expectations. And just what distinguishes a growth stock from a value stock anyway? Will the definitions or criteria change either from institution to institution or from month to month? Different buzzwords will develop from time to time, giving rise to tremendous low risk opportunities in the group or groups that are currently out of favor. Such changes will also continue to produce hundreds of new specialty mutual funds, all of which will be statistically proven best in class, just like all automobiles, expensive restaurants, and New York radio stations. Wall Street is a buy-high world.

Keep in mind that The Street knows (is certain about) only one thing. It can market absolutely anything (even companies that don't exist) to the speculating public. Did I say speculating? You bet I did. Maybe they live in the land of certainty after all.

Fixed and Variable Costs
Any viable enterprise studies its costs carefully to determine just how much of a markup is needed for profitability. Just what do I have to spend to keep this business producing the units I want to sell? Fixed costs, such as some labor, rent, property taxes, and insurances are, for the most part, fixed. You have to pay them whether or not you sell even one widget, muffler, topcoat, sled, lawn chair, or staple gun. Management goes gray trying to manage their fixed costs. The profits from your product sales have to pay these costs, in addition to production costs, just to break even and to stay in business.

Smart managers pay their top sales people big commission bucks to keep them motivated (ever seen the Amway yacht?). Expense accounts are fine. Entertaining clients is encouraged. Advertising and marketing budget numbers boggle the mind. Why? Because they lead to increases in sales, and sales produce profits. You don't ever want to restrict your variable investment costs artificially. This is the seed money that grows your profits.

Fortunately, investing involves very few fixed costs. Some brokerage firms and most banks get some form of sadistic pleasure from charging nuisance fees of all shapes and sizes for anything other than bare-bones services. They then add insult to injury by making you deal with telephone robots when you want to get a question answered. The list of special charges seems endless, but when they charge for inactivity, or assign you to a call center, they've gone too far. But most costs can be avoided or negotiated if you really work at it.

The stronger your relationship with the brokerage firm and the more commissions you generate through trading, the more likely it is that your account executive will be able to waive these onerous and insulting fees. Online brokers, discounters, and lower-cost independents won't be able to help you as much because (a) there is not as much fat in the commission schedule and, (b) they aren't given special slush funds to use for the benefit of their bigger clients. There are also exchange fees and SEC fees that you are pretty much stuck with no matter where you trade. So, depending on the level of service you require to run your account, your fixed costs are fairly easy to identify and to control. But what about the variable costs?

Commissions and Taxes Are Variable Costs
Please take a deep breath, slow yourself down, and go through this section with your mind wide open. You may not agree with me here, but if you can hypnotize yourself into thinking this way, and then manage your portfolio using this approach, you will avoid most of the more common mistakes that even the most experienced investors make. Just keep your eye on the gold watch.

Commissions are absolutely variable costs, but only when they are paid within an actual buy or sell transaction. Paid in any other form, they are as much a fixed cost as your car payment, mortgage, or gym membership. And by the way, unless you are in the business of buying and selling them, neither automobiles, nor houses are investment portfolio assets. Investment management fees, incidentally, are fixed costs.

Many people try to separate the cost basis of their securities into two parts: the amount paid for the stock and the amount paid as a commission. And then they fixate on the total cost of their trading efforts. As an active trader in both equities and income CEFs, I feel that it is much more important to focus on buying the security at a reasonable price, and at a commission rate that is fair to me, and to the person I rely upon for the execution of my trades. This is one area where I actually agree with the tax code, without agreeing that there should be a tax on investment income. The proceeds of a sale – the cost basis of security sold = taxable gain or loss... a proper calculation of a bad tax.

There are three ways to pay commissions: (a) the old-fashioned pay-as-you-go way, (b) a flat fee expressed as an annual percentage of the portfolio market value, and (c) using one of two forms of wrap account programs. Standard wrap accounts are a sham—they charge for personalized management but don't provide it. However, there is an acceptable form of wrap account that may solve chronic-commission-fixation syndrome while providing the personal portfolio management that Wall Street's version does not. They're out there, but if you can't communicate directly with your portfolio manager, or if you wind up with odd lot positions in your portfolio, you probably don't have one.

If I paid a lot of commissions in the form of an annual fee, because I bought a lot of securities and held on to them, I probably acted foolishly. If I paid a lot of commissions because I traded a lot of different positions profitably, I probably made a lot of money. You want to do all you can to hold fixed costs in line, but variable costs are generally the result of some action that is intended to produce a financial gain. You have to spend money to make money!

Taxes are variable costs too, and as much as we hate to pay them, they are a very good thing because of what they represent, i.e., the realization of profits. If I have made a lot of money, even after making every legal effort to shelter that income, I will certainly pay a lot in taxes. But what is better: $70,000 net after taxes on $100,000 in profits, or nothing at all? In your long-range planning, do two things: (1) develop a tax-exempt income portfolio in addition to your tax-deferred IRAs, 401(k)s, etc., and (2) actively seek out politicians who favor investor-friendly tax reform.

The Invasion of the Business Snatchers
Sometime during the '90s, Wall Street moved into the personal investment management business in a big way by marketing plain-vanilla mutual funds disguised as wrap account programs. These are popular investment products offered under a variety of sexy names by practically all brokerage firms. They are sold to investors as a way to obtain personal, private, individually designed, professional portfolio management programs with positively no commissions... you just pay a small annual fee.

I think I mentioned that investors should be suspicious of anything that Wall Street recommends. Remember, no matter how they try to disguise it, they will absolutely never do anything that will reduce their revenues or profits. Yours, yes; theirs, no! Institutional brokerage firms like the investment management business because they can reduce their fixed overhead expenses (staff salaries and the broker's share of commissions) and because they can develop a captive, dependent market (the money management firms they hire) for other products that their empires produce. They also can collect huge fees for doing absolutely nothing.

The cost of this type of arrangement for most investors is going to be 3 percent per year or a bit less, depending upon portfolio size alone, but with a lower annual rate for income portfolios, which must be managed separately. The individually managed portfolios are available in all the standard mutual fund flavors: growth/income, value, mid-cap, emerging markets, small cap, technology, you name it. The idea seems simple. The management fee replaces all charges to the client and never again is there a discussion about commissions, exchange fees, inappropriate securities, or churning. If I call a commission a management fee, is it really no longer a commission? Just what is it that the brokerage firms are asking their clients to do, and just how personally managed are these programs? And do you really believe that your financial advisor is not getting a cut?

They Do It with Mirrors

Let's say that you have $100,000 (probably the minimum allowed) and you agree to pay the 3 percent annual fee to enter a wrap account arrangement. You have just added $3,000 to the fixed costs of running your portfolio. Assume further that there are twenty-five trades during the year, that the average gain per trade is 10 percent (for a total profit of $10,000), and that the portfolio generates an additional 2 percent in dividends and interest. What is the keep? Is it a 12 percent growth in working capital? Right? Nope.

Amount Invested	$	100,000
Minus Total Fees Paid	- $	3,000
Net Amount Invested	= $	97,000
Plus Capital Gains	+ $	10,000
Plus Dividends & Interest	+ $	2,000
Total Working Capital	= $	109,000 (approx.)

First of all, your fixed costs are deducted quarterly in advance, and they are calculated on the value of the portfolio, not the investment that you made. In the illustration above, your year-end market value would not be $112,000 as you would like it to be. You would wind up with less than $109,000 or a growth rate of approximately 9 percent! What if there were no capital gains? (The underlying assumption is that the value of each security held at year end is equal to its purchase price.)

Now let's look at the full commission scenario with less of an increase in fixed costs. The account is managed in the same way: a 10-percent average gain per trade for a total of $10,000 in profits and a 2- percent interest and dividend kicker, with the same year-end market value assumption. There are the same twenty-five trades, but now the commissions are paid in the normal manner and are thus included in the stock's cost basis. They are not deducted from the 10-percent profit. You are the manager of the portfolio so there are no fixed overhead charges at all! It's obvious that you have to sell at a slightly higher price to realize the target of 10 percent net. Let's further assume that commissions and charges were a whopping $100 per trade! The result? You Keep $112,000 in working capital and enjoy a growth rate of more than 12 percent because your gains are after commissions which have become what they should always be, after all, a variable cost! If there were no profits, you're in the black by two grand. This math is better, really.

Amount Invested	$	100,000
Minus Total Fees Paid	- $	0.00
Net Amount Invested	= $	100,000
Plus Capital Gains	+ $	10,000
Plus Dividends & Interest	+ $	2,000
Total Working Capital	= $	112,000 (approx.)

WOW, you say, just think how much I would make at a discount broker if I paid just $250 dollars in commissions instead of $2,500. Guess again, the results are precisely the same. $10,000 in profits + $2,000 in other income, $0.00 in Management Fees = $12,000 or 12 percent. So much for the discount brokerage industry. Plug the figures in above to make this crystal clear. Your trades would not be more profitable because the manager is still shooting at a target of 10 percent above your cost basis. Your dollar gain would actually be less! Comprendez?

Note: I have managed hundreds of accounts through dozens of brokerage firms and with various types of flat fee or discounted commission arrangements. There is absolutely no correlation between the amount of commissions paid and the long-term rate of capital growth in the portfolio. Take a look at the trading results illustrated in Table 3, at the end of chapter 3. Can you determine if this was: (a) a discount brokerage account, (b) a flat fee arrangement, or (c) a regular pay as you trade account? Only your investment manager (you) knows for sure.

Is Bigger Really Better?

Now let's examine the process undertaken by Wall Street to determine just who is qualified to be an approved wrap account portfolio manager for the brokerage firms. Requirement number one is size. No manager with under $100,000,000 in managed assets need apply. No manager without subordinate decision makers is eligible. Don't bother us either, if you don't have a variety of investment products to offer. What does this sound like to you? Got it! A mutual fund store with a new wrinkle: monthly or quarterly personalized account statements that list the positions owned by the fund. And that, my gullible friends, is the limit of the personal investment management you will receive from your private investment manager.

Not only will you never meet the person that is managing your investment portfolio, you will never even have a conversation with her. It is likely that the management firm itself will not even know your name...but they will sure know the name of the brokerage firm that sent your money in. They probably won't even know the name of the personal wealth executive (stockbroker or other financial advisor) who sold you the program. Would that kind of a relationship be acceptable in any other profession? Your financial advisor will act as the middleman throughout the entire process of selecting an appropriate manager, reviewing the objectives of the program (actually, the mutual fund), and analyzing the manager's investment performance. If he's an honest person, he'll tell you that he has never met or had a conversation with the investment manager either. Just for kicks, ask him how he gets paid on the sale of this kind of ar-rangement. He absolutely does get paid, but it's not called a commis-sion. I know that you've seen those TV ads that imply that you will meet with the manager. Sorry, the meetings will only be with your financial advisor. Please, give us a break.

Had enough? There's more, further adding to the wool that is slowly being drawn down over your eyes. Your $100,000 will be in-vested in exactly the same stocks as those who signed up yesterday, last month, and last year. You'll have odd lots of up to one hundred different issues—some at their all time highest levels and very few that are in a buy-low(er) posture. Yup, you have just purchased another mutual fund. I understand that you can even get a wrap account program where the investment manager actually puts the money into a selection of mutual funds. It's hard to believe that even the super salespersons of Wall Street could find buyers for that. There is no individuality, no personal attention, and no real chance of investing in a program suited to your financial objectives. Have they no shame?

This is simply just another one-size-fits-all product. How many different managers would you need to run a 70-percent equity, 30-percent income, asset allocation and to diversify either of the two buckets...certainly no less than two. Who coordinates and re-allo-cates? I guess you are really still the manager, huh?

Want more? The investment management company must run its trades through your brokerage firm and, believe me when I tell you that they don't provide the service for free. Additionally, because of the size of the total fund relationship, the fund manager receives the low end of his billing schedule (probably .5 percent or less), allowing the brokerage firm to keep the lion's share of the up-front manage-ment fees you are paying. Not quite greedy enough for you yet? For directing this traffic to the manager, the brokerage firm steals (oops, I'm sorry, collects) an additional 10 percent of the management fee for its sales efforts.

Note: Registered investment advisors (RIAs) are required to disclose to their clients precisely how they are compensated for what they do and sell. Was any of this information shared with you when you started up your wrap account? You don't have to ask, you must be told! Feel abused? You should.

Still, most investment managers would kill for this kind of business because it is an endless source of new clients, and a relationship that they will do practically anything to continue. Integrity anyone? If ever there was a blatant conflict of interest, like an accountant selling mutual funds and collecting commissions, this is the place.

Fact or fiction, you decide: approved wrap account investment managers obtain thousands of clients and millions of fee dollars from the major brokerage firms every year. There is no way they can generate the dollars, achieve the recognition, and become popular with the media without this type of business. The CEO of Your Money and Us Brokerage, LLC, recognizes this dependency, and suggests that the investment management company form an alliance with his firm's underwriting department, thus assuring a captive market for new issues being brought public. Wouldn't it also be nice if the manager removed stocks from YM & Us managed portfolios if we lower our opinion and added those that we are pushing?

Why do you think Congress cuts the SEC's budget practically every year? Less money, fewer investigations of institutional practices like these. Additionally, I'm sure you won't be surprised to learn that few small and/or private brokerage or investment management firms act as advisors to regulatory bodies like the SEC. Similarly, it is rumored that the big guys purposely seek ways to influence and support regulations that are prohibitively expensive and time consuming for small businesses (see chapter 7).

Note: In 2007, news stories indicated that the SEC had finally taken note of these fraudulent wrap account products, albeit through a technicality. As I understand it, the brokerage firms are (allegedly) illegally charging clients investment advisory fees without having a signed investment advisory agreement on file.

A Word about Day Trading

Day trading refers to the practice of buying and selling stocks within the same trading day, with all positions being closed by the end of the day. Day trading is a common practice among professionals, but it is becoming more and more popular among individual non-pros for myriad reasons that make the practice extremely speculative. There is no evidence that Wall Street is encouraging clients to use these techniques, but whoever creates and distributes the hot-stock-tip lists and research reports must be up to something. Because it has no foundation in the basic QDI principals of investing (i.e., quality, diversification, and income generation), it is speculation of the same type as IPOs, junk bonds, and roulette. Basically, if the deal is that you will get rich quicker and easier, it's just another type of gambling, and not true investing at all. Plus, think of the commissions it generates, even at $7.00 per trade.

Recently, business news radio stations have been carrying advertisements for computer software that can spot hot movers that can be turned over rapidly to let you make big bucks even more quickly. It just can't fail; we're led to believe. Really, who is doing the programming?

If you are fortunate enough to buy a stock that meets all of your QDI investment criteria, and that achieves your target price within twenty-four hours, that's just great, and it may happen. Most day trading schemes are based on large numbers of shares and very small price movements, and you won't find too many experienced/wealthy investors involved in the exercise.

A Personalized Set of Rules

Every investor is different from every other investor. Risk tolerance varies with age, financial position, and/or experience. There are optimists and pessimists out there, making dissimilar decisions in similar environments. Each of us has our own investment equation and it is important that we make an effort to understand who we are and how we act in times either of stress or of elation. This needs to be done before we develop our personal investment plans and strategies. Knowing who we are, what we are trying to accomplish, and how we deal with the very emotional thing called money is an important foundation for an investment program.

Successful businessmen and women work within a personalized set of rules and procedures developed over time to help them achieve a defined set of objectives. Each of us must come up with an action plan, appropriate guidelines, and practices, and monitoring devices if we expect our investment program to produce the desired results. We have to be able to establish an investment plan, organize our portfolios in a manner that will help achieve our objectives, and focus on the plan in a disciplined decision-making environment. We must implement the plan consistently over an extended period of time, with only occasional and minor fine-tuning adjustments allowed.

Investing absolutely involves financial risk. If there is no risk of any kind (market or price movement, interest rate, deadline expiration, etc.), there is no investment. A CD (certificate of deposit) or a money market fund, by this definition, is not an investment, but the interest rates available from either are useful tools in performance evaluation. In looking at performance, beat the bank is a worthy investment benchmark, because if you can't beat the bank, why even bother to assume the risk? Most brokerage firms will ask you to select a benchmark that you want to use to gauge your portfolio performance. The very idea is ludicrous, unless your self-esteem is so low that you think an average or index, even the CPI, mirrors the objectives, design, and content of your investment portfolio. Investors deal with risk through the hierarchy of investment rules that they set for themselves. Investment rules can and will be different at times in a person's investment life, but there are really just three principles of investing that need to be mastered. Interestingly, each of them deals essentially with risk minimization.

An in-depth discussion of QDI follows in chapter 2, but first it's important to deal with another Wall Streetism that you will find more and more insidious as you gain knowledge and experience. The Street has established itself as an icon whose knowledge is unquestionable. On a daily basis, radio and television commentary will quote Wall Street analysts who will explain away the events of the day, the week, or the quarter as reactions in either direction to heightened or lessened uncertainty in the marketplace. Well sure, that makes a lot of sense. But does it really?

What is certainty, and does it exist at all in the stock market? Wall Street firms want you to believe that they know what is going to happen in the future. Their analysts are so smart that they can predict the future. As far as I know, the last crystal ball lost its power centuries ago. We can be certain of only one thing in the investment world, and in life, and that one thing is that we will always function within an environment of uncertainty.

A little later on, during the same show, you might hear another opinion that tells you money managers are placing their bets on something. Is this the statement of an omniscient entity or an admission of ignorance on the part of an institution with too many mouths to muzzle?

Have we progressed so far backward that it is acceptable for professional investment managers to be compared to blackjack players? (You're right. These guys would be playing baccarat.) Is the media being irresponsible (for insinuating that investing is, after all, just gambling) or altruistic (for warning us that serious risk of loss is involved)? Maybe they are just being realistic, recognizing that the bulk of their drooling audience is just looking for a play anyway. Maybe they are just more ignorant than we would like to believe. In any event, if you're looking for a game to play, you should try one that's a bit less expensive when you lose.

Obviously, there's a lot more to investing than just picking a winner and riding it over the horizon. Successful investing over the long haul requires understanding a short list of common-sense principles from several disciplines: management, investing, and psychology. But it also requires a consistent methodology for both portfolio construction and performance monitoring. Wall Street speaks volumes about asset allocation but doesn't know how to do it because they have obfuscated its purpose. Even more disconcerting is the fact that they have manipulated performance-evaluation techniques in a manner that fails to distinguish between the two classes of investment securities and the cyclical nature of both. Call me cynical, but it's hard to believe that this wasn't phase one of the systematic brainwashing of the American investor. Investors require a personal, goal-oriented, portfolio-specific asset allocation and performance-assessment methodology.

Break Time: Fundamentals of Asset Allocation and the Working Capital Model

Asset allocation is a personal planning tool, not an investment strategy. Few investors take the time to appreciate the distinction between the two. Various strategies, substrategies, and routine procedures can be used to implement the plan. But asset allocation itself is most important because it is derived from the investor's own perspective of his financial position translated into a unique set of goals, objectives, time frames, what ifs, etc.

Asset Allocation is the most important and most frequently misunderstood concept in the investment lexicon. One of the most confusing aspects of asset allocation is the idea that it and diversification are the same or complementary concepts. Diversification is actually part of the separate selection and control functions that take place within each of the asset allocation divisions, or securities buckets. Next in line would be the fallacy that asset allocation is a sophisticated technique used to soften the bottom line impact of movements in stock and bond prices. A similar idea proposes that asset allocation is a process that automatically (and foolishly) moves investment dollars from a weakening asset classification to a stronger one, a subtle market timing device. Finally, there is the widely accepted myth that a properly designed asset allocation formula must include a percentage of cash.

Because of its buzz-word status and general acceptance as a valid investment concept, a warehouse full of asset allocation models, programs, software products, mutual funds, seminars, books, gurus, and worksheets have evolved. These sophisticated applications will process your personal data and then (after a few days so you'll think it is more than just boilerplate) spew out a glossy personalized asset allocation presentation that could have as many as twenty different decimal-pointed classifications and subclassifications that your financial advisor will be pleased to fill up with his favorite investment products. This is unnecessary.

The basic asset allocation formula can be a kitchen-table plan, developed by crunching very few numbers in tandem with a consideration of very few ballpark answers to some basic, common-sense questions. At retirement, for example:

1. How much will you have to invest?
2. How much income will you have from pensions, Social Security, rental properties, etc.? and
3. How much additional income will you need?

The income need should always be identified first. Never count on the stock market to provide you with spending money. Read that again, out loud. Assets not needed to ensure that there is adequate income can be invested within the equities bucket.

Asset allocation need not be complicated or mysterious, nor does the development of a workable asset allocation formula require the fee-based assistance of an RIA, CPA, CFA, CFPC, or any other similarly designated sales representative or fee-based asset allocation specialist. I don't mean to diminish the importance of having an experienced and skilled advisor to help you with your asset allocation decisions. Just be careful not to use someone who either has products to sell or a referral-fee arrangement with someone who does.

An asset allocation formula needs to be flexible over the years, and flexibility is easier to achieve with individual securities than it is with products and contracts. Most advisors have a good working knowledge of packaged products, and very little experience with individual securities and their goal-directed management.

The problem that most investors don't realize they have is that they use the wrong numbers and time frames to make their secondary asset allocation decisions. The initial allocation decision is simple, particularly if the portfolio starts with a bundle of cash that has been intellectually separated into the two standard buckets. It really does need to be in one brokerage account. Once fully invested, we have, for example, $60,000 invested in equities and $40,000 invested in income securities.

This original cost basis percentage relationship (60/40), is the allocation of our initial working capital, and it will remain the same until a change is made to our income requirements in either direction. Now this is the key element of asset allocation using the working capital model. It, the total investment, is not impacted directly by changes in market value. It increases through deposits, dividends, interest, and capital gains and decreases through withdrawals and capital losses. Gains and losses are a function of what we do about changes in market value—an action number, not a planning number. Every net dollar received, while held in your money market fund, is eventually directed to the two buckets so that the 60/40 cost- basis relationship is maintained. Close is fine, but don't even think in terms of market timing. Remember, KISS.

Think about the impact of various real-world experiences (a trading loss or gain, an IRA contribution, etc.) on the amount of working capital in each bucket. The asset allocation can be kept on target without ever considering either the market value of the portfolio or where we are in the calendar year. No more year-end rebalancing or ignoring the income bucket when interest rates are low. The only way of offsetting the impact of inflation on your income is to grow that income by maintaining your asset allocation using the working capital model.

Working capital, then, could be defined as the productive capability of the securities in the portfolio. Based on its purpose as an income provider, and assuming no serious change in quality, a municipal bond at 90 percent of face value has the same productive capability as one at par. Similarly, an investment-grade equity maintains its ability to produce a capital gain regardless of where it is in its price or popularity cycle. Historically, these relationships are well illustrated.

Chapter 2
The Big Three

I t is likely that the three most often repeated concepts in this book are quality, diversification, and income generation (QDI), or the three principles of investing. If this is the last chapter you read and you come away from the effort understanding their importance in a successful investment program, you will probably do pretty well in the minors. But if you want to make it to the majors, you'll still have a ways to go...

Note that the big three investment principles apply to income securities just as completely as they do to equities. We'll get into that area in chapter 5.

Standards of Quality

Each of us deals with investing differently and there certainly are many perfectly acceptable ways of doing so. I suspect that there are some methods of speculation that I would find more acceptable than others, but the important thing is to know which of the two (investing or speculating) you are doing. In the long run (and anything less than five years is not the long run), the inherent quality of the securities we buy will be the primary determinant of how successful our investment program becomes. The second determinant is the amount of time we allow to get an investment strategy or methodology up and running, operating routinely, and moving through market and interest-rate cycles before judging its effectiveness. If you're thinking in terms of a year, don't even bother trying the strategy, and that applies to any strategy at all. Obviously, the higher the quality of the stocks we own, the lower the risk of loss in the portfolio. But how does one go about measuring the quality of a Home Depot, an Amazon.com, a General Motors, an ETF, or a mutual fund?

One of the basic relationships we deal with while investing is the one between financial risk and reward. The higher the potential reward, the greater the risk. If the reward seems high and the risk isn't up front and personal, right in your face, keep looking. It's in there. If you can't afford to lose the amount you invest, you should not allow yourself to accept the risk. (Some commodity speculators fail to realize that they could actually lose more than they invest in many programs... or wind up with a lifetime supply of pork bellies in their freezer.) Controlling the overall risk level of your portfolio is your very own personal responsibility. You have the power to decide. You da man! How would one assess the risk level of an ETF or of any mutual fund?

Some people will do their own research (and be wrong more often than they'll admit out of love for their own analytical ability), or they'll "sheep"ishly follow the advice of some self-proclaimed guru or wire house suit. Neither of these approaches will work consistently because their basic premise is flawed. It is just not possible for anyone, no matter how smart, to predict the future movement of individual stock prices. Good managers rely on others to do the grunt work (research) and on fundamental numbers to assess the viability of the companies in which they invest.

Fundamental Analysis vs. Technical Analysis
Fundamental and technical analysis are the two main disciplines used by Wall Street analysts to gather data in support of their guesswork (or purchased opinions). Fundamental factors include: profitability, debt-to-equity ratios, P/E ratios, dividend history, etc. These numbers are used to describe the present or last reported corporate financial reality. Technical analysis involves the use of trend numbers, averages, lines, graphs, tea leaves, and haughty British accents to (attempt to) predict the future movements of stock prices.

Most predictions of the future are wrong, particularly those that are based upon input from (drum roll please) those masters of hindsight, those monuments to meaningless numerical trivia, Wall Street's answer to David Copperfield, the technical analysts. I mean, really, why should we care if May or October are historically the worst months of the year? My personal feeling is that most research is simply the intellectual rationalization for the particular speculation being offered, just shined up a bit for public consumption via the financial media. What percentage of IPOs, for example, lives up to the promise expressed in the research? The financial risk is purposely well hidden within the legalese and mind numbing verbiage of the prospectus.

There are many services that provide all the fundamental analysis anyone could ever need to make well informed investment decisions. Pick one. Understand the information it is providing, and set your own quality standards. I use the very simplistic information provided in the small (5" x 8" x 3/8") monthly stock guide published by Standard & Poor's International. Then, of course, there is the 418-pound Value Line Investment Survey, with its 5-pound weekly updates... both guaranteed only to produce analysis paralysis. Could you imagine trying to carry that thing around in your briefcase? There are many similar services, but be particularly wary of the naturally biased and self-serving preparations of Wall Street institutions. After what you've read so far, I'm certain (oops) that you'll never look at another wire house research report. If I'm wrong, return to "Go" and don't place any orders.

Most investors have received confirmation notices with notations on them that "XYZ brokerage makes a market in this security," or you've heard talking-head commentary with regard to brokerage firms trading their own accounts. Just how unbiased do you think their research will be? The Wall Street hydra has many heads. Each time regulators lop one off, two new ones appear. Slow as they are, corporations are quicker than governments. I suppose it's easier to direct high-priced in-house counsel to develop new semi-legal products than it is to get a government overrun by attorneys-turned-politicians to agree on how to regulate the beast (or on anything at all, for that matter). It is true, by the way, that it is the institutions who give advice to the regulators.

The S&P Stock Guide

The S&P Stock Guide rates the financial viability and relative quality of companies from as low as D (for a "dog" in bankruptcy) to as high as A+. Standard & Poor's doesn't even know that I exist, and I get nothing at all for this endorsement or any others that appear in this book. Pity.

TABLE 2: S&P ratings of the thirty stocks in the DJIA (7/11/07)

SYMBOL	S&P RATING	DIVIDEND PAYING	BLUE CHIP	SYMBOL	S&P RATING	Dividend Paying	BLUE CHIP
T	B+	Yes	No	HON	B	Yes	No
AA	B+	Yes	No	IBM	A	Yes	Yes
AXP	A-	Yes	No	INTC	B+	Yes	No
BA	B+	Yes	No	VZ	B	Yes	No
CAT	A-	Yes	No	JNJ	A+	Yes	Yes
C	A+	Yes	Yes	JPM	B	Yes	No
KO	A-	Yes	No	MCD	A	Yes	Yes
DIS	B+	Yes	No	MRK	A-	Yes	No
DD	B	Yes	No	MSFT	B+	Yes	No
PFE	A-	Yes	No	MMM	A	Yes	Yes
XOM	A-	Yes	No	MO	A+	Yes	Yes
GE	A+	Yes	Yes	PG	A	Yes	Yes
GM	B-	Yes	No	AIG	A+	Yes	Yes
HWP	B+	Yes	No	UTX	A+	Yes	Yes
HD	A+	Yes	Yes	WMT	A+	Yes	Yes

Full-service brokers no longer pass these out to customers, probably because their bosses would rather that they push investment products.

S&P earnings and dividend ratings of B+ through A+ identify investment-grade equities, or stocks that they consider to be lower risk, higher quality companies. These letter ratings should not be confused with the rankings of possible future market performance published a la Value Line or via the latest brokerage house recommended list. They are analyses of fundamental survival statistics like current and P/E ratios. Note that they also have absolutely nothing to do with the S&P Market Performance Star Rating System. Also, just for the reality-slap-in the-face fun of it, check the rating on each of the stocks in the S&P 500 Average...hmmm.

Even more surprising are the ratings of the companies that comprise the closely watched, highly respected, Dow Jones Industrial Average (DJIA), which I've analyzed for you above. The majority of investors believe that all of these blue chip companies carry the highest possible ratings. Isn't that what blue chip is supposed to mean? Would you bet on it? Check it out now and think about it for a while before reading further. I've arbitrarily (generously) assigned blue chip status to only the top two categories.

Although most are investment-grade securities, 40 percent are B+ or lower. Only eight are in the elite A+ category, while five are rated B or worse. The term, "blue chip" has an ironic twist. Here's a type of gaming chip being used to describe what is defined in some circles as a high-priced, value security with good earnings and a stable price.

You'll find that most millionaires focus on stocks that fall within the investment-grade classifications. This is because they understand the concept of risk and how to go about the important task of risk minimization. Eliminating risk is impossible; managing or minimizing risk is essential. You'll also find that most professional investors—those who are not investment company employees—pay little attention to what Wall Street strategists conclude from their analysis of the DJIA and other averages, the purported consensus being that institutional reporting is just a bit biased in favor of the firm and its interests. But do independent professionals take advantage of the market gyrations caused by Wall Street prognosticators? Do we ever!

Keep in mind that employees have personal agendas that absolutely influence the opinions and predictions they publicize. Wall Street propaganda is designed to fill consumers with confidence in the products that they are selling (remember, consumers buy products, investors buy securities). If you were to pool all the institutional expert analytical opinion, you would have a high priced serving of bull...chowder.

It should be patently obvious that quality is an integral part of buying decisions in most aspects of life. Yet, mysteriously, millions of people throw billions of dollars at every manner of investment product and get-rich-quick scheme without even thinking about what's inside. Most people are more selective filling their shopping carts with high-quality products than they are when filling their portfolios with securities. We are all looking for sale prices on quality merchandise. I'll never know why such logical behavior can't compute when it comes to investment decisions, where a whole lot more zeros are involved. Brainwashing?

Here's a Wall Street buzzword you're probably unfamiliar with: coverage. I'm not exactly sure what coverage is, but I get several cold calls a week from representatives of research firms, bond houses, and well known brokerage firms who want to make sure that I have coverage with or by them. Sometimes I'm not sure that the caller knows either, but they seem to expect that I will. Thank goodness for a good secretary (and a delete key when it comes to the more recent barrage of stock-pick emails). Sometimes a caller breaks through the screen and I have the time to play along to see what he is selling. I always ask why I would want their particular coverage. Naturally they are all the very best at what they do, be it research, bond pricing, or stock picking. However, they all start to mumble when I ask how much of the security they own personally, or what special risks are associated with the 12-percent bond that they want me to buy for my clients in a 5-percent environment.

The point is that you have to find the quality: in things you buy for consumption, in investments you make for your future, and in the people with whom you have business relationships. In investing, quality is job one.

Also, in response to the unanswered question above, there is no easy way to assess the quality of mutual funds, closed or open ended, and there can be no such thing as a quality index fund. Ah, two more questions. Why?

Elements of Diversification

Several years ago, I was speaking at an IAFP (International Association of Financial Planners) meeting in Florida on the basic principles outlined here. [I am not a financial planner. I am a registered investment advisor (RIA), and my practice is solely investment management.] It was around the time that Wall Street was touting junk bond funds as a great new investment idea. These securities were safe because they were a diversified group of bonds that surely, the marketers hoped, would not all default. How many savvy investors do you think fell for this proposition? If I own twenty different pieces of junk in my portfolio, does it in some way make the portfolio un-junk? Still, greedy investors stood in line to buy the things in spite of the incredible risk involved.

I was the first speaker that day, and my presentation was intended to be a disembowelment of the Junk Bond product: "perhaps the biggest scam orchestrated by Wall Street, ever" were the words I used. The next speaker (a representative of a Wall Street bond firm) was late, missing my entire presentation. It was a bit tense in the room when he got into his story about the outstanding investment merits of his firm's brand new junk bond funds.

Years later, a similar product based on foreign government debt became even more popular than the junk bonds. The interest rate on these wonderful instruments was about twice the going rate in the U.S. and was guaranteed by the full faith and credit of Columbia, Peru, or Madagascar, for example. The fine print pointed out innocently enough, that it was the return of principal that was not guaranteed. But don't worry Mr. Client, all you have to do is hold on for eight or nine years and you'll be sure to break even. Is that a good thing?

Diversification is not just the presence of many different names, products, categories, countries, and industries. Rather, it is a manageable portfolio of purpose-directed investments, each of which can stand on its own merits as a profitable venture. Every investor must organize his or her portfolio recognizing several different types of diversification.

Just as asset-allocation formulae are personal and need periodic reviews for suitability, diversification needs constant monitoring. One of the few behaviors I would support among life insurance salespeople is their constant review of a person's circumstances to see if their current plan remains sound. Of course their motivation is to sell more product. Mine would be to see if fine-tuning adjustments are necessary.

Fine tuning is an important concept for another reason. People who live on commission are generally uncomfortable with minor portfolio changes because fine-tuning a portfolio for a new customer doesn't generate enough commissionable change. It is unlikely that your present investment plan is so terrible that nothing you own deserves to be kept. Still, most financial planners and investment advisors will recommend that everything be sold and that you start out fresh with a whole new collection of securities. Remember to question the motivation of any advisor who benefits directly from his or her advice. Be wary of a recommendation that includes the immediate sale of your holdings and/or purchase of either annuities and/or mutual funds. These two products occupy the highest rungs on the commission ladder.

Have a look at the new guy's personal investment portfolio before you trust him or her to design your own. You would be surprised just how often there isn't one. You deserve an experienced person. It's not your responsibility to train the new and the hungry, even if they happen to be related to you!

I was managing an income portfolio for a young widow for several years before she began dating a newly annointed financial advisor. The new guy had no love for her stodgy income portfolio and quickly changed it into growth income funds—just before the NASDAQ bubble burst. You just can't make this stuff up!

The financial industry is large and growing larger every day, creating excellent career opportunities for people who just might become a part of your life. Your gut will tell you to help your loved ones' progress by letting them handle your investment program.

Of course, your [insert child, fiancé, niece, lover, etc.] is the best and the brightest! If so they will survive and prosper without your product or securities purchases. Remember that the survival rate in the securities business is about the same as in the restaurant business. If you want to help, just write a check when they need to pay the rent. Don't let them blow their own inheritance while you still need to use it.

Asset Allocation Revisited: Income Securities

No matter how complicated we have been brainwashed into thinking the investment world is, there are really only two classes of investment securities: income and equity. Dependent primarily on your age and your plans for retirement, your portfolio should consciously be allocated between that class of securities whose primary role is income production (the former) and the other class, whose primary purpose is to generate growth in capital. Regardless of age and salary level, any six-figure investment portfolio should have a portion allocated toward income production.

The primary purpose of fixed income securities is the production of a safe and consistent flow of income. Corporate and municipal bonds, government securities, preferred shares, debenture-like preferreds, unit trusts, royalty trusts, and income CEFs are among the securities (and products) that fit within this category. Any realized growth in capital is simply gravy, resulting from a willingness to take advantage of changes in the perceived direction of interest rates and other market factors. Surprisingly, this concept is difficult to grasp for many investors. But the wealthy person's portfolio is always well stocked with income producers, especially municipal bonds. The income bucket can be viewed like an insurance policy for the equity or growth bucket of the portfolio, even though that is not the purpose of the securities in the overall scheme of things. For example, if the market value of your securities falls by 7 percent but you have generated 8 percent in dividends, interest, and capital gains, you will show a net gain for the period. Right?

Wall Street Thrives on Action

Why aren't fixed income securities popular with investors, commissioned financial advisors, or the Wall Street media? Probably because of the horse-race mentality that Wall Street nourishes so successfully. Fixed income is not nearly as exciting at the personal portfolio level as it is among professional institutional bond traders where the pressures for performance are incredible. Fixed income filters down to the investing public either in the form of odd-lot individual bonds, investment products called closed-end and open-end bond funds, and various types of unit trusts (see chapter 8).

These investment products can play a valuable role in portfolio development and management, but they too are not something you hear a whole lot about. Other than for professional managers and traders, they are just plain boring. Prices don't jump around as they do with other securities. There is little chance for exponential growth, and thus, there is less likelihood of media attention. Still, a profit on a fixed income security can add a lot to portfolio productivity over the long run.

But Wall Street thrives on action! It's a lot like Las Vegas—the casinos don't care if you win or lose. They want your action: hours played and average amounts wagered. Losers get the same comps and benefits as winners. The croupiers just get tips. Eventually, Wall Street will be even smarter.

Wall Street Salespeople Thrive on Ignorance

Commissioned sales people have little use for fixed income investment products because they are traded so infrequently. Most people are reluctant to trade them at all. Thus, the commissions per dollar of investment over the life of a thirty-year bond are low compared with the same amount of money churned about in equities. But I have had many experiences where financial advisors use the public's ignorance of fixed income security behavior to encourage unnecessary transactions. I'm sure that many of you have heard this one, which nearly dropped me from my chair at a meeting with a

CFP and his client many years ago: "Your bond fund isn't doing very well. I want you to sell it and buy this bond fund, which has performed much better." What was the fund supposed to be doing, and how should one measure the performance of an income security?

The only thing a bond fund is supposed to do is generate a regular stream of income. That's it. At any point in time, bonds of the same quality and duration will produce similar interest rates. Switching from one bond fund to another generates nothing but penalties for the investor and commissions for the salesperson. The same is true of fixed annuities. Unless you are totally changing your financial plan, be careful about drastic changes in your fixed-income portfolio. In the scenario above, the salesperson was seeking to unload an average-paying fund at a small loss in order to purchase a fund that had risen nicely in price, but was yielding just about the same amount of income. The incentive? The commission.

The market price of a fixed-income security varies inversely with the perceived direction of short-term interest rates, with the emphasis on perceived. (Prices go up when lower rates are expected and down when higher rates seem to be on the horizon.) Investors don't like fixed-income securities because they know so little about them, and because of their price movements. Prices of safer securities just aren't supposed to fluctuate; it's not fair! Actually, if you invest in the right types of fixed-income securities, interest rate movement in either direction will be your friend. If you or your financial advisor have no tradable income securities in your portfolio, you are letting an outstanding long-term growth opportunity pass you by.

The Magic of Municipal Bonds

There is magic in your municipal bond portfolio. Many people of means fail to recognize the usefulness of a well diversified, income-producing fixed-income portfolio. Once you have one, never let it go. Here's a real life example. When I was building my house in South Carolina and then my office a few years later, I needed to raise a significant sum of money to buy the property and get the infrastructure started. Financing possibilities were endless; partial portfolio liquidation, was, of course, the last possible choice. The cost of the money had to be minimized.

If we can borrow money for less than what we make with our assets, and if it is a short term-proposition, why not? This concept, by the way, which people use regularly in determining the economic viability of, for example, a rental property, is known as leveraging the assets, and it's used as well by most closed end fund managers. The problem with using equities for leverage is simply the fact that you cannot be sure of your income level. Using your bonds as collateral for a short-term margin loan to avoid liquidating an important asset can provide extremely cheap financing.

My municipal bonds were producing nearly 7 percent, or $42,000 tax-free per year. My margin rate was about 8 percent at the time. Are your gears starting to whirr? It gets better. The interest paid is deductible from my taxable portfolio income, making my actual cost of money a (theoretically) negative number, with an actual negative cash flow of only 1 percent. One more thing, the loan is self-liquidating because the monthly cash flow is greater than the monthly interest charges. You are never too young to develop a municipal bond portfolio. Fire anyone who advises you to liquidate it. One other point you need to know about this particular financing method: you must own the municipal bonds first. The IRS frowns on borrowing to purchase a tax-exempt cash flow, and deducting the interest on the loan.

Trading fixed-income securities profitably is a bonus. If you are managing your asset allocation properly, you will be purchasing fixed-income securities periodically at whatever prevailing interest rates happen to be. This is a real-life example of compounding, regardless of the interest rate received. In a falling-interest-rate environment, you will discover that some of your preferred stocks or closed-end income funds have moved up in price to the point where a considerable profit can be realized (10 percent, or a year's interest in advance). If you can find a reinvestment opportunity with a comparable current yield, take the profit and increase your cash flow. Once again, there's no such thing as a bad profit.

Asset Allocation Revisited: Equity Securities

The purpose of equity securities (which include common stocks, closed-end stock funds, and equity mutual funds) is to produce capital gains income. Any other income (the dividends) is simply gravy and is the direct result of a firm belief that dividend-paying securities are

safer than those that pay nothing and a conservative portfolio management rule that insists upon cash flow from every security owned.

In order to pay regular quarterly dividends, several important
fundamentals must be solidly in place. First of all there must be
sufficient cash flow to pay out the money. Secondly, the firm must be
operating profitably in order to support the payments for any length
of time. Both are signs of strength and stability in a company, and
add to the inherent safety of the stock.

On a personal level, if you ever start your own business, you'll know
that a certain amount of financial strength and steady cash flow is needed before you even think of paying yourself a salary. (It was six or seven
years before I felt comfortable doing so in my little start-up business.)

Now doesn't this simple little explanation point to something else?
Is it anything short of crazy to bet on unknown new companies? And
what about those growth companies and their plowing-back-earnings-
into-the-company rhetoric? What they really are doing is plowing back
earnings into executive salaries (check the public records) while their
debt continues to rise. It pays to stick with companies that boast sound
fundamentals, and paying a regular dividend is one of them.

Here's a research project for you. Check out the executive salaries of any of the growth companies you own that say they are operating profitably but don't pay dividends. Aren't you an owner that
deserves some spending money too?

The equity portion of the portfolio can be as high as 100 percent
for the young person just starting out. But as the size of the portfolio
and/or the age of the investor increases, the proportion at risk must
be reduced. No matter how solid the equities, they are still more risky
than high-quality fixed income securities. There were many investors, particularly in the hot NASDAQ stock market of the late '90s,
who felt that their growing portfolio market values allowed them the
luxury of undertaking greater risks. On the contrary, it is the wise investor who understands that real wealth has been secured when you
no longer have to put serious dollars at risk.

Diversification Level 1: The Size of Individual Positions
A perfectly diversified portfolio will have no more than 5 percent
of its assets in any one individual security, either fixed income
or equity. This determination is based upon the amount actually

invested in the security, not the current market value. (This is one tenet of the working capital model, explained in chapter 7.) The 5-percent figure is certainly just a guideline, but it is of vital importance to never let the amount invested in any one security get out of line. Disasters must be avoided, and this is the easiest way to keep the risk associated with any one investment under control. The operative question should be an easy one to answer: if the market value of this security goes to zero, will the level of portfolio pain be acceptable? Yes or no!

This could be the most difficult aspect of diversification strategy to manage because of the outside influences that heap pressure upon the investor. More often than not, the buying decision was the result either of some brainstorm concocted by a hungry financial advisor or a media story that has pushed the person's greed button. To manage money successfully you must be disciplined, and you must develop a good filtering system. If you can't just say no, you at least have to limit the size of the yes.

Some investment theorists would say that a controlled percentage allocation to speculation is acceptable. My contention is that speculation is as addictive as nicotine or heroin, and must be stopped cold turkey even before it begins. The worst thing that can happen is for the speculator to get lucky and make money. I've seen the speculative portion of a portfolio grow and grow until it takes over the program. I've seen clients finance their addiction by liquidating the income-producing assets they had taken years to accumulate. I've seen the implosion of one bubble after another...

Recognize speculation as a cancer in your investment portfolio and you will magnify your chances for a successful experience. Any idea that sounds like a sure thing or that is predicated upon knowledge of the future is a speculation.

Where did the "5 percent in speculation is OK" idea come from anyway? Just who is selling these speculations? Wall Street and its cronies have got to push these high-risk ventures somehow, so they try to make you believe that some speculation is OK. It's a lot like the junk-bond scenario described earlier. If I go to the racetrack and place equal bets on all the horses, I'm going to have some winners, but will I make any money? Get the idea? The possibility of loss exists to a certain extent in all securities. Don't add to the problem by overindulging. Here's a thought: instead of allowing class action suits for catastrophic losses like Enron (which actually was rated investment grade by S&P), why not direct the lawsuit against the financial advisors and accountants who failed to advise their clients against holding disproportionate positions in the stock? Now that would create smarter investors and less self-serving professionals.

Any time you are tempted to bet the farm on a hot tip, remember Whoops, IBM at $40 per share, W. T. Grant at $0.00, or First Jersey Securities. [For those unfamiliar with these names or prices, they are classic stories of: (1) a AAA municipal bond failure; (2) the saga of IBM going from an A+ to a B rating (it's now back to an A); (3) a bankruptcy in a major retailer; (4) a big discount securities firm that succeeded for years selling fraudulent story stocks to unsuspecting speculators.]

The late '70s-early '80s Whoops fiasco is perhaps the best example of the lot. These AAA (the highest possible quality rating) Washington Public Power Supply System bonds were brought public by several major wire houses and were instantly gobbled up by investors. The eventual default had something to do with gross mismanagement of a nuclear power plant development project. However, my point is that some slick attorneys were able to get the company off the hook for the interest and most of the principal. Neither the bank trustees, nor the Wall Street institutions were able to save the investors from major losses. It never really seemed like they tried very hard either. Basic contract law was tossed out the window. Politics? No one is talking. Investors eventually received just pennies on the dollar; the lawyers did better.

One of my relatives had just received a significant insurance settlement from a near-fatal accident around the time of the Whoops offering. His unsuspecting and inexperienced-investor father placed the entire sum in the bonds. Ouch! But that's not as disturbing as the fact that some supposedly experienced financial professional allowed (even encouraged) him to do so. Now there was a justifiable lawsuit that never happened.

Diversification Level 2: Industry Representation

I've pointed out before that the market is a "groupie" kind of place, in the sense that one group or another is always falling from grace for whatever contrived reason Wall Street comes up with. Rarely will you hear the big guys identify a flight from the financials, drug stocks, or the tech sector simply as profit taking by investors who are switching to under-priced bargains somewhere else. When The Street pans one sector or group, they normally will find a reason to play up another. Coincidentally, they'll have plenty of the new favorites in their trading accounts. Once you have implemented your trading strategy, you will appreciate the help. You will already have taken your profits in some previous hot group, and should have plenty of smart cash available for investment in the new pariah. (Smart cash balances result when dividends, interest, and capital gains come in faster than new investment opportunities arise.)

Wall Street never encourages the purchase of stocks that are going down in value. Ninety percent of Wall Street analysts' recommendations are buys. They only want you to buy stocks that are strong because they will probably go up forever and you'll feel stupid if you don't own them. This chain-letter mentality sinks a lot of IRAs and 401k programs every year because it just doesn't work that way. Professionals take their profits and move on to other opportunities. The new opportunities are generally in the group or groups we all hated last year and into which those rich guys put their money before their puppet wire houses gave you the OK to follow suit.

Group Rotation Is a Fact of Investment Life
Sell recommendations from Wall Street gurus are scarce for at least three reasons: (a) Self-proclaimed geniuses hate to be proven wrong so they avoid telling their clients to give up on securities they've touted so strongly in the recent past. (b) On the other side of the scales, they are afraid to recommend taking profits (until after their in-house mutual fund managers do) for fear that the stock will continue to go up. Do they know human nature or what? Someone in the media could point out that they sold too soon and their reputation as a guru could suffer. (c) Major firms can't say sell or take profits because of the investment banking relationship they have with the company in question.

Instead, The Street will just lose interest for a while and inertia will move a group of stocks to lower price levels. Look for the new orphans to reach your buy target and add a few to your portfolio...slowly. Apply patience, assign a reasonable sell target, and relax. (Targeting is a management function and is discussed in chapters 4 through 6.)

The Circle of Gold

The DJIA has put together a 2.75-year hot streak by doubling in value. This is far more impressive than the rally that preceded the market break that occurred several years ago. I don't see much similarity between the economic environments that existed then and now, but investor attitudes are identical: greed, invulnerability, recklessness, and certainty.

Over the last few months we've seen periods of significant weakness and a shift of dollars into ever-more speculative investments. It's unusual to find such large numbers of quality investments (good companies down in price) at such high market levels.

This is probably a good time to remind you that paper profits do little to produce productive wealth and even less to prepare you for (the inevitable) correction. Anything that goes up in price for an extended period of time becomes vulnerable, particularly when the pace of the rise has been fast. For the mutual fund investor, the similarity to a chain letter is very real. Someone is going to be left holding a bag full of securities purchased at the highest price in the history of mankind!

It's natural to want to milk the last dollar out of a rally, but it's foolish to leave all your chips on the table indefinitely. Mutual fund results are uncorrected numbers, an illusion of brilliance that fades with each downturn. These managers cannot take profits in the face of greed, and are unable to buy bargains when the greed becomes panic. Always remember to sell too soon!

I have periodically discussed this behavior with coverage callers, and it has never been denied. Just business as usual on The Street, and what's your point? I believe the point was summed up succinctly by one of the Vanderbilts, who said that the secret of his great wealth was selling too soon. So in diversifying by industry group, try to position yourself in the next popular group. More often than not, hints will come from bad news and from lists of stocks that are moving lower.

I remember a situation a few years ago when a hotel chain owned by a number of my clients was the target of a takeover. Well the stock price shot up and I instantly made the calls to sell all and to reel in a considerable profit. A few days later, I got a call from a client who was extremely upset that I didn't wait around for the offer to be sweetened. I didn't even think about it. Had I done so and the deal had fallen though, who do you think would have called? There is no room for hindsight in management situations, and there is no such thing as a bad profit. Interestingly, stocks of similar companies rose as well and profits, smaller of course, could be taken on all of them.

In constructing your portfolio, 15 percent or so should be the high end for representation in any one industry—not as much for fear of total loss, but for a lessening of your ability to take advantage of opportunities elsewhere. One really never knows which groups will move in which direction, or when such movements will occur.

Diversification Level 3: By Country
Investing overseas demands a level of knowledge that is beyond the expertise of most investors, private and professional. Investment textbooks single out this type of investing as particularly speculative. Still, Wall Street provides whatever the addicts want to snort; in fact, they create the demand. Someone should produce a documentary to tell the story of the development of foreign country mutual funds. Packaged products from a thousand different vendors appeared almost overnight, just so you could feel like you've done your duty and properly covered this slice of your financial advisor's multi-colored pie-chart diversification plan.

Here are a few clues:

1. An asset-allocation formula needs only two percentage figures (income and equity).
2. An asset-allocation formula that includes a target for cash is the confused creation of someone who thinks he can predict the future or who is waiting for his boss to tell him what to think.
3. An asset-allocation formula with multiple cap classifications, precious metals, or decimal point percentage breakdowns is the work of a sick mind. The same goes for diversification: try to keep your decision making as simple as possible.

There is an easier and more fruitful way to invest in the global economy with considerably less risk. The vast majority of investment-grade companies are international players with proven track records of success in foreign markets. Additionally, the very best foreign companies trade their ADRs (American Depository Receipts) on our own hometown stock exchanges. Don't make this more difficult then it needs to be. Boutique funds for foreign investing won't find a home in most sophisticated portfolios. When global investing first became popular in the form of mutual funds, there was a frequently aired TV commercial where a mutual fund big shot is poking around the streets of Hong Kong or Manila. "This proves, Mr. Investor, that we know how to find the very best overseas investment opportunities." Now there's one to test your GQ (Gullibility Quotient).

Here's a true or false Wall Street quiz: the following mutual funds could be sold to the public, legally, and successfully as worthy foreign investments.

1. The South American Political Stability Fund.
2. The Arctic Refrigeration Industrial Reclamation Fund.
3. The Middle East Peace and Security Fund.
4. The Tiger Woods Absolutely Anything Anywhere Fund.

Flip back to Table 2 earlier in this chapter. How many of these companies do not have a worldwide presence? We all need to accept the fact that our Congressional leaders continue to ignore: we exist in a global economy and may actually be losing our leadership position in global markets. But our multi-national companies are out there anyway. Few investment-grade companies are likely to be unaware of these realities.

Additionally, if you must invest in foreign companies, apply the same quality tests that you would to domestic companies. Stick with the best and you'll rarely lose money. Try Phillips, Royal Dutch, Sony, Unilever, and others of similar stature. (No don't drop everything and call your broker...you're not ready yet and these are not current stock tips.) Overseas investing is not a new idea; it's just the hype and the ETFs that are new. My very first profit more than thirty years ago was on a foreign company. Since I first sold my Royal Dutch, I've probably traded it fifty additional times.

The Case for Income
Maybe it's the tax code or perhaps just a misconception people have about investing, but I've always gotten a chuckle out of seriously well employed people who direct me to "just invest for growth, I don't need any more income." This is a widely held misconception. Income is

good. It pays the bills, particularly at retirement time. Never discount the importance of cash flow, especially if you can arrange for the bulk of it to be tax-free! What's better, tax-free or tax-deferred? BOTH.

Pretend you are a corporate executive, making and spending a large salary while you accumulate expensive toys and enjoy the good life. You have millions of dollars in company stock that you are reluctant to sell and much more in stock options that you don't want to exercise until the company splits a few more times. BANG! Suddenly, your company's buggy whip is replaced with the new and improved Pentium 12 buggy whip perfected by your competition. Surprise! Now how does the million in municipals you shunned last month sound? That $60,000 in tax-free income would certainly pay a few bills while you find a new employer. QDI strikes again!

My father was big into real estate. He didn't trust the stock market and hated the thought of anyone else earning a commission from him. He said that he had no use for things that fluctuated wildly in market value. Actually, he was more of a trader than he would ever admit. It was not uncommon for him to sell a house or a property before he even owned it, and cry about the taxes all the way to his accountant's office.

You can behave similarly in the stock market with a transaction called a short sale. You are guessing that the price of a stock will fall so you effectively borrow the shares from the brokerage firm as they sell it from their inventory. You cannot collect interest on the proceeds of the sale, so the cash sits idle in your account, and any dividends that are declared by the company belong to the brokerage firm. You then buy the stock back after the price falls to cover your short position. This is an extremely speculative and dangerous strategy that must be avoided, no matter what you think you know. It could be where the expression, "lose your shorts" comes from, or is that your shirt?

Many rallies are temporarily magnified toward their end as speculators rush in to cover their short positions and to cut their losses. I don't think I've every heard any one report that a rally has been started as a result of profitable short covering.

So in bad real estate markets, brought about by recession, high interest rates, whatever, Dad would feel broke. I never cared for developing real estate. There are just too many rules and regulations, an illiquid market, not to mention having to deal with the petty dictators who live on local planning boards, etc. Still, over the years, I have grown to appreciate the usefulness and profitability of well-positioned real estate, as a portion of a person's fixed income investment portfolio. Here's another area where a seasoned professional is worth every dollar you pay him or her in fees or commission. Find someone you can trust, check references, and apply the same rules as you now do in your equity selections.

Once our family was out for a fancy dinner, and Dad thought that we should all pass up those wonderful lobster and crabmeat cocktails because they were so expensive. Real estate wasn't selling, and cash flow wasn't nearly at normal levels. Corporations, on the other hand, weren't stopping, or even cutting, their quarterly dividend payments. Municipalities didn't default on their bond interest payments, and there were still trading opportunities in the equity markets. I was happy to pay for the fancy appetizers.

The lesson is simple. I can buy a lot more meals with my municipal bond interest and trading profits than I can with a vacant rental property, or with a thousand acres of raw land. I can pay for more vacations with interest, dividends, and capital gains than I can with a portfolio full of securities that don't produce income or that are subject to a buy and hold mentality. I also can't buy more growth stocks without cash flow from somewhere else. Just what is a growth stock anyway? It must be one of those stocks that only go up in price, because its numbers go up every quarter and will forever.

Liquidity

Note that the liquidity of an investment is a factor in determining its inherent quality. A portfolio comprised solely of even the highest quality real estate is as poorly diversified as the junk bond portfolio mentioned earlier. Liquidity is definitely a factor that must be considered when developing the fixed income side of the portfolio. Don't load up on securities with a thin (non-liquid) market. But, at the same time, you should be purchasing fixed-income securities with an I-may-never-sell-this-investment mindset.

In other words, find securities that can be sold easily and not at a big discount. Stay away from odd lots of even the best individual bonds and recognize that there are more efficient ways to invest in real estate than owning land and buildings. Even though you may never sell that closed-end municipal bond fund, you want to be able to in an emergency.

Real Estate Investing:
No Lawyers, No Debt, No Plungers

Real estate investing is not nearly as complicated or time consuming as you might think. In fact, it is easy to add raw land, shopping centers, apartment complexes, and private homes to your portfolio without brokers, bankers, attorneys, and a rolodex full of maintenance professionals' phone numbers. Even better, you can blend your real estate investments into your security portfolio for ease of management, income monitoring, diversification analysis, etc.

All of the basic types of real estate investing are available through closed-end funds (CEFs) and real estate investment trusts (REITs), and both can be purchased in the same manner as any common stock. And for me, this has always been their single most attractive feature. You can own a piece of the action without the big commitment of time and resources. You can take advantage of changes in the real estate market cycle in precisely the same manner as you can deal with the volatility and fluctuations in the stock and fixed income markets.

Real estate CEFs and REITs are safer investments than outright purchases of shopping centers and apartment complexes. They are also somewhat less risky than owning the common stock of individual real estate companies. The size of the numbers may be less exciting, but the net income and capital gains potential are comparable and the turnover rate much more impressive. Both methods of participation in the Real Estate market should be considered as you add to your investment portfolio… but to which asset allocation bucket? I've always included REITs and real estate CEFs in the fixed income bucket while the common stock of a plain vanilla real estate company would properly fit within the equity portion. You must establish a reasonable profit-taking target on any investment. Real estate is no exception.

On the income side of the portfolio, make sure you look at a lot of REITs and even more CEFs of various kinds to get a feel for the levels of income they produce. REITs must pay out a certain percentage of their earnings, but CEFs may not have the same restriction. Either can be leveraged, which simply means that management may choose to borrow some of the money they invest. Leverage is not a four-letter word when used properly, and (in my opinion) it is more likely to help your results than it is to hurt them. It's always good practice to stay within the normal income range, assuming that there is either a risk or a management reason for the highest and lowest yields, respectively. Be careful not to create a poorly diversified income portfolio. Bonds, preferred stocks, and mortgages deserve your attention as well and should be represented. Monthly income is available and more attractive than any other.

The major distinction between the two types of investing needs some re-emphasis. When purchasing stock in any company, your main objective should be to sell the stock for a reasonable profit as quickly as possible. You will then select some other stock and repeat the process. It is likely that you will return to the same companies over and over again. Any dividend income is gravy. When purchasing a REIT or a real estate CEF, you are depending on the managers of these entities to generate income and capital gains and to pass it on to you every month. You have the capability either of selling the REIT or CEF shares when they rise to an acceptable profit level (more gravy), or of buying more shares to increase your income level. The distinctions (benefits?) of this form of real estate investing vs. ownership of the properties themselves should be clear as well. No attorneys, no debt, no maintenance, no problem.

Income Must Increase Annually

Not only must a portfolio generate income, it is important that a conscious effort be made to increase the base income level each year. Base income is the sum of dividends and interest only, exclusive of capital gains, because you cannot actually plan on any particular level of capital gains. This is certainly a conservative way of planning your cash flow, but it seriously reduces your risk level in a very important area.

The easy way to increase annual income is through an asset allocation formula that has a fixed-income element of at least 30 percent, which is applied in investment decision making. The formula itself need never be changed and the base income will still increase, absolutely.

Make sure you understand the math. Here goes: a $100,000 portfolio produces $7,000 of base income in 2006. None of the income is spent, and it is all reinvested in fixed-income securities at a 5-percent interest rate. Our base income would increase to approximately $7,350. Right? ($100,000 x .07) + ($7,000 x .05) = $7,000 + $350.

The classical portfolio objective is to have enough base income at retirement to preclude the need to invade principal. You just can't do it with a Microsoft home run and nothing else, and you don't want to wait too long to get started.

Risk Management

An awful lot of wisdom has been packed into the education phase of this book. Your appreciation of how Wall Street functions; your understanding of how easily the media is manipulated to suit the long-range plans and objectives of the institutions; and some familiarity with what makes a commissioned financial advisor tick are all elements of risk management. An insistence on quality, strict adherence to the fundamental rules of diversification, and a constant pursuit of increased annual income are the fundamental tools you should use to protect yourself, not only from the bad guys, but also from yourself. Humans are very much alike; they can resist anything except temptation. Wall Street owns about the sweetest smelling candy store on the planet—temptation is the cornerstone of their business plan.

It's important to understand that investing is in no way an intellectual pursuit in which research, information, and business degrees are more important than common sense, greed control, discipline, and experience. Every investment involves some element of risk, and you would be well advised to stay far away from any person or institution that even suggests to you that they have solved that problem. You just can't eliminate risk. Forget about it! But you absolutely must manage it.

This section has provided much of the investment insight that you need to preserve the wealth you accumulate. You would do well to review the preceding sections periodically as a wake-up call for your portfolio. Here are the key words and concepts: trading, fixed and variable costs, quality, diversification, income, and liquidity. If you're confused, nobody is looking, go back and read it again. Look at your portfolio structure frequently to make sure it is positioned in accordance with the plan.

Break Time: Financial Professionals and You

It's nearly as important to distinguish between financial services professionals as it is to understand the motivations lurking beneath the recommendations they make and the advice that they give. Most of us will need the assistance of some form of financial pro at some time in our investment life. We'll look at a few of these very superficially, just so you will know to whom I am referring throughout the remainder of the book. You'll find that several categories of professionals are missing: accountants, doctors, attorneys, bankers, and media commentators among them. They are professionals who are certainly worthy of your respect for their professional opinions, but the vast majority of them are absolutely not qualified as financial professionals no matter how wealthy or influential they happen to be. Even a license to sell securities is not qualification, in and of itself.

I have a great deal of respect for the honest financial professionals I have been fortunate enough to work with over the years but, unhappily, I have found that most are less than interested in what is best for you. It's easy to test your professional with money. Tell your life insurance agent that you want a million-dollar policy and see if he tries to talk you out of it. Tell your stockbroker to sell all your municipal bonds and buy a foreign aggressive growth fund. I'm sure you get the picture; what was that oldest profession again?

Every brokerage firm has some euphemistic title that they use to describe their retail stockbrokers. Many stockbrokers are also given a vice president title to further impress you and gain your trust. When I use these terms, I am referring to the person you speak with when you are placing orders to buy or to sell securities. If you are not speaking to someone, you emphasis is on the wrong syl-la-ble.

These are also the people who cold call you at dinnertime to sell specific stocks, funds, or other investment products. Some of these people can, and often do, fall into other categories since they are encouraged to learn as much as possible. Learning is geared toward passing specific tests that (you guessed it) qualify them to sell additional products.

Stockbroker types often try to achieve additional status by becoming either a chartered or certified financial planner; most are required to become RIAs. Anyone, even a plumber can call himself or herself a financial planner or an investment advisor. Qualified financial planners and registered investment advisors will have a designation such as CFP and RIA after their name that sets them apart from the unqualified variety. They have education.

Most financial planners are also registered investment advisors, which merely means that they have passed some securities examinations, and that they have registered with the Securities and Exchange Commission. If they haven't gone to the trouble to obtain the education, I would question their ability to fully understand their own experience, since that has to be their primary claim to fame. Your first search should be for a financial planner or investment advisor with the official designations.

That group can then be divided into three sub-groups. First there are those that simply plan and advise, and for a fee only. They make generic recommendations that you can implement on your own with whomever you like. If you ask them to point you to a salesperson, and they do, remind them that they are legally bound to disclose any financial arrangement that they have with that person. It would be unethical, and illegal in some circumstances, for any of these professionals, not to disclose such a financial arrangement. It's best if you don't ask for names.

One of my clients introduced me to her accountant. He had been impressed with my handling of her accounts and wanted to recommend me to some of his other clients. How much of my fee would I be able to share with him as a referral fee, he asked? Investment management fees are much smaller than mutual fund commissions, I explained, and, I could legally make such an arrangement only if I disclosed it to the SEC and if he disclosed it to the client. This was fine until I told him that I had to have a disclosure document signed by his client in my files and that my client files were subject to SEC audit. The arrangement never happened, and the client was eventually moved into load mutual funds.

Other financial planner-investment advisor types will primarily be product salespersons. They want to sell you whatever benefits them most from among the many products they have in their bag that will absolutely satisfy your goals. Unlike the stockbroker group, these people always sell life insurance and annuities. In fact, no self respecting life insurance salesman would ever refer to his profession as anything but financial planning. It has a very respectful and confidence-building ring to it, doesn't it?

Finally, there are planners and advisors who are fee based if you want them to be, or commission only if that's what you would prefer. These guys and gals want it both ways, and should be avoided at all costs. There is no need for you to deal with a person who is having such an identity crisis.

Note that all of the professionals listed above (stockbrokers and financial planners) think of themselves as investment managers and will try to convince you that they are literally managing large sums of money for their clients. They aren't. They sell investment management services that are provided by others.

Investment Managers, Money Managers, Asset Managers, and Fund Managers

One word separates these professionals from all of the others. Manage! They run the investment program in a manner that they hope will achieve certain identifiable objectives and goals. Even a mutual fund prospectus talks the talk as though a certain directional strategy will be adhered to. Managers make all of the decisions with regard to securities selection, buying and selling, and so on. They may or may not be involved in planning the program itself with the client, but they absolutely run it! For some reason that is unintelligible to me—packaged money management is much more popular with investors than individualized management. Somehow people think it's safer to trust people they've never met than to meet with people to determine if they should be trusted.

Personal investment management is facilitated by a legal document called either a trading authorization or a limited power of attorney, either of which allow the brokerage firm to take the Manager's directions with regard to a specific investment portfolio. It is very specific and very protective of the owner of the securities. A mutual fund manager is tacitly given exactly the same powers, but with none of the protection.

Mutual fund managers have one other serious and often fatal problem: when the going gets tough, they get fired. That's right ladies and gentlemen, and it's the mutual fund shareholders that do the firing. Deep Pockets will tell you all about it:

> *Being in the right place at the right time often provides some of life's greatest opportunities. Agree? We all know stories where someone got the "buy of a lifetime" on a boat, plane, house, or whatever. Sometimes, just by chance, life gives us a shot at making the really big deal at a cheap price. We often pass these opportunities up because of ignorance, fear, or lack of money.*
>
> *The most frustrating reason to forego great opportunity is lack of money. In the case of ignorance you don't feel bad because you have*

no idea that you are missing out on anything. Fear makes one more comfortable to pass up the big deal. Lack of money haunts you for a lifetime as the only-if scenario plays over and over again in your head.

Peter Lynch, manager of the famed Magellan Fund, expressed that frustration after the crash in October 1987. On one of those research trips on the other side of the Atlantic, he got the news on the faltering markets. Oh yes, it was the end of the world back then also. Life as we knew it at the time was over and we were on our way to economic disaster with no way out. The lemmings were very busy selling all of their stocks at any price, running as fast as they could from the Capitalism monster. It was the biggest one-day drop in terms of points and I believe also in percentage. The party was over as the selling pressure was so great that even the specialists on the NYSE panicked. We were close to a meltdown.

Old Peter wasn't fooled. He was a seasoned professional who saw the glass as half full, soon to be refilled. What did he see in all of the chaos? Opportunity. What did he do? Buy up all the bargains? Wrong. Knowing that the stocks of the greatest companies, in the greatest economy the world had ever seen, were at fire-sale prices, what did he do? Sell! Sell! Sell! But why?

Because the lemmings were giving orders to exit the market. As redemptions come in, even the brightest fund managers were forced to sell stock. But what about buying all that cheap stock at once-in-a-lifetime prices? Managers have to wait for the lemmings to reverse course and buy when the prices are high. Why? Because that's what the lemmings think is best.

The fund managers can't buy low...lack of money. I read somewhere that Mr. Lynch said it was one of the most frustrating times of his life. Not the crash, but the inability to take advantage of the opportunity. When the going gets tough...the manager gets fired.

All these professionals are required to pass securities tests similar to those required of the other financial professionals. But, those who are running their own investment management businesses must achieve a higher grade to become a registered principal. What don't they do? They don't sell products, or anything else, other than their own skills and experience. How are they compensated? They get a fee based on the market value of the assets they manage. Obviously, their incentive is to make the value increase. Any commissions or similar compensation they receive for directing investments to particular places or products would be considered an illegal conflict of interest. Also, there are specific rules that prohibit performance- or profit-based incentives for smaller investment clients.

Most professional money managers are employed by the major Wall Street institutions because they can't survive the early years of building this type of business from scratch without commissions. A million dollars under management generates less than $10,000 in gross annual income for the manager. Selling a million dollars worth of annuities and mutual funds would produce between $40,000 and $60,000 in commissions. Does that help explain why your accountant obtained a securities license?

Additionally, major firms will pay big salary bucks to recruit fund managers, experienced or not, while the independent manager route will take years to develop a meaningful cash flow. The big firms also pay big advertising bucks to promote the management business, making for a competitive environment that most independents can't survive.

Another reason many investors choose in-house or wrap account managers is because they are affiliated with institutional entities. These investors want to have someone with serious money to sue if something goes wrong! It's a sad statement, but a true one.

Very few people can afford to become independent managers and even fewer are able to survive. Those that do survive, sacrifice more and more of their independence as they grow, and most do want to grow as much as possible. Competition in this field has become so fierce that most managers have had to become fund managers. Many allow themselves to be used as wrap account managers; most eventually become pawns or employees of the Institutions. Pity.

The bigger and more important they get, the less accessible they become. If you can't meet with the person who is managing your portfolio, or at least get references from other clients for whom he manages similar accounts, you should be looking elsewhere. Learn how to be underwhelmed by the hype of institutional advertising. Commercial minutes at major sports events cost millions, and many of those minutes are purchased by financial institutions solely to tell you about their no-commission, personal money management services.

Would you spend billions promoting a service that you expect to lose money on? I don't think so! Find yourself a totally independent investment manager, with no affiliations or dependencies on any other entity or professional! Talk to the real live person who will be making the decisions in your account, look her in the eye, and shake her hand. Get references and check them out. Formulate a plan and monitor the transactions. There are only two "don'ts." Don't be impatient and don't compare your performance with indices and averages that have absolutely no correlation with the structure of your portfolio.

I'd Like to Test the Program

Mutual funds have minimal requirements for starting an account, and that's perfectly fine because every unit or share that is purchased theoretically represents a fraction of the fund's assets. Thus, you will experience the same performance with a $2,000 test investment, as you will with a $2,000,000 commitment.

But, you can't do that with a real investment manager because of the rules we've already discussed. You have to give the manager enough of a commitment so that he or she can put your program into operation effectively. A mutual fund manager really doesn't care. They have no idea what your plan is, and they do only one thing that is supposed to satisfy a million owners.

A personal manager, though, has to set up a portfolio with a definite asset allocation and make appropriate selections of companies that you will actually own. You will see what he is doing immediately. With a mutual fund, what you don't see is what you get. There is absolutely no way you can determine what you own at any point in time. If something is done that is improper for whatever reason, or not in line with what you would expect, you'll just never know.

With a personal manager, the more of your program you allow him to control and to supervise, the better job he will be able to do to meet your goals and expectations. And, of course, you'll be able to talk to him about what he's doing for you, if you happen to have a question. There's always been a difference between fine dining and fast food. You may get less indigestion with a private investment manager, even if he is you.

Chapter 3
Waltzing around Wall Street

I f you accept the premise that Wall Street institutions are a financial superpower that can take over our investment lives and manipulate us invisibly and effortlessly, read on and learn how to harness that incredible power for your own advantage. Yes, you can become and remain wealthy investing on Wall Street, but only if you control the process using the institutions and the media as your own private investment counterresource. We've begun your know-thy-enemy training, the process continues below. If you disagree, turn off the TV or your computer monitor, stop kidding yourself, and re-read the introductory portion of the book.

Management of anything involves: planning how to achieve stated goals and objectives; organizing the work and the workers; controlling to see that things are done according to defined procedures; and directing resources in a goal-oriented manner. Mastering these four management principles, and combining them with the QDI investment principles will go a long way to getting you where you want to be. We've talked about developing an investment plan as a basic first step in the process of organizing your investment program. Although the investment plan can be part of a broader financial plan, it need not be developed at the same time, nor by the same people. In fact, since most financial planners have no handson investment experience, it is likely that their only investment ideas will involve investment products. As important as an overall financial plan may be, a well thought out investment plan can operate just fine without one. For our purposes here, we'll use the investment plan that I've been using to manage investment programs for more than three decades.

Wall Street Would Be Boring Without Corrections

Every now and then the stock market retrenches for a while as the experts in the media and on Wall Street try to sort out political, economic, social, and atmospheric events. Hey, it's their job to make you think that they can predict the financial future and that takes time. Monthly portfolio market values begin to erode, as does consumer confidence, and the familiar fear products become popular because of the uncertainty of the shock market. When will they learn? Corrections are quite simply the flip sides of rallies—every bit as necessary and even more attractive than their more popular alter egos. Try to take comfort in the fact that there has never been a correction that has not succumbed to another rally, however short in amplitude or duration.

The quality of the securities you own has not and should not change just because share price has declined. Similarly, falling fixed income security prices have no qualitative significance. All things being equal, your income will either remain the same or increase. Your working capital value is growing every day, regardless of what your portfolio market value is doing. Corrections provide investors with the opportunity to add equity inventory less expensively and to increase their overall yield from fixed income securities by purchasing additional shares at lower prices.

As you move further and further from the ancient buy and hold or the modern (and even more ridiculous) core portfolio concepts, and as you appreciate the fact that open-ended mutual funds and index funds are really not managed entities, you will begin to realize that both corrections and rallies are beautiful things. Both are often too short lived in investment time, but each requires your close attention and appropriate action. Embrace each of them with enthusiasm and you will succeed. If you feel that you have taken profits too soon during a rally, or that you have gotten yourself totally reinvested while the markets are still falling...you are doing it properly. Why? Because market turning points are only visible in rear-view mirrors. Sprinkle on a little patience, and everything will turn out just fine.

You must learn to buy profitable, dividend-paying companies when prices decline 20 percent or more from their highs and to add to your existing holdings to produce a lower cost-per-share. You must learn to establish reasonable selling targets for profit taking without worrying about stuff like commissions or taxes. After all, how many times have your unrealized gains become realized losses? You need to be willing to take even smaller profits when buying opportunities are abundant.

You cannot do anything about changes in market value in either direction, and selling high quality securities at a loss is almost never acceptable or necessary. The market is just too big and the hysteria generated by slight changes in expectations just too pervasive, producing changes that are more emotional than economic. This is the known world of investing, and it can be dealt with sanely by purchasing only within the investment-grade category. Never let fear cloud your judgment and jump on the opportunities created by those who do. Sure it's easier to fantasize that your market value will rise every month and, frankly, it sure is more fun to take profits. But if you don't buy during the corrections, the thrill of profit taking will escape you. So relax and enjoy the opportunity to buy less expensively just as enthusiastically as you will enjoy new profit-taking opportunities when it is their turn to regain the media limelight.

Anytime now, the Wall Street media will alert you to the obvious: the rally is coming! The rally is coming! You'll see the normal charts, figures, rationales, and estimations, all designed to make you feel safe again and to encourage you to run out there and buy the stock market, particularly those issues and funds that have surged ahead faster than their not-quite-as-wonderful competitors. Please step back and think a minute. The only thing that has changed is the price of the shares they want you to buy—they've gone higher.

You could be thinking that there really is a fourth basic principle of investing, just from the emphasis it has been given above. You're absolutely correct. I consider profit taking an integral part of the investment process, but it is an operational principle as opposed to a design principle. Sure it's as important as the big three, but you're not going to have much use for it if you don't fully implement the others.

If someone were to approach you with an offer to give you twice the value of your Benz, or three times what you paid recently for your living room furniture, what would you do? Hold out for more or take the money and run? Only in the securities markets do most people take the wrong course of action most of the time. Conversely, what if you could buy that Mercedes at half price? Now there's a no-brainer. Right? So why does the whole mindset change when we talk in terms of Daimler Chrysler common stock

Dealing with Market Rallies: 10 Do's & Don'ts

This is a list of ten things to do and think about right now to protect yourself more than you did last time.

1. Your present asset allocation should have been tuned in to your goals and objectives. Resist the urge to increase your equity allocation because you expect a rise in stock prices. That would be an attempt to time the market, which is, rather obviously, impossible.
2. Take a look at the past. There has never been a rally that has not succumbed to the next correction, so set reasonable profit-taking targets and pull the trigger.
3. After taking a profit, don't look back and get yourself agitated. There's no such thing as a bad profit and no place for hindsight in an investment program.
4. Take a look at the future. Nope, you can't tell when the correction will come or how long it will last. If you are taking profits during the rally, you will be able to love the correction just as much.
5. As the rally continues, sell more quickly as opposed to less quickly, and establish new positions slowly and incompletely. Hope for a short and steep decline, but prepare for a longer one.
6. Understand and embrace the "smart cash" concept, an integral part of the investor's creed.
7. Since your portfolio is at, or very close to, an all-time high-value level, examine your holdings to cull the weakest position now, while it will be least painful. Examine both fundamentals and price, giving significantly more weight to the former. Don't force the issue.
8. Identify new positions using a consistent set of rules, rally, or correction. That way you will always know which of the two you are dealing with in spite of what the Wall Street propaganda mill spits out.
9. Examine your portfolio's performance with your asset allocation and investment objectives clearly in focus; in terms of market and interest rate cycles as opposed to calendar quarters and years; and only with the use of the working capital model, because it tunes in to your personal asset allocation.
10. Remember that there is no single index number to use for comparison purposes with a properly designed value portfolio.

at a 30-percent discount to its highest price of the last fifty-two weeks? In general, the markets (both equity and fixed income) have always provided us with two basic scenarios. A successful investment strategy will deal with them as the normal sequence of market events.

Developing A Selection Universe

Knowing what to expect from something is always better than being clueless, but it's equally important to know that many things are just not knowable. Don't confuse the self-fulfilling prophesies of market gurus with an ability to predict the future. Having valid expectations is about as good as it gets on Wall Street, and we should be able to live with that. So with plan in hand, and a few strategic filters in place, let's get into the process of filling up those asset allocation buckets with s_c_r_t__s.

Universe is about as all-inclusive a word as we really need to deal with, isn't it? Its use here, in a counter-Wall Street culture training guide about the process of investing, is interesting because the infinite size, scope, and mystery of the universe is not unlike the infinite potential, confusion, and mystery of investing. Perhaps the most important bit of learning the investor can acquire is an appreciation of just how vast the possibilities are. And, the investment universe is growing every day.

What to do first is one consideration. How to go about gathering an understanding of the variables that affect each of the different types of securities, commodities, options, indices, funds, new issues, and other investment products is another. Is it even possible to understand all this stuff? The secret to becoming unconfused is to operate only within defined limits. For example, if you are looking for investment-grade stocks that pay a dividend of any size for your equity bucket, and tax-free municipal bonds for your income bucket, you can eliminate a whole lot of product that just doesn't fit. The less you intend to speculate the less confusion there will be in your investment future. My experience has been that no speculation at all is necessary for success out there.

And then there's the problem of who to listen to. There are bulls, bears, stockbrokers, financial planners, discount brokers, radio and TV personalities, miscellaneous celebrities, co-workers, government officials, shoe-shine boys, cousins, online brokers, sports personalities, Bloomberg, CNBC, accountants, attorneys, and of course, spouses. No two of these bastions of learning and expertise will agree regularly on any particular subject and most have an agenda that does not include you anyway! They all have one or two things in common: selling products, analyzing the past, or predicting the future. And their investment experience is a question mark. The products will change periodically, the analysis and predictions daily.

Independent investment professionals, on the other hand, are few in number, particularly if you emphasize the independent. They recognize that investing is a long-term process, and they don't make their living making predictions. It is not suggested that you need to become one, a professional, that is. It is strongly recommended, however, that you learn how to distinguish an investor from a salesperson, and to ask the right questions of either.

There's another problem with the information and/or advice that you receive from the usual sources, and that is its inconsistency. The same people will advise one thing today and then a totally different approach will be recommended next week. Before you begin to act on something spread through the normal Wall Street media channels, find a spokesperson that seems to be heading in the same direction consistently. This sounds logical, I know, but you're not going to be able to do it. Consistency doesn't promote transactions, and The Street's objective is to keep that money moving. You'll have to keep your filters active and only take actions that are in line with your stated objectives. Good luck. I've found that Wall Street institutions are a lot like politicians. They try to satisfy everyone by changing either the story or the emphasis depending on the audience. Neither cares about you as an individual. Tax cut and tax relief. Insured tax-exempt bonds and foreign government non-guaranteed notes. You want it, they've got it.

Our Mutual Funds are "Best in Class"

Finally, what do we really have to read to understand what's going on as we try to fill up our portfolio with securities? The list of research and news services is endless. There are nearly as many experts as there are mutual funds. Incidentally, have you ever noticed that every mutual fund is the best performer in its class, whatever that means? If not, they just make up a new class.

Most investment managers, either independently or through their mutual fund companies, submit performance statistics to rating services. A standard form is completed where the managers indicate the types of products they are reporting on, performance figures for various quarterly and annual periods, and other general questions that give a picture of their management style. All of the above are submitted in standard mutual fund jargon.

Early in my career, I submitted data to one of the major reporting entities for all of my clients on a working capital, annual figures only basis. The portfolio asset allocation at the time was 65-percent equity and 35-percent fixed income. Wow, was I impressed with myself when I learned I was third in the country in my class (diversified managers with ten years or more of statistics and a proven track record—one of the things I didn't realize at the time was how few managers there actually were with ten years of experience). I immediately ran out and purchased several thousand dollars worth of glossies to distribute at seminars and trade shows and sent them to every lead, relative, and financial professional I could think of.

The following year was weak in the quality sector of the market and trading wasn't as productive as usual. Working capital growth fell to about 12 percent and my rating moved down. It was then that I noticed that one firm's results were based on their top five portfolios and another's was based on portfolios over $1,000,000. But, there was another, bigger, surprise. I was number two in foreign equity investing!

Time out. I traded a few ADRs, but that's hardly foreign investing. Picture a light bulb clicking on. These guys are selling printing services. No matter who you are, what you do, or how you do it, they make sure that you are good at something. Free services don't pay the bills, they've got to sell those glossies. I don't submit data to these services any longer, but Wall Street firms love them to death.

My college statistics professor said it best: there are liars, there are damn liars, and there are statisticians. Yes, you can add politicians, and Wall Street research analysts, but you get the point. Talk to the clients. Get live references, as you would for a babysitter. This baby is your money.

What we really need is a manuscript written by a millionaire who has made the millions investing—not selling, predicting, writing, reporting, representing, or calculating. Just doing it. Every day. Up markets, down markets. Rallies, corrections. All those truly unfathomable, unpredictable things that comprise the enterprise we refer to so nonchalantly as investing.

How many Wall Street experts, fund managers, brokers, and the like have been into investing for more than ten years? What does it tell you when you realize that there are literally more mutual funds out there than there are stocks listed on the New York Stock Exchange? There are also more mutual funds than there are money managers with five years of investment management experience. Interesting...beware of glossies.

Applying the KISS Principle

A basic principal of life applies equally well to the investment world: the future is totally and completely unknown and unpredictable. I've always gotten a kick out of the incredible amount of useless information that is circulated. Why should I care that certain months are historically good or bad in the market? Technical analysts are often interviewed and frequently tell us when a rally or correction will begin, and why. Now if you could tell me with absolute certainty what's going to happen tomorrow or even next week, and to which particular stocks, I'd be interested.

Once you separate yourself from this preoccupation with predicting; once you start to appreciate that the information you really want, but can't get, would only get you thrown in jail anyway; once you appreciate the absolute fact that you can make money and preserve your wealth in the market; then and only then will you be able to adopt this millionaire's proven method of investing in the stock market. I use the KISS Principle extensively as I try to avoid most of the investment land mines that have been buried in my brain by our friendly institutional Streetwalkers.

It's important to note that the stock market is the world's largest breeding ground for hindsight, even larger than sports news desks. Most users of investment hindsight are addicts, a product of the human need for certainty that has been cultivated mercilessly by Wall Street. But more important by far is the fact that hindsight is useless and counterproductive. Shoulda, woulda, and coulda must be stricken from your investment vocabulary. Any manager of anything real

TABLE 3: A sample stock worksheet

S&P RATING	SHARES HELD	TICKER SYMBOL	DEC 2000	MAY 2001	JUNE 2001	JULY 2001	CURRENT + OR -	DOWN %	CURRENT YIELD
A+	700	AFL	36.09	32.43	31.49	29.58	-.49	22%	0.7%
A+	2700	ADP	33.61	53.74	49.70	50.95	-4.01	33%	0.9%
A+	2300	AVY	54.88	58.48	51.05	51.26	-.18		
A	1600	BK	55.18	54.61	48.00	44.86	.27	24%	1.6%
A	600	BSC	50.68	54.35	58.97	58.15	2.45		
A-	3100	BLS	40.94	41.23	40.27	40.70	-.08	20%	1.9%
A	2200	BMY	73.93	54.24	52.30	59.14	-1.34	23%	1.9%
A+	2000	CSL	42.93	39.30	34.87	36.14	.09	22%	2.3%
A	1900	CLX	35.51	34.64	33.85	37.68	-1.28	23%	2.3%
B+	3400	CA	19.51	28.36	36.00	34.48	1.51		
B+	3000	DIS	28.94	31.62	28.89	26.35	.25	40%	0.8%
A+	900	HD	45.69	49.29	47.24	50.37	-1.25		
A-	1300	ICN	30.69	30.23	31.72	30.75	2.72	20%	0.9%
A-	2300	KMB	70.69	60.45	55.90	60.81	.29		
A-	1100	MEL	49.18	45.82	44.81	38.02	1.28	24%	2.4%
A+	2700	PFE	46.00	42.89	40.05	41.22	-.48		

Developing an effective stock worksheet will help you implement the investment principles that will help you make solid investment decisions.

will tell you that decision making is always done under conditions of uncertainty, no matter how accurate they believe their information to be. It's similar to risk. It's out there. Get used to it. More importantly, learn to manage it!

Developing A Stock Worksheet
The first step in organizing your attack on Wall Street is the development of an effective stock worksheet. Get some good software, a fast computer, and set up a spreadsheet that will help you implement the investment principles that you are going to use as your decision-making model. Your spreadsheet should look something like the one above, and please don't concern yourself with the actual symbols, prices and ratings in the table. The important thing is that this format has not changed in many years (I actually used to do it by hand).

Column 1 should contain the S&P rating of the stocks contained in the stock selection universe. Quality is the most important investment principle, and this placement assures that it will always be the first thing considered. This should also be a reminder to obtain the current month's S&P Stock Guide. Ratings change regularly and you need to know about the direction of these changes. Some stocks will need to be removed from the selection universe and others may occasionally beg to be added.

As a trader, you will become a bigger-than-usual brokerage client. Your broker may still be happy to give you the latest copy of the stock guide, but it's just as likely these days that he won't be familiar with it.

When a rating changes to below investment grade (you should know what that is), only remove the issue if you don't own any. If it's in a profit position, sell it; if not, wait for an opportune exit point. Because I manage multiple securities portfolios, I only keep track of securities that I actually own. If you are in the same boat, you'll need a separate inventory report to keep track of your holdings, which should have different purchase prices and dates.

Equity CEFs may or may not be included in the stock worksheet, depending on your time constraints and personal circumstances. It is unlikely that they will trade as frequently as individual issues.

Column 2 is where you record the number of shares owned of each stock currently in your portfolios. Those that are owned must be looked at every day to see if they've attained either their target selling price or their buy-more price. Notice that there is no place for a stop-loss price. Similarly, there is no need to make any purchase lot or ownership distinctions on this worksheet. Those stocks that are being watched closely each day, but are not yet owned, may also be listed. But in honor of the KISS principle, limit the number of stocks on your list. My list for hundreds of portfolios rarely exceeds 110 issues, and during extensive rallies will fall to as few as seventy or so. I can usually go though it and make all buy and sell decision plans in less than two hours, and I try to do this in the evening, right after the market closes.

Let's observe a moment of silence for the stop loss order, an artificial tool developed by Wall Street brokerage firms to increase trading activity. There is no need for this device in a portfolio of high quality securities. We know that prices of stocks we are buying may go down, since we are buying them when they are in a

down-trend, and we do not pretend that we know where or when
the down-trend will end. Wall Street technicians will try to dazzle
you with talk of support levels and so forth. This simply defines
a price point where more shares would be sold at a loss than at a
profit. Since professionals are in this for the profits, the likelihood
of continued weakness is said to diminish. New support levels form
all the time. Understand? You can confidently buy more of, or average down on a stock that has fallen in price since you originally
purchased it, if you haven't maxed-out your allocation percentage too quickly and if your confidence in the fundamentals of the
company remains intact. Has the S&P rating changed? Has the
dividend been cut? Is the company making money? All of this important information is at your fingertips on the Internet, or in your
broker's database. But, you must avoid bringing the total invested
in any security above 5 percent.

Column 3 contains an alphabetical listing of the stocks that
you have chosen to include in your selection universe. This is
where the fun begins because now you actually have to identify
companies that fit those very exacting selection criteria. It's really
much easier than you think, unless you do it the old-fashioned,
newspaper listing, way. There are hundreds of stocks that meet
the selection criteria as to quality, profitability, and payment of
dividends. Table 4 lists the symbols of 105 of the companies that
met my criteria back in 1999. Again, it's imperative that you follow the rating changes that are included in the S&P guide each
month! Note that many of the listed companies from 1999 were
no longer listed in my selection universe just two years later, for
many different reasons. Many that would be listed today will be
gone next year, so you would be foolish to skip this important,
educational, and creative step by just copying the list of symbols
in Table 4.

Columns 4 through 7 will contain month-end closing prices,
starting with the last December 31st closing price. I use this figure
as a point of reference for informational purposes, nothing else. The
next three show closing prices for the three most recent months (i.e.,
May through July 2001 in Table 3).

If it is impossible to get your hands on a newspaper, use the
Internet, the next issue of the S&P guide, or some other reliable

source. Don't discount the importance of accuracy in this data. It's the stuff from which decisions are made, but not for the reasons you might think.

This is another test of your "brainwashed level." Do you think that these three months of price data are used for trend analysis or to trigger some kind of buy signal? Be honest now, this is like golf. Recording a better score than you really achieved is only kidding yourself and will eventually cost you money. Actually, neither answer is correct, but the data is used in the decision-making process and is covered in more detail later.

Column 8 is the current month column and will be used to show this month's price in positive or negative terms compared with last month's closing price. This column gets updated every day and is probably the most important decision-making column on the spreadsheet. As you update this column each morning or evening, you will create your buy list for the day and determine which of your current holdings, if any, are in profit-taking range. Regularly updating this column will also help you appreciate your sixth grade math teacher...finally, a chance to work with decimals.

Column 9 reflects the relationship between today's stock price and the twelve-month high for each of the stocks you are watching. Any stock that is 20 percent or more below its twelve-month high, for example, is considered a candidate for new buying. But there are other criteria to be considered, such as diversification and the price relationship with previous month-end closing figures.

Additionally, a stock that is down more than 20 percent, or ten or more points, from your original cost-basis per share is considered a candidate for additional buying, or averaging down. You will find that the averaging down decision is one of the most difficult you will have to make, ever.

This process, which reduces the average cost of your holdings, allows you to escape from a weak holding far sooner than would be the case if you just held on and waited. For example, if my original purchase of General Electric was at $47 per share, down 22 percent from its twelve-month high of $60.50, I would consider buying more GE below $38. If I succeed, I can then sell the entire position for a 10-percent profit at around $47, as opposed to $52. Buy more decisions should be avoided on B+ companies and those

TABLE 4: A changing selection universe

1999	2001	1999	2001	1999	2001	1999	2001	1999	2001
AFL	AFL	T	T	ABT		APD		ABS	ABS
ALD		ALL	ALL	AHP		ADM	ADM	ADP	ADP
AVY	AVY	AVT	AVT	AVP		ONE		BCR	
BSC	BSC	BLS	BLS	BMY	BMY	CWP	CWP	CPB	CPB
CCL	CCL	CBC		CTL	CTL	CB		C	
CC	CC	CLE	CLE	CLX	CLX	KO	KO	CL	
CAG	CAG	CA	CA	CDD		DH		DIS	DIS
DG		DLJ		DOV	DOV	DJ		DD	DD
EMR		EFX		BEN		FTU	FTU	GPU	GPU
GCI		GPS	GPS	GE	GE	G	G	GSK	GSK
GWW		HDI		HRS		HNZ	HNZ	HSY	
HRZ		HWP	HWP	HB		HOE		HD	HD
ITW		IFF		JNJ		JCI		K	K
KEY	KEY	KMB	KMB	KRI		LEH		LNR	
LTD	LTD	LOW		LU	LU	KRB		MRD	MRD
MCD	MCD	MDT	MDT	MRK	MRK	MOT	MOT	MYL	
NSC		NUE		PWJ		PEP		PFE	PFE
PNU		MO		ROK	ROK	ROH	ROH	RD	
SLE	SLE	SGP	SGP	SLB		SCH	SCH	VO	
SHW	SHW	SBH		LUV	LUV	TNB	TNB	TR	TR
UST		UL		VFC		WMT	WMT	WLA	

The selection universe changed nearly 50 percent in just two years for reasons that included: profit taking, mergers and acquisitions, downgrading by S&P. Of the fifty-one stocks that were no longer listed, twenty-five were still looked at regularly for new buying (bull pen residents) and thirteen were taken over by other companies.

that you have not had at least one profitable experience with previously. In all cases, double check the fundamentals of the company before proceeding.

Column 10. The final column of the spreadsheet is for the dividend yield of any stock that is being considered for purchase. The importance of the dividend information is absolutely not the dividend yield in and of itself. Rather, it is the fact that the company pays a dividend that is a symbol of the fundamental strength of the company.

When interest rates rise or are expected to rise, utility stocks often become great trading vehicles, although the time between the buy and the sell will certainly be longer than normal. Don't hesitate to add these boring stocks to your portfolio. They pay great income while you wait for interest rates to move back down.

TABLE 5: Companies joining the selection universe

AXP	ASO	BUD	BDG	BK	CTS	CAJ	CSL	DCX	DCN
DDS	DNY	EK	AGE	AJG	GT	HLT	ICN	IPG	JPM
LM	LZ	MAY	MCK	MEL	MER	NWS	NOK	NT	PHG
P	PBI	PCP	STR	RJF	RTN	REY	ROP	RCL	SBC
SFA	SNA	SON	SNE	TIF	USB	VOD	WAG	WCS	WFC

By 2001, these fifty companies had replaced those that had left the selection universe for various reasons.

You may want to consider categorizing them as income securities rather than as equities, but only if trading statistics are the only numbers that push your pleasure button. It is unlikely that you will be able to achieve your normal trading objectives with these stocks, and they won't help your statistics at all. Quality and diversification rules absolutely apply!

Today's list would be significantly different from either of these presented here, but the point should be clear. Investment opportunities are constantly changing, even in a very specialized, well defined, conservative, value-orientated, selection universe. That's enough excitement for me.

No, this listing doesn't include every stock that fits the criteria because it would require much too much time to review every possible issue every day. And yes, it includes only New York Stock Exchange companies. One of my personal rules is NYSE only; it need not be one of yours, but it suits the KISS principle well. The list includes many companies that have been excellent trading vehicles in recent years and a few excellent companies that haven't been tradable at all recently.

There is no good reason to list every possible candidate on your worksheet. Only those that you own, and those that are getting close to the initial buy target, need to be listed. Periodically, you should scan a newspaper with a complete stock listing to search for new prospects, and, much as I hate to admit it, there is really no reason to exclude good quality companies that are traded on other exchanges, so long as you are able to keep things simple and manageable. But they must meet all of the selection criteria. Liking a stock just because it hits you as a good idea or because the story on The Street is fascinating will bring your investment program to DEFCOM I. It's called discipline—without it there is no program.

By the time we reach the third fairway, any person who knows my profession will invariably ask me a stock market question. The brainwashing is a virus. It's everywhere! This is one installment:

> "Hey Steve, Do you like Intel here? Do you think we're at the bottom of this downturn?"

> "Are you buying or selling Intel, John? You're retired aren't you? Should you own it at all? Why do you think there has been a downturn? Did you know that advancing issues have exceeded decliners over the past eighteen months, and that new twelve-month highs have exceeded new twelve-month lows by a huge margin for more than a year? Haven't your fixed-income securities risen in market value?"

> "But they say it's been a terrible year—don't you listen to CNBC? Just yesterday they were predicting..."
> "I watch the tape on CNBC occasionally, John. But I avoid listening to the commentary like I try to avoid the flu...what did you have on number 2?"

Time Management

Organize your schedule so that all of your routine daily investment decisions are made and ready for implementation before the stock market opens at 9:30 a.m. EST. This allows for the calm and quiet that most people find better for decision making. If you're only looking at a few portfolios (personal, pension, IRAs, and your mom's), only an hour or two is needed. You will find that sell and buy-more decisions are more time consuming than buy decisions. Lately, I've found that I save a lot of precious morning time if I deal with those two decision types in the evening, after the market closes at 4:00 p.m. EST. There are many places on the Internet where accurate closing price information can be found.

Record your planned decisions separately for each portfolio on a daily order log that separates buys from sells, indicates approximately how much cash is available in each portfolio, and distinguishes between cash which is allocated to stocks and that which will be invested solely for income.

The order log worksheet should be completed in pencil, because it will be changed to reflect the actual prices of orders submitted. You should plan on checking in with your market contact from two to four times a day to see if any of your planned decisions will be changed into actual orders and to determine if any of your actual orders have been executed. You must be committed to spend the time necessary to do this properly. Opportunities will be missed. This is inevitable. But the number missed is reduced in direct proportion to the attention you bring to the exercise!

One of the standard buzz words used by Wall Street firms that are trying to steal your business is the promise of best executions. Just what kind of silliness is this? Don't believe any of it. You are the master of your own executions simply with the way you place your orders, which we will cover in the next chapter. But the idea of best executions is a story you may enjoy shaking your head about. Regulators are hammering investment advisors about best executions to such an extent that their position would force all investment managers to trade through discount brokers, even those whose client agreements specifically state that they do not attempt to obtain best execution. Do the major institutions mind? Not at all—the rules don't apply where the commission and the management fee are combined into one lump...at the present rate, we will regulate ourselves into economic chaos.

The order log can easily be used to control for the receipt of brokerage house confirmation notices, paper or electronic, which you should check for accuracy. It will be helpful to you at tax preparation time if you have recorded all of your transactions in a computer program designed to deal with securities transactions. The program I use provides a Schedule D-like form that probably could be used directly in a tax return but can't because...that's right, regulations. But you're not regulated, and you can provide your CPA with all the info he or she needs to file with the push of the right button.

If you have the proper software, all of the required tax information will be there. If your accountant asks to see the confirmation notices, either to check them out, or to get more detail than that which is provided on the brokerage firm year-end summary report, he or she is: (a) padding your bill unnecessarily, or (b) trying to find a way to suggest that something else would be a better investment.

If your discount or online broker doesn't give you this information for free, you're stuck. In life, what you get cheaply is usually worth it.

Stability vs. Volatility

The brilliance of trading is using market volatility for your personal advantage. You are looking for those stocks that are constantly making fairly significant gyrations so that you can buy them when they are low and sell them when they are higher. Trading is the process of implementing this most trite of all investment sayings. The more often we can do this, the more money we make. Being cliché is not a bad thing.

Volatility has become more a function of media reports and spin than it is a function of the fundamentals of companies and economies. This is precisely what creates the opportunity for profit. So long as Wall Street and the media continue to pay too many people too much money to pretend that they know the impact of hundreds of different variables on one simple weighted average of thirty not-nearly-as-wonderful-as-you-might-think companies, these truths will exist. Appreciating this, and avoiding the temptation to take any action based on Wall Street's self-serving interpretation of events, can help you become a successful investor. For example:

Most forms of market analysis and reporting are two to three steps ahead of themselves. The predicted end result depends upon a chain of uncertain events. Caveats are always expressed in a please-ignore-me manner, or not expressed at all. This is standard operating procedure. The same analyst will often express a totally different opinion within days of his original statement.

The market always overreacts to news, good or bad, global or individual. Always. This is one thing you actually can rely upon with some degree of certainty.

Defining Low and Higher

We have to define low and higher to establish our trading rules. We also have to come up with some standard for measuring volatility. We can do all of this rather simply, and you should be starting

TABLE 6: Nine months of trading

BOUGHT	SOLD	#	SYM-BOL	COST	REC'D	SHORT TERM	LONG TERM	MONEY STREAM	# OF TRADES
12/21/98	1/4/99	100	BDX	3,863	4,338	475		1	
10/28/97	1/5/99	100	MOT	5,864	6,119		255	2	
12/14/98	1/11/99	100	C	4,850	5,800	950		3	
10/28/97	1/11/99	100	MOT	5,864	6,725		861	4	
8/26/98	1/15/99	100	DIS	3,256	3,731	475		5	
1/12/99	1/27/99	100	EFX	3,348	3,881	443		2	2
5/21/98	2/2/99	100	HWP	6,612	7,225	613		6	
5/27/98	2/6/99	200	UPC	9,425	10,338	913		7	
6/24/98	2/9/99	100	ROK	4,319	4,575	256		8	
1/4/99	2/11/99	200	BFI	5,675	6,225	550		1	2
12/23/98	2/19/99	100	CDD	3,550	3,875	325		9	
1/31/99	2/22/99	100	UHC	4,150	4,700	550		2	3
3/1/99	3/10/99	200	BBC	5,012	5,713	701		2	4
12/7/98	3/17/99	100	RD	4,519	5,018	499		10	
3/11/99	3/19/99	100	JEF	3,712	4,756	1,044		2	5
8/6/98	3/19/99	100	PNC	5,262	5,906	644		11	
8/7/98	3/22/99	100	[GWW]	4,325	4,625	300		12	
3/25/99	4/9/99	100	LEH	5,775	6,350	575		2	6
4/7/99	4/13/99	100	EMR	5,200	5,725	525		5	2
2/9/99	4/19/99	100	BWA	4,575	5,100	525		3	2
7/8/98	4/19/99	100	NUE	4,594	5,568	974		13	
11/27/98	4/20/99	100	DCN	4,113	4,663	550		14	
3/13/98	4/20/99	100	DS	4,000	4,538		538	15	
3/24/99	4/20/99	100	PPG	5,075	5,850	775		4	2
12/1/98	4/22/99	200	AME	4,100	4,563	463		16	
2/16/99	4/22/99	200	BEN	6,550	7,550	1,000		1	3
6/16/98	4/22/99	100	HAL	4,231	4,488	257		17	
10/16/97	4/26/99	300	SHI	5,148	5,175		27	18	
10/28/97	4/30/99	300	TUP	6,736	6,993		257	19	
2/25/99	5/7/99	200	[RAL]	5,575	6,118	613			
5/18/98	5/11/99	300	ELY	5,181	4,519	-662		20	
1/22/99	5/12/99	100	CB	5,994	6,962	968			
3/26/99	5/17/99	100	HNZ	4,819	5,362	543			
5/14/99	5/28/99	200	PEP	6,875	7,675	800		1	4
4/1/99	5/28/99	200	TRW	9,050	9,962	912			
2/22/99	5/28/99	200	UST	5,538	6,113	575			
1/22/99	6/1/99	100	KO	6,325	6,887	562			
4/2/98	6/1/99	200	SNT	7,075	7,100		25	21	

TABLE 6: Nine months of trading (Continued)

BOUGHT	SOLD	#	SYM-BOL	COST	REC'D	SHORT TERM	LONG TERM	MONEY STREAM	# OF TRADES
5/19/99	6/7/99	300	PLL	5,250	6,038	788		2	7
5/24/99	6/8/99	100	GLW	5,369	5,500	131		3	3
5/17/99	6/11/99	200	[LBY]	6,025	6,575	550		4	3
5/18/99	6/15/99	100	GPS	6,106	6,538	432		5	3
6/11/99	6/25/99	200	[RAL]	5,350	5,863	513		2	8
6/7/99	7/8/99	100	BSC	4,056	4,756	700		1	5
5/21/99	7/8/99	100	SGP	4,656	5,344	688			
5/27/99	7/12/99	100	CAH	6,250	6,944	694			
6/29/99	7/23/00	300	FSS	6,037	6,693	656		2	9
6/25/99	7/23/99	100	G	4,188	4,706	518		3	4
6/30/99	7/29/99	200	[LBY]	5,700	6,350	650		4	4
7/13/99	7/30/99	300	SUT	7,500	8,850	1,350		1	6
1/14/99	8/2/99	100	DF	4,044	4,313	269			
8/12/99	8/30/99	100	CA	4,500	5,275	775		1	7
7/23/99	9/2/99	200	PFE	7,150	7,825	675		2	10
6/26/98	9/13/99	100	TNB	4,888	5,100		212	22	
8/16/99	9/20/99	100	[GWW]	4,500	4,900	400		3	5
9/10/99	9/27/99	200	CC	7,400	8,275	875		1	8

This analysis of money streams shows how a series of small profits can build large annual returns.

to realize now that you don't need to be a rocket scientist to make money trading stocks. You also do not need fancy or expensive computer programs, schools, trading floor simulators, newsletters, momentum analyzers, or witch doctors! Managerial skills are much more important than finance degrees, technical data, and research reports.

Low is a price that is at least 20 percent below the high point achieved by an issue during the past twelve months. Higher is a selling price at which we will realize a 10 percent net/net profit, where net/net means after all variable expenses. Why variable only? Because fixed expenses cannot be allocated easily to individual security holdings, and the KISS principle rules. Remember that, as traders, we hope to realize such 10-percent gains several times per year on many different stocks. At times when the vast majority of stocks are 20 percent or more below their twelve-month high, a higher number than 20 percent may be appropriate. But absolutely never buy at a price that is less than 20 percent below the benchmark figure.

TABLE 7: Trades from money stream 1

BOUGHT	SOLD	#	SYMBOL	COST	REC'D	SHORT TERM	LONG TERM	MONEY STREAM	# OF TRADES
12/21/98	1/4/99	100	BDX	3,863	4,338	475		1	
1/4/99	2/11/99	200	BFI	5,675	6,225	550		1	2
2/16/99	4/22/99	200	BEN	6,550	7,550	1,000		1	3
5/14/99	5/28/99	200	PEP	6,875	7,675	800		1	4
6/7/99	7/8/99	100	BSC	4,056	4,756	700		1	5
7/13/99	7/30/99	300	SUT	7,500	8,850	1,350		1	6
8/12/99	8/30/99	100	CA	4,500	5,275	775		1	7
9/10/99	9/27/99	200	CC	7,400	8,275	875		1	8

Power trading in low-risk securities: eight trades in nine months with an average net/net gain of 14 percent and an average holding period of just over one month.

I know this sounds a bit boring and out of line with the type of gains that some individual issues will certainly make if held for longer periods. But if you apply these decision parameters to nearly every equity success story, you will find that more money would have been made trading the issue than just holding it. (Go ahead, review some charts.) Another issue is involved here: hindsight, the great Wall Street greed and guilt producer. Don't use it or allow it to influence your decision-making process in any way. Second guessing your disciplined trading, decision model will bring your program to DEFCOM II.

Identify if you can ten stocks, traded anywhere, that will increase 100 percent in the next two years with absolute certainty. You can't, of course. On the other hand, it's pretty easy to come up with a list of fifty or sixty stocks that you can trade over and over again for reasonable gains during the same time frame. Trading is not a one-decision enterprise. It is a process of finding a potential short-term gain opportunity, capitalizing on it, and then finding another and doing it all over again. Actually, when you become an experienced trader, or a professional, you could have more than one hundred trades in process at any given time. Get it?

Money Streams

Table 6 shows the actual trading activity in a managed portfolio during most of 1999. I don't usually recommend the hindsightful type of analysis that money streams report upon, but this illustration is useful to exhibit the raw power of a fresh trading concept. It would be foolish and pointless to try to do this type of analysis in the course of managing a portfolio. Follow the theoretical money trails and the power of this strategy becomes abundantly clear. Here's how it works: take a marker and highlight the trades with a number 1 in the money stream column. Highlight money stream 2 in another color and number 3 in another color, etc. The total number of trades in each money stream is indicated in the last column. Money stream 1 includes eight trades, which are presented for analysis in Table 7.

Assume that money stream 1 started on January 1, 1999, with one hundred shares of Becton Dickinson (BDX) and some spare cash. Get a feel for the cash flow from trading. The first trade took fourteen days and produced a 12.3-percent gain. Proceeds plus some cash reinvested in two hundred Browning Ferris (BFI) and sold five weeks later for a 9.7-percent gain. Trade 3, Franklin Resources (BEN) took nine weeks and produced 15.3 percent. Similarly, Pepsi, Bear Sterns, a stock with Symbol SUT, Computer Associates, and Circuit City were purchased and sold before the end of September.

Nine trades in nine months with an average net/net (after commissions) gain of 14.1 percent, or an annualized rate of 18.7 percent, without considering dividends and interest received. The average at risk throughout the period was $5,800 and a total trading profit of $6,525 was realized. BDX, BEN, PEP, and BSC remain in my selection universe today.

Similar analysis of the other money streams would show equally impressive results, but more importantly, look at the quality of the companies traded and the diversification of the portfolio. This is low risk and high yield without investing in anything other than investment-grade securities.

Combining all twenty-two money streams produced: total net/net gains of approximately $31,500; an average gain of 10.5 percent; an average holding period of less than four months; an annualized yield on investment of roughly 25 percent. Kind of takes the boring out of quality, diversification, and income, doesn't it?

Stability Is Not Welcome Here!

We are looking for volatility, which is generally defined as frequent (two or more times per year) movement within our buy and sell parameters. Unwanted stability is identified by using a portfolio-management technique called aging. Since the objective is to trade frequently, a security that refuses to cooperate by going up 10 percent or more in a reasonable amount of time must be considered for sale, even at a below-average profit. What is a reasonable amount of time? If you can't sell a stock within twelve months, it really should be culled from your portfolio and replaced with a more cooperative issue.

A trader's portfolio is different in appearance from a buy and hold portfolio in a number of ways. The most important difference is the average age of the positions held. The objective is to move the stuff off the shelves and out of the warehouse as quickly as possible. If it isn't selling at the original markup it goes on sale at any profit. Finally, and on rare occasions, a loss may have to be taken. I generally use new all-time highs in market value to cull losers from a portfolio, but a serious amount of patience must be applied before a loss is taken. Start with stocks that have fallen below investment grade, and don't take a loss on a solid, but out-of-favor, company.

Traders crave volatility, and they learn to love major movements, particularly to the downside. The worst environment for a trader is one where prices move broadly lower very slowly. Although we want to get invested too soon, it's better for quicker trading when the market moves in big gaps. Always buy into panic selling, and use your day-limit orders wisely (see chapter 4).

Let's say you are driving down the highway when the radio program you are listening to is interrupted by an announcement of a five hundred-point decline in the DJIA. What do you do about it? Don't waste time going to Bloomberg or searching the airwaves for analysis and explanation. All you need to know is how much money you have available and where it is. Call your broker and determine the price of your favorite trading stocks, even if you just sold them days ago. If they are in range, down 20 percent from their one-year highs, throw in a day-limit order well below the bid and see what happens.

Performance, Tools, and Rules
The performance of a trader's equity portfolio must be appraised in a different manner as well, which is the subject of chapter 7.

Think about it. There could be forty or more different investment entities in operation at the same time, without even considering the Income side of the portfolio. Table 6 identified twenty-three distinct start-up points for new investment/trading entities. Very few of these would have the same starting point and, most importantly, the ending point is totally uncertain. How could it possibly be appropriate to look at such a portfolio through the same lens as we would a portfolio that held the same securities throughout the entire period? It is likely that up to half of the equities are still just works in process.

Wall Street uses models to measure market performance. Their favorite models are the Dow Jones Industrial and the S&P 500 averages. Both are just computer games that track buy and hold portfolios. Such analytical comparisons are totally misleading in evaluating the performance of actively traded mutual funds and individual securities portfolios, especially those where trading is relatively frequent—it just has to be. The content of the averages and indices being used as benchmarks may not change at all from one year to the next. Trading portfolios change up to hundreds of times in a year. Mutual funds fight back by using model portfolios themselves, and their performance numbers reflect the opportunity for manipulation.

A trading portfolio rarely compares favorably to a market index when the index is on the rise—and nearly always performs better than such an average when the index tanks. This is an observation that really has little or no relevance, but it may just "learn you" what your expectations should be. Trading portfolios need to be analyzed differently, and you have to be able to explain this to your investment buddies, or they may succeed in undermining your resolve. Remember that if you are trading, you've already proven that you are operationally smarter than they are.

In fact, any planned investment portfolio with its goals, objectives, rules, constraints, and individual personality is just not measurable by normal Wall Street standards and procedures, whether or not it's traded frequently. Blasphemy, you shout. Absolutely. By what stretch of the imagination is your portfolio anything like any average or index created by Wall Street to make you transact? Investing is an objective directed exercise and the only valid performance analysis is one that compares your personal results with your own personally stated objectives...end of story.

I hope you've seen now that, with some readily available and not so complex tools (a newspaper, an S&P guide, and a spreadsheet), we can gather and synthesize all of the data we need to create a selection universe. With an equally simple and precise set of rules, we can manage an investment portfolio quite productively and in an unusually low-risk environment. There are three distinct types of decisions to make about every holding, every day: buy, sell, and hold. The hold or do-nothing decision is actually the most common of all, and even though we go through the daily ritual of preparing a buy list and identifying stocks that are to be sold, nothing is forcing us to actually do something every day. Sometimes, even with fifty or more potential trades on my worksheets, no orders are actually submitted. In chapter 4, you will learn how to develop a buy list and to prepare to do some trading, but the trades you actually submit will depend upon how well you cope with volatility.

A Volatile Stock Market Is Your Dearest Friend

Most people never forget their first love. I'll never forget my first trading profit. But the $600 I pocketed on Royal Dutch Petroleum was not nearly as significant as the conceptual realization it signaled. I was amazed that someone would pay me that much more for my stock than the newspaper said it was worth just a few weeks earlier. What had changed? What had happened to make the stock go up, and why had it been down in the first place? Without ever needing to know the answers, I've been trading RD for more than thirty years.

Looking at scores of similarly profitable, high quality companies in this manner, you would find that:

1. most move up and down regularly (if not predictably) with an upward long-term bias, and
2. there is little, if any, similarity in the timing of the movements between the stocks themselves.

This is the volatility that most people fear and that Wall Street loves them to fear. It can be narrowly confined to certain sectors, or much broader, encompassing practically everything. The broader it becomes, the more likely it is to be categorized as either a rally or a correction. Most years will feature one or two of each. This is the natural condition of things in the stock market—Mother Nature, Inc.—if you will. Don't take her for granted when she gets high, and never ignore her when she feels low. Embrace her volatile moods, work with them in whatever direction they travel, and she will become your love as well.

Ironically, it is this natural volatility (caused by hundreds of variables: human, economic, political, natural, etc.) that is the only real certainty existent in the financial markets. And, as absurd as this may sound until you experience the reality of it all, it is this one and only certainty that makes mutual funds in general (and index funds in particular) totally unsuitable as investment vehicles for anyone within seven to ten years of retirement. There will always be rallies and corrections. In the last forty years, there have been no less than ten 20-percent-or-greater corrections followed by rallies that brought the market to significantly higher levels. The DJIA peaked at 2700 before its record 40-percent crash in 1987. But at 1700, it was still 70 percent above the 1000 barrier that it danced around for decades before... always a higher high, rarely a lower low. The '87 debacle was followed by several slightly less exciting corrections, but the case was being made for a more flexible and realistic investment strategy. Mutual funds were spawned by a buy-and-hold mentality; Mother Nature, Inc., is a much more complicated enterprise.

Call it foresight, or hindsight if you want to be argumentative, but a long-term view of the investment process eliminates the guesswork and points pretty clearly toward a trading mentality that keys on the natural volatility of hundreds of investment-grade equities. During corrections, consider these simple truths:

1. Although there are more sellers than buyers, the buyers intend to make money on their purchases.
2. So long as everything is down, don't worry so much about the price of individual holdings.
3. Fast and steep corrections are better than the slow attrition variety.
4. Always accept even half your normal profit target while buying opportunities are plentiful.
5. Don't be in a rush to fill your portfolio, but if cash dries up before it's over, you are doing it correctly.

Most of the problems with mutual funds and much of the increased opportunity in individual stock trading are functions of growing non-professional equity ownership. Everyone is in the stock market these days whether they like it or not, and when the media fans the emotions of the masses, the masses create volatility that always overreacts to market conditions. Rarely will unit owners take profits, particularly if they have to pay withdrawal penalties or taxes. Even more unusual are expert advisors who encourage investors to move into the markets when prices are falling.

A volatile market creates opportunities with every gyration, but you have to be willing to transact to reap the benefits. A necessary first step is to recognize that both up and down markets are forces of nature with abundant potential. The proper attitude toward the latter will make you much more appreciative of the former. Most investment strategies require answers to unanswerable questions, in an effort to be in the right place at the right time. Indecisiveness doesn't cut it with Mama... in or out too soon is not an issue with her. But wasting the opportunities she provides really ticks her off. Successful investment strategies require an understanding of the forces of nature and disciplined rules of portfolio management. If you can make the transition back to individual securities, you will do better at moving toward your goals, most of the time, because the opportunities are out there... all of the time.

More Inside Information

By Wall Street broker, "Deep Pockets"

What are the basics of the stock-recommendation process at most major retail firms? At the start of the month every broker's paycheck is zero. Each day, he comes in and looks at the money run of uninvested cash or money market. The next step is review of the firm's hot list—the research department's list of stocks that shine above all of their other buy recommendations. Surely everyone with cash needs one of these stocks. Calls are made to clients explaining just how perfectly the stock compliments their portfolio. Keep in mind that every other broker at the firm has been chasing the stock over the past few weeks. No regard is given to recent price movement, and the lucky client probably buys it somewhere near the high for the year.

When the client has no cash available for the purchase, an imaginative broker can come up with a dozen reasons why one of the current holdings should be sold, and a beautiful thing happens for the broker: double commissions. This is not to say that all brokers are bad or that all recommendations are based on the broker's greed, just most of them. Most firms would disagree with this scenario, but that raises some interesting questions: Why is it that 60 percent of most firms' revenue occurs during the last week of the commission month, and the largest day, invariably, is the last day of the month?

Were the good ol' days really all so good? Is tomorrow quite as bad as it seems? During the good old days of '98 and '99, the growth rates suggested for earnings and revenue were outrageous. The price targets for stocks were laughable. Everyone wanted in on the party. Some professionals resisted the temptation to join in the festivities and were punished by greedy clients who now knew everything about investing, from financial television shows and Internet chat rooms. They left to go it alone. Over the last fifty years the return on common stock has averaged eleven per cent.

The bottom line is that none of the party crowd was smart enough to go home and the fortunes made on paper turned into financial disasters. From April 2000 through June 2001, five trillion dollars was lost in the stock market. People who bought Juniper at $120 soon held it at $8. Priceline.com went from $100 to $1, and the beat went on. What were people thinking? Oh, it's happened before. The 1920s and the late 1960s lost fortunes for the masses.

How about all of those safe mutual funds? The gurus who run the trillions in Mutual Funds did no better. They were busy pumping up their funds with all the latest growth names. Drunk with power, they tried to lead the pack in performance. Complete disregard for the safety of client capital was the order of the day as they tried to squeeze the returns to higher and higher levels. When the scam unraveled, growth funds dropped in value by half, technology funds by three quarters. Many of the new Wall Street darlings just disappeared into bankruptcy. Once again a new generation of investors had been duped. Quite frankly, greed is greed and those who ran with the fast crowd got just what they deserved.

How can The Street bounce back from this embarrassment? If your broker makes recommendations for selfish reasons and the mutual fund thrill rides don't seem appropriate, what should one do? Hire someone to do it all for you, an investment manager. It's logical. With the vast amount of information that flows through the system and all of the conflicting views, why not hire someone to filter through it all and make informed decisions? Take the emotion out of what should be a business process. You're in luck. Wall Street's new scam: managed money.

There isn't a firm on The Street not trying to garner a share of this action. Charge a flat fee and do it all: asset allocation, security selection and management with no transaction costs. Put yourself and the brokerage firm on the same side of the table. Perfect. Wrong. Most registered representatives (stockbrokers) have no skills relating to money management. Then who manages it? Of course, an elite group of hand-chosen investment professionals. The firms charge up to 3 percent of the value of the client's account and basically do nothing. Let's look at this one.

Just as trying to walk in someone else's shoes that are four sizes too big would prove to be difficult, one-size-fits-all portfolio management doesn't work either. Once again Wall Street has taken a legitimate process and turned it into a scam. What is represented as individualized portfolio management is nothing more than a mutual fund. In most cases, the performance has been even worse.

How do they disguise this so that it's sellable? Clients are invited to complete applications to be accepted into managed money programs. The questions are probing, giving the impression that this is truly a personalized program. Goals and objectives are established along with risk-tolerance guidelines. An asset allocation is established and finally an investment management search picks just the right manager for you. Sounds individualized so far, right? Wrong again. The information is fed into a computer program at the broker's desk and all of that personal probing information spits out a boiler plate proposal that, in most cases, invests along only one investment style (growth, value, mid-cap, small-cap, large-cap, international, fixed income, etc.). The minimum account is $100,000 with any one manager. A typical investor tries it out with $100,000 because of the minimum requirements. The entire amount is invested in one style.

Doesn't that negate all the asset allocation work that was just done? Let's follow the process for a typical investor, Mrs. Jones. Mrs. Jones filled out the long questionnaire and received a beautiful proposal that showed an optimal asset allocation personalized to her needs and risk tolerance. The allocation suggested 50 percent fixed income and 50 percent equities, with the equity portion balanced between large-cap value and large-cap growth. Mrs. Jones has $150,000 available for investment—her only $150,000. Remember that each manager only manages one style with a minimum size of $100,000. By the book, this account is not suitable for a wrap account.

The broker reviews the situation and gives careful consideration to the client's needs and the suggested asset allocation that he has prepared for the client, and comes to the following conclusions: I need the commissions, and the manager is putting pressure on me to market our wrap programs. By dangling the impressive returns of last year's hot growth manager, he convinces Mrs. Jones to bet the entire $150,000 on one growth manager. Keep in mind that the computer generated plan suggested that only a 25-percent growth weighting was appropriate.

The forms are completed and signed by both Mrs. Jones and the broker. Her only hope is that the office manager will realize this aggressive investment style is inappropriate and it completely ignores the firm's own suggested allocation. Wrong a third time! When the broker presents the new account form to the manager, he is praised for going with the flow and marketing the wrap program. The manager is particularly happy because his salary is increased for each dollar of wrap program business produced by his office. He doesn't even look at the new account form or the allocation model. The broker is patted on the head, and the manager signs off to open the account. From here the scam becomes even larger...

Chapter 4
Buy Low

The decision to become your own investment manager is a major breakthrough in your thinking. It should not be done because you think you know something that others don't, because you've either done or intend to do your own research, or because you've purchased some fancy software that gives you special trading signals. You should not be attempting to beat the market or to reduce your investment costs. The reasons for managing your own assets are much more personal. You're doing this to achieve the financial objectives that you have identified, prioritized, and organized within your investment plan. And you're doing this because you don't want your financial progress to be in the hands of the non-professionals who control the fate of every open-ended mutual fund on the planet.

You are taking on responsibilities that the mutual fund glossies profess are being dealt with personally by their superstar investment managers—each earning millions per year to make you money. You should actually be a lot better and much faster than they are. You don't have to answer to an investment committee or buy and sell under the pressure of what one of the company's analysts has to say. You are not competing with other managers, either in-house or out-house (you're supposed to smile at that one) or with the market averages. You aren't directed what to do by the emotional decisions of shareholders. You are free to do it a better way. If you aim at your own targets you just might hit them; if you follow your rules religiously you will succeed. The only individual authorized (if not qualified) to second-guess you is your spouse.

What's in a Trade?

There are two components to every trade, with or without the analysis that inevitably follows. This chapter covers the buy portion with a mindset that is totally different from both the instant gratification mentality of the Wall Street media and the footrace with the averages mentality of the financial institutions. Be prepared for the admonitions, the blank stares, and the attitude. But rest assured, at the end of the trade, you'll be the one who is smiling—most of the time.

Developing a Buy List

Before you implement this new approach to your investment portfolio, buy yourself a reliable alarm clock. There's a lot of wisdom in the early-bird-gets-the-worm adage, particularly when planning your trading day. Getting an early start will allow you to find the nearest coffeeshop and newsstand. Better yet, make your own coffee and find yourself a financial website where you can get your mouse into all the data, statistics, and market information discussed below.

Contrary to popular belief, daily investment decisions can be made from a well constructed selection universe without forty-seven pages of listings, statistics, and drum beating. Pick a publication that you know you can get your hands on early in the day. Barron's, the Wall Street Journal, and Investors Business Daily (IBD) are excellent publications, but you just don't need that level of detail on a day-to-day basis. And why spend a buck per day when you can get the job done for 35 cents? Sure they are impressive, and I'm confident that every subscriber to IBD is now a mega-millionaire. In reality, you don't need the majority of the stuff they publish at all. If you pay too much attention to the stories, you will develop investment-decision impotence. Stick to the numbers you require and filter out all the opinion, prognostication, and hype. Sorry guys.

Have you heard the rumor about the real cause of that recent brokerage firm failure? It seems that every employee was required to keep current by reading the WSJ, Barron's, IBD, the International Herald Tribune, and the local rag. Nothing ever got done. I've seen too many people develop the dreaded analysis-paralysis dementia from spending the bulk of their time trying to interpret, categorize, and synthesize all the investment-related materials they can get their hot little laptops on. They don't wind up prepared, they become confused, mesmerized, and indecisive. The condition is curable but excessive analysis is extremely dangerous. Chronic indecisiveness limits a person's ability to identify investment opportunities. Just before financial collapse, it may cause irrational, knee-jerk like, loss-taking behavior accompanied by many symptoms of panic!

The three-step cure is a simple one, but the withdrawal period is susceptible both to self-doubt and to occasional bouts of speculative relapsia. Step 1: limit the daily intake of business news and information to thirty minutes. Step 2: cancel all business newsletter and research subscriptions. Step 3: establish reasonable, personalized goals and objectives. You know the rest.

The purpose of most analysis is to explain the past somewhat intelligently, a worthy endeavor. The purpose of Wall Street-flavored analysis is to create an image of a wisdom so profound that it can predict the future and help you pick the right time either to invest, liquidate, or to just wait and see. What you must learn to accept is that investing is not an either/or proposition. Buying, selling, and holding are daily decisions, and they get along really well together, operating as they do, in the land of ignorance. Investing is not something that one should do at a certain time; it's something that just has to be done all of the time.

Barron's, by the way, is complete overkill. It lives by snob appeal alone. All you really need is a newspaper or websites that list all of the stocks that were traded yesterday in a convenient manner of presentation. Incomplete listings are inconvenient at best, and you just have to question their reliability. Obviously, a news resource that doesn't provide all of the decision-making data you need is undesirable. As the Internet takes over as the preferred source of information, these tree killers will fuel future tar pits for sure. I haven't used a newspaper in years, except when I'm traveling or lose access for some other reason. But just for your information, the New York Times still doesn't include symbols in its quotations and the Wall Street Journal, which I used to subscribe to, has become about useless. You do need to be online; you do not need to trade online.

To be at all useful, your information source must provide all of this information for all securities:

- The fifty-two-week high and low.
- The amount of dividend paid.
- The daily sales volume.
- The daily high, low, and last trade prices.
- The amount of daily change.
- Daily market statistics

The dividend yield and the P/E ratio are also helpful.

My Streetscape software provides all of this information in real-time, plus a whole lot more. AOL Finance provides great advancing, declining, and most active issue lists. In time, you'll learn where to go for the information you need.

A Daily Ritual

Trading in the stock market is a unique enterprise because it is different every day. And every day we have to study yesterday's action in order to develop an action plan for today. There are two key thoughts here: this is a required daily exercise that must be completed before the market opens for two reasons. It relieves the pressure that comes from knowing what type of day it is on the trading floor, and, generally, you should avoid making inter-day buy decisions on stocks that you already own, but which were not on the action plan list. Secondly, it is simply that, an action plan based on the last day's results in the marketplace. We are merely creating a list of stocks that we will consider buying should the market price cooperate.

This does not mean that you have to reinvent the wheel every day. Most often, the same selection decisions will be appropriate for the portfolio in question, with a slight change in target price. There is never a huge urgency to buy.

Let's assume that we have money to invest in equities right now and that our portfolios are all properly diversified so that we don't have to make a conscious effort to avoid a certain industry or issue. We will also assume that our selection universe contains about one hundred names. Our goal is to come up with a list of between ten and fifteen buying opportunities. We select opportunities from the universe by applying a very strict set of rules. Never force the issue. There is no guarantee that as many as ten opportunities will exist, and there is also no requirement that we buy something every day. The larger the portfolio, the more likely it is that something will be going on all of the time, but there is no pressure to transact.

Buy Low

The stock market is the only place in the world where the standard sales pitch is something like this: We like this stock a lot. It has been attaining new highs nearly every day, and we expect that trend to continue. My interpretation is: If you buy this stock right now Mr. Investor, you will pay more per share than anyone in the entire world has ever paid. Additionally, you will be encouraged to buy the issue immediately before it goes any higher. Note that your financial advisor will buy you as much of it as you want, without question.

I wonder how this approach would fly with someone investing in a business, a piece of real estate, or a child's education. Ever hear this one at the mall: Attention shoppers. Prices for our most popular fashions have just been raised to their highest levels of the year—literally twice what you paid for them last season. Hurry to the ladies' department now. Certainly, there are people who feel good about themselves when they pay too much for something, but try to stay real when you're considering an investment strategy.

You should only be looking for stocks that are down in price by at least 20 percent from their highest level over the past twelve months. All this requires is a simple comparison of the last trade price with the price listed today as the fifty-two-week high. Depending on an enormous number of factors, this alone may not be enough to identify the absolute best opportunities. Frankly, there is no best way to do that, because "best" connotes a level of knowledge that we humans, and our electro-mechanical creations, are incapable of achieving. Selecting the stocks we feel have the best short-term gain potential involves a study of the month-to-month data on your worksheet, your personal experience, and good judgment.

Even if you do not listen regularly to the popular business radio stations, you have undoubtedly heard advertisements for software, systems, or training guides that will let you trade like the pros, with faster, smoother, cleaner executions. The software includes the latest and greatest information, facts, and opinions culled from all over the virtual universe so that you can trade better. Wow, I'm excited just writing about it. Don't get caught up in this. Information of any kind is out-of-date the moment you receive it. Stick with the fundamental trading rules described here and you'll make fewer mistakes. Didn't some human just like you and me program that computer? If you are serious about investing, you are not in the market for what they are selling. Remember, shortcuts lead only to speculation.

I have a friend who has purchased every conceivable gimmick possible in an effort to improve his golf game (training tapes, fancy new clubs, swing trainers, special golf balls, hypnosis, you name it). If they all worked, we'd be watching him every weekend on The Golf Channel. They haven't, and neither will myriad investment tools you can buy to improve your investment performance. Stick to the fundamentals for the best possible results.

Good judgment—that quality our teachers and parents knew we would never have any of—now has to be exercised. How do we determine which of these investment opportunities we should be looking at today? I once worked as a manager in a large life insurance company. My boss was the same one that most of you have worked for as someone's employee. This guy would constantly give me assignments and projects that were the highest priority. So I went into his office one day, after dutifully trying to organize my time among my list of projects and assignments, asking for guidance, "Which of these projects should I attack first since each will take several days and each has to be done ASAP?"

He just didn't get it or take it well when I pointed out to him that I really had no high-priority projects at all. Poor judgment strikes again. The point is this: if all or most of the stocks in the selection universe are down 20 percent or more, we need a way to distinguish the better opportunities from the other opportunities. This will happen quite often, and there are other times that you will wish that it would.

The buy list creation process is technical, but it should not become mechanical. There are stocks on my list today that meet my criteria but that I'm not interested in buying. The sell identification process is also technical, but it must become human/mechanical, as you will see in a later chapter. You must never, ever, let a known target-profit pass you by. Is there anything that you don't understand about never?

Good Buys vs. Best Buys

The next step involves selecting which of the securities on the buy list you are going to try to add to your portfolio when the market opens its eyes to the trading day. No, you don't go after all of them, thinking that this is the best time to buy them. You selectively go after two or three, or ten to fifteen, depending on two factors: the number of accounts you are managing, and the number of dollars you have to invest. For example, with several hundred portfolios and nearly $100 million being managed, I never shop for more than twenty different equity issues per day and I limit the number of orders placed for each at five under normal conditions, i.e., where there is abundant supply. The original *"Curb Your Enthusiasm."*

I have used two different methods to make the important distinction between those that meet the selection criteria and those that I'll actually put on the final buy list. As the number of stocks meeting the basic buy parameters rose above 15 percent of the selection universe, I would ratchet the parameter up 1 percent at a time until the list of opportunities falls back within the acceptable range of twenty issues. During the market meltdown/computer loop in October 1987, for example, I was buying only those stocks that had fallen 40 percent or more from their high. If you're basically a technician, or an engineer type, that approach should satisfy your need for structure, but I found it too limiting. I now use another, more KISS-like approach, that is less structured and which seems to produce superior results.

For the past several years, I've been exercising that good judgment thing by matching my success experience against the raw list of stocks down 20 percent or more. I select the opportunities that my past experience tells me offer the fastest turn around times. For example, from the partial list in Table 3, I would have (at the time) preferred to buy AFLAC (down 22 percent) before Disney (down 40 percent) or Bank of New York (down 24 percent) before Automatic Data Processing (down 31 percent). This approach worked particularly well in the mid-1998 to early-2000 crash in high quality securities that was engineered so beautifully by the wizards of Wall Street.

There are no guarantees that either approach will work. But applied consistently, they have both worked consistently. You may want to use the first approach for a cycle or two to gain some experience before switching to the second. Have no fear; your best opportunities are a lot like your children… they make their presence known when they need attention.

Bulls and Bears, Pigs, Sheep, and Sharks

You're right! That is too easy. There are two types of investment animals out there and I don't mean bulls and bears. I'm referring to the buy and holders and us, the traders.

Actually there are several other animals that you should learn to identify. Pigs and sheep come to mind instantly and there will always be schools of sharks (not attorneys) out there ready to swallow anything you have in your wallet. Pigs are investors who refuse to take profits because of their greed. It can take a while, but they always wind up slaughtered. Sheep are investors who buy whatever becomes popular on The Street. They just have to have those zero coupon Venezuela hyper inflation notes or Hong Kong 500 index fund futures, particularly if one of their buddies owns it. Shish kabob anyone?

Now who are the sharks? They are the ones who fuel the avarice of the pigs and the vanity of the sheep. You know who they are, and they know what you are. We're going to change all that.

We are walking our way through a managed trading strategy, so temper your good judgment with your knowledge of what the average trader is likely to do. He or she is going to take profits. When adopting a trading strategy, you accept all the responsibilities of membership in what really is a club for enlightened, independent investors. One of these responsibilities is to become one of those fearsome Wall Street villains, the profit takers! I know that the media has taught you to hate these people—those dirty rats, blankety-blank, rally killers. But hate them for the right reasons. They will always make money while you lament in your beer, or single-malt whatever, about what coulda or shoulda been. Yes, they made money as a result of the '87 crash and the clink that followed a few years later. While you were flushing your dot.coms down the commode in 2001, they were taking profits on the rebounding quality stocks. Come on in, this is a success club that anyone can join, even if you drive an old rambler. And with human nature what it is, we'll always be the minority that roars.

Trading is really profit taking, and these guys, the professional, big-ticket traders are probably going to set their profit goals a bit lower than the 10 percent I recommend. Their target turn-around time is likely to be a bit shorter than the average below six months that I expect you to exceed. They are trading hundreds of thousands of shares in their own commission-free trading accounts. A small dollar move can mean a serious profit.

So look at your spreadsheet carefully and eliminate from the qualifying buy candidates any stock that:

- Went up a point or more yesterday.
- Is up a point or more from last month's closing price.
- Is up two or more points from the previous month's close.
- Is up three or more points from the close three months ago.

So now you see why it is important to track those three months of closing prices… no trend analysis, no buy signal, just another risk-minimization exercise. The approach to selection and trading I'm describing here is unique, but the idea of trading large quantities for relatively small per-share gains is not. These simple rules will keep you from paying too much more often than they will cause you to miss a best buy opportunity, and there absolutely will always be another buying opportunity. Have I mentioned that successful investment management requires discipline and patience?

I know that you think that you're ready to rock 'n roll, but be patient there as well—you haven't even taken the mid-term exam yet. Here are some cautionary thoughts for right now: (1) You should be developing a list of important words, not Streetese buzz words but human emotion control words like discipline and patience, as well as management words like objective, strategy, and planning. (2) Keep in mind that this is not a get-rich-quick trading scheme or program. It is a conservative, practical approach to making more money with less risk by applying simple selection techniques to a very limited group of high-quality, dividend-paying, historically profitable, (preferably) NYSE equities.

What's in a List?
Smile if you were just about to kick back, print the buy list, log on to some discount broker, and submit a bunch of market orders. First of all, no self-respecting trader or (old money) millionaire will ever submit a market order so erase those words from your investment vocabulary forever. Secondly, the buy list is not a damn-the-torpedoes, full-speed ahead, fill-up-the-portfolio-today shopping list. It is a presentation of possible actions that we may or may not choose to implement during the trading day. Most of you are going to have a little trouble with this, depending on your brainwashing quotient, or BQ. The idea that there is

a rush to buy or sell is part of the hysteria Wall Street has programmed within you. This devil must be exorcised for success to be possible. You are the decision maker. You have set the rules and you will implement the strategy. As an aside, you will no longer listen to we-thinkisms from account executives either. Contrary to what the Street (and your accountant) wants you to believe, your investment life doesn't run from January 1 to December 31. If you choose not to pull the trigger today, there's always tomorrow. Here's how you do it:

From the buy list, you will select no more than three stocks to purchase in any one of your portfolios. The guideline is: one potential selection for every 10 percent or more of the portfolio that is not invested (i.e., in cash and/or money market). However, there's no reason to select three if the total cash is less than $100,000. But never submit more than three equity orders on any day, ever. You have to put the brakes on your enthusiasm. There are no good reasons to fill up your portfolio quickly (particularly since you know now that you do not know just how low the prices of your selections will go). Usually they will continue to go down after you have purchased them. Mr. Murphy wouldn't have it any other way and, most often, the outcome will be the same. Additionally, the less available cash you have, the more selective you have to become. Beginning to see why cash flow is so important?

One test that you will eventually, over the cycles, apply to determine how well you are doing is a cash-availability test. Stop! How well you are doing means how well you are doing compared with:

a. market averages,
b. the consensus of expert Street opinion,
c. the objectives of the trading strategy,
d. none of the above.

If you are thinking (a) or (b), you know what to do...back to "Go" again.

You should be running out of available cash while there are still a large number of stocks on your buy list. Why? Because it proves that you are not caught up in any type of market-timing fantasy. Market timers are plentiful, but I dare you to find a satisfied client who would refer you to one. Not even Wall Street, which really does sell anything and everything it can conceive of, tries to sell the market-timing story. I'm not even sure if a market-timing fund exists, but I know that it would sell, and eventually fail.

It's OK To Be Arbitrary

Why is three the magic selection maximum? This is absolutely arbitrary, but it is based on a principle that has been flowing between the lines all along. This is the principle of ignorance that will be addressed in more detail in chapter 8. In a nutshell, we don't ever want to make a decision that even appears to be made under conditions of knowledge or certainty about the future, either of the stock market, or of the individual stocks we are thinking of buying. Such knowledge does not exist, period. It may well be a great time to buy the listed stocks, but we really cannot know this. It is extremely unlikely that we will ever buy a stock at its low and we have no intention of even trying to sell them at a new high. Therefore, we will control our enthusiasm by establishing easily managed constraints (rules).

Here are more arbitrary but time-tested buying guidelines. On an order sheet or log, make a notation of the stock or stocks to be selected for each portfolio today. Yes, in pencil. Since we are only interested in buying stocks as they move down in price, the price we are willing to pay today must be below yesterday's closing price by:

- $.35 or more if the stock is trading below $20 per share.
- $.50 or more for stocks between $20 and $49 per share.
- $.75 or more for stocks ranging from $50 through $70.
- $1.00 or more for stocks above $70 per share. (Which of these portfolio sizes could support the purchase of a $70 stock: $70,000; $140,000; or $235,000?)
- Don't even think about buying a stock selling for $90 a share or more. It just has to be overpriced.
- It goes without saying that odd lots are never purchased.

The Daily Routine

About two to three times per day, check in with your broker to see if any of the planned decisions is ready for implementation. This involves an examination of the three prices that make up the trading range of the stock for the day. Isn't new information fun? Most of you are used to this: "Hi George, I want to buy one hundred shares of

Pfizer. If your broker doesn't know the symbol for a stock like Pfizer, he's either a mutual fund salesman or a speculator. Find another guy.

"Sure, Steve, just hold on a minute and I'll be able to confirm that purchase at-the-market." This sounds like great service, doesn't it? That bell you hear is sounding Portfolio DEFCOM Three; it sounds on market orders.

A market order is what Wall Street wants you to use to buy or to sell securities. It simply means that you are willing to pay whatever price the owner of the stock is willing to sell it for. Consequently, you always get what you want, but at a price over which you have no control. The same is true with a sell order at-the-market; you get whatever the next buyer is willing to pay. If it's me, you're going to get less than you might expect.

Do I hear the whirr of those gears? Of course you wouldn't transact business in this manner anywhere else.

"Hey, George, I want to buy a hot new yellow Corvette."

"Sure, Steve, just hold on a minute and I'll be able to confirm that purchase for you, at-the-market."

"OK, Steve, we got the yellow "vette" you wanted for just $225,000. It was the only one for sale today."
"Thanks, George, that was sure a great execution."

Here's the new way you will communicate with your broker:
"Hi, George, give me a quote on Pfizer, please."

"Sure, Steve, just a second. Pfizer is at $37.50, last trade. That's down $.88 for the day. The bid is $37.10 and the asked is $37.75."

"Great, get me one hundred shares at $37.40, Day. Thanks."

This is called a day-limit order, and it will save or make you thousands of dollars. It precisely specifies the maximum you are willing to pay and for how long your offer is valid. Thus you will try, and succeed most of the time, to buy the Pfizer for less than you would have paid otherwise, with one of those other orders. Your broker absolutely has all of this complete stock quote information at his fingertips. These days, you can check details yourself while you have him on the phone. Most often, market orders will go off (be executed) at the asked price, but they can execute at higher or lower prices and often will. Most often, a higher price will be paid because the security is being aggressively marketed by Wall Street and even more furiously reported upon by the media. This creates a demand far in excess of supply and results in an upward price spiral. This is why people often get abused when attempting to buy a new issue.

True or false: (a) Buying currently less popular issues using day-limit orders frequently produces executions that are below the limit price; (b) Selling currently more popular issues using day-limit orders frequently produces executions that are above the limit price. Eureka!

Heed the Voice of Experience:
Any time the market seems to be in a state of freefall, for whatever reason, throw in some limit orders well below the bid price and see what happens—only for stocks on today's buy list, of course. I've used this tactic on several occasions in the past to pick up some real bargains. You'll know when to do it; the Wall Street media will report that the sky is falling!

The bid price is what buyers like you are offering to pay for the stock. The asked price is what sellers want you to pay for their stock. Somewhere at or between these two numbers there will be a last trade figure and this is the number we are most likely to use in our d_y l_m_t buy order most frequently.

Yes, Virginia, There Is a Seller for Every Buyer
Believe it or not, there are people out there who think you can just sell something to the market. Not so. Wall Street specialists in a particular security match the buy and sell orders (electronically, of course) to create the auction market that we all misunderstand so thoroughly. The matching takes place at very specific prices and with very detailed rules of behavior that I will not attempt to explain because I have really never needed to understand them. But this is one of the reasons that you should stay away from securities that have a limited float, or number of shares outstanding, and are therefore not very actively traded (local bank shares, for example). Just like crude oil, low country hand-woven baskets, and Maine lobster, stock market prices are a function of supply and demand. Day-limit orders prevent you from being on the wrong side of the equation.

The high-quality stocks that we trade have enormous daily volume, so we can often enter orders below the bid price and be filled. A day-limit buy order can execute below the limit but never above. On the sell side, the order can execute above the limit but never below. If you place such an order and it is either entered or executed improperly, you have a right to have it busted at the broker's expense, not at yours!

As you might have guessed, brokers are trained to have you place market orders. Many sales assistants that I've dealt with in the past have entered market orders on my trades because they had never placed a limit order before. I understand that at some broker-ages, limit orders and day orders are more expensive than market orders. Make sure your broker understands that every order you submit is a day-limit order—even if you forget to say so. Send him a certified letter if you have to.

Day-limit orders are the only type of order that should be placed. The price of the order must be at or below the price we planned to pay before the market opened. There is never a reason to pay more, ever. Day orders expire automatically at the end of the trading day if they are not filled. Limit orders may only be filled at the price indicated on the order-ticket or at a better price for you—not a better price for the brokerage firm. Wall Street discourages this type of order because it requires more effort to control and because it is not an automatic com-mission. Do not let this concern you. If you cannot simply and quickly obtain all the information you require and submit your orders within a matter of seconds, find a different service or a new broker. If the broker (or the online prompt) says market, it is not a day-limit order.

Another type of order that must be avoided is the open order, an order that never expires but just hangs out in the computer until ex-ecuted. Stop-loss orders are one form of open order. Open orders do have another interesting (insidious may be a better word) wrinkle. When the price on the order is reached, it miraculously becomes a market order. In the trading methodology we are discussing here, there is no need for a stop-loss order because? (Answer provided below, with the usual penalty for a wrong answer.)

I Once Had A Client

I once had a client who insisted on using a well-known discount broker to take advantage of the lower commissions. The order entry process was complicated, cumbersome, and time consuming, even before a salesperson became involved. The annoying recorded message just kept repeating how it was all for my protection. Finally, a real person would come on the line and I would have to repeat the same account number and password information.

By the time they get done checking passwords and names, reading back numbers, and realizing that you want a complete quotation, the price on the order may no longer be realistic. Then they end their spiel with:

"Is this correct, sir?"

"Well," I respond, "I really don't know. Have those prices we spoke about earlier changed in the last few minutes?" They just don't get it, but you better.

Personal Relationships Are Worth It

Service, I've heard, can often be a more important consideration than price, especially since this particular price, the commission, is simply a variable cost of the merchandise you eventually will be selling. If you value your time more than most discount firms do, either arrange for a direct inside line, if the relationship is large enough, or move your account to a stockbroker who really does want your business. On general principles, you should never be forced to do business with a telephone menu monster. Enough said?

Sometime before the end of the trading day, the brokerage firm should let you know whether or not your order was executed. You can then update your cash position and prepare for tomorrow. If your broker, or online service doesn't provide a verbal confirmation for either result, find one that does. You need this information before you can proceed to the next day's decisions.

Now let's say that something goes wrong: you typed in XZY for the symbol instead of XYZ; you said buy to your broker at Cheapskates, Inc. instead of sell; the stock you just sold profitably last month has fallen big time today, and you're on the way to the golf course. If you have a relationship with an intelligent professional, these problems will disappear. It's called capitalism, an informal partnership, friendship, or just plain common sense. My broker just called me to point out that I had three clients with 10-percent net/

net profits in closed-end income funds. Will he get a commission? Will my client make 10 percent? Will these transactions be good for all concerned? Are you a rotarian? Develop a win/win relationship with your broker and get the service you need to prosper.

Never Violate the Rules
But first, the answer to the question raised above. No stop-loss orders, ever, because:

a. We own high-quality stocks purchased in a down-trend and we fully expect them to move lower;
b. If the price falls far enough, we want to add to our position, and we have allowed for that in the original purchase amount;
c. Using the stop loss to protect a profit doesn't apply either because we religiously pull the profit trigger. That's right, immediately.

In the investment world, there are deadly emotions that we have to recognize and protect ourselves against. Fear is one. Greed is another. Pride can also be financially fatal. Emotions have about as much use in an investment strategy as multiple swing thoughts have in a tee shot. Investment decisions have to be made objectively, so make sure that your judgment is not being influenced by outside forces. If you find yourself thinking something like this: issue breadth has been negative for three months, maybe I'll just hang loose for a while and see what happens. Stop, do the opposite. This is a day-to-day exercise; don't allow your emotions to complicate things!

You must develop a new buy list every day, using all of the rules we've discussed, without exception. The down-20-percent-from-the-fifty-two-week-high rule itself is inviolate. But, don't be an engineer about it either; I just use the whole numbers, particularly when I'm dealing with a really short buy list. Of equal importance are the rules about big daily movements and month-to-month changes in price. Weather you agree or disagree with the rules and guidelines in the methodology, it is the total entity that has stood the test of time. There are no buttons to click on to program your own system... it's all or none.

Out of town, overslept, tied up in meetings? If you haven't been able to do the work, either don't do anything at all, or look at the same securities you planned to look at the day before. Then, base your decisions on the previous day's closing price, not yesterday's. You'll wind up paying less than you originally intended if you do actually place an order. Issues you may be ready to sell? Remember those crib sheets that those other guys (never the Fijis) used in college? Write down the pertinent information, and call your full-service broker between flights, nines, meetings, etc.

What about Vacation?

Your money works every day; your equity portfolio is in business five days per week. Even though we human beings do require some R & R, the equity side of an investment portfolio needs to be managed regardless of where in the world you happen to be. You could do this even before the Internet made it a piece of cake. I've traded from Athens, London, Rome, Hong Kong, and other neat places without missing a beat. Rarely do my clients even know that I'm on vacation. This is your money, remember, and your responsibility. None of your traveling companions, whomever they may be, will begrudge you the few minutes a day you spend taking care of business. Actually, they'll be impressed.

All you need to do is have an inventory of what you own, a relatively current newspaper or Internet access for current quotations, and a telephone. You should be able to get an international 800 number from your broker or insist that he take your collect calls and e-mails. If your relationship with your broker is strong, you'll be able to get the job done. No excuses! You absolutely need to be able to trade from anywhere you happen to be. Profit-taking opportunities just can't be allowed to slip away, even if you have. Your performance will absolutely suffer if you fail to take care of business when you're away from home.

There is one other thing, specifically for mutual fund owners and wrap account participants to understand. None of these investment managers or your accountant, financial planner, or investment executive, would even consider doing this while they are on vacation.

Don't Rush to Fill Your Portfolio

There will always be new opportunities. Think about it. If there are no new opportunities, your account should be full of profit-taking smart cash. If it's not, you are not following your rules. I have never experienced a time when there were both no buying and no selling opportunities in the stock market. (The smaller the portfolio though, the more likely it is that this could occur.) Don't press yourself to find new opportunities just because you feel that you have too much cash in your portfolio. You'll wind up adding marginal issues to your selection universe for the wrong reasons. There is no harm at all in holding smart cash. The more of it you accumulate, the more likely it is that some serious institutional profit taking will happen soon, giving you plenty of new investment opportunities. Think of it as a form of compounding: You've already made around 10 percent on this money, and now it will compound at money market rates until you find a new home for it. That's not so bad when you consider that the historic growth rate of Wall Street's favorite benchmark is slightly less.

The selection universe is hallowed ground and it will prove to be counterproductive if you become less selective for any reason. Be patient, your investment life is a long one. The shorter your buy list becomes, the more likely it is that your type of securities are becoming overpriced. In August 1987, for example, a month or so before what proved to be the best buying opportunity in the history of the financial markets, my buy list contained only two stocks. My inventory of stocks owned amounted to only forty or so, with 50 percent of those being utility stocks, because interest rates were very high at the time. Continue to take your profits and smile a lot. New opportunities will be along soon enough.

Just what is this smart cash I'm talking about? The oracle of Wall Street always recommends that a portion of your investment portfolio remain in cash. Banks will advertise their CD (Certificates of Deposit) and money market interest rates and suggest that you invest in these high-yield vehicles. Other financial types will tell you to move into cash quickly because this or that is about to happen. You should wait and see what is going on before you make any further commitments.

None of that cash is smart cash for two basic, and I mean extremely basic, reasons. This direct from the oracle of reality, so make sure you thoroughly understand it: (a) By definition, cash is never an investment, because an investment always involves risk. Cash is a temporary holding area for dollars that are destined for placement in either the equity or fixed-income portions of the investment portfolio. (b) The future is an unknown.

Even those superstar Harvard or Wharton MBAs, with their million dollar salaries, have no more of a clue about tomorrow's stock market than you or me. A recommendation without a cash percent would be an admission of ignorance about the future, and they can't afford to admit to that. Actually, their fixed vs. equity numbers have nothing to do with asset allocation either. It is pure guesswork about what these two classes of investments are going to do (in terms of market value performance) in the short-run.

They advise you to hold cash until they tell you that the time is right to do something with it. Don't take the bait. Put your right hand over your heart and recite "the investor's creed" (see sidebar). There is another, subtler, motivation for Wall Street firms to recommend a change in the cash portion of the portfolio: transactions. Right? Right! Something either has to be sold to raise cash, or purchased (the latest product idea) to alter the amount of cash in the portfolio.

Smart cash, on the other hand, is simply that which results from the taking of profits, plus the cash flow produced by dividends and interest on securities. The only reason it is in cash is because we haven't gotten around to doing anything with it yet. We don't rush around doing things that are outside the plan, just because the pinstriped piper of Wall Street is playing a different song than he did last month. The investor's creed summarizes the overall concept at work, and it is the answer you should learn to use when asked about the amount of cash in your portfolio. I call it:

The Investor's Creed

My intention is to be fully invested in accordance with my planned equity/fixed income asset allocation. On the other hand, every security I own is for sale, and every security I own generates some form of cash flow that cannot be reinvested immediately. I am happy when my cash position is nearly 0 percent because all of my money is then working as hard as it possibly can to meet my objectives. But, I am ecstatic when my cash position approaches 100 percent because that means I've sold everything at a profit, and that I am in a position to take advantage of any new investment opportunities, that fit my guidelines, as soon as I become aware of them."

Put this on your refrigerator and recite it often.

How Much to Buy

We've talked quite a bit about diversification. What are the three basic principles of investing? If you don't spit out this answer instantly, return to chapter 1, do not pass Go, do not place any orders!

It goes without saying that the big three are inviolate. But in smaller portfolios, keeping positions below 5 percent can become difficult since purchases must be limited to round lots. Remember that the 5-percent rule is a total investment program consideration, which means that three separate $70,000 portfolios = one $210,000 program. Ten percent might just have to be acceptable in extremely small portfolios, but you can always raise your quality parameter to A- or better to offset some of the increased risk in the diversification element. Portfolios of less than $30,000 should be started in closed-end equity mutual funds. Check the back of your S&P guide, and/or find your way to one of several websites that present excellent detail with respect to hundreds of managed, non-index, CEFs that are available for equities, tax-free, and taxable income investing.

Closed-end funds are much less complicated than the open-end variety. They generally produce nice dividends and capital-gains distributions, and they trade like normal equities. They provide instant diversification, and it is relatively safe to have higher than normal portfolio percentages in them. But you must know what is inside, and build on the most conservative (least risky) base first. The best features are that they are not affected by mob hysteria like open-ended funds, and they can be sold without penalties, back-end loads or anything else. You should be aware of the fact that the bulk of the dividend may come after January 1. One slight drawback is the fact that (as recently as 2007) most brokerage statements (especially those from lower-cost entities) list them as equities—even if they contain a managed portfolio of municipal bonds.

As soon as the portfolio working capital (cost basis) exceeds $30,000, commence the move into individual stocks. Even though the fund itself is a diversified entity, be careful not to establish any one position that represents as much as 20 percent of the portfolio.

A move from one type of security within a class to another (CEF to individual equities), or from one class to another (fixed income to equity) is orchestrated over time and in accordance with our basic trading standards. Take profits or accumulate income in one area and then reinvest in the other.

Averaging Down

Since we are buying stocks that have moved down 20 percent or more from their twelve-month highs, it is likely that they will continue to move down after we have purchased them. This is a fact of life that is dealt with through a strategy called averaging down, which simply refers to the purchase of additional shares of a stock you already own, but at a lower price. Some of the profits in Table 6 are on issues that involved the purchase of additional shares at lower prices. Please don't confuse this strategy with either of two popular concepts: dollar-cost averaging or dividend reinvestment plans (DRIPs). Their popularity should be your first clue that they are bad for your financial health. Think about it.

Dollar-cost averaging is a mechanical process where a fixed sum of money is invested in the same security or fund at a regular time interval (monthly, for example) either through direct deduction from a bank account, payroll, or by regular cash payments. I can't think of a single reason why this type of investing makes any sense. It certainly doesn't fit into a program that involves any kind of personal decision making. Obviously, it doesn't fit into a program that is based on quality and diversification, nor does it allow for a selection process based on price. Finally, there's no provision to sell. This is probably an idea that developed through the life insurance industry, where systematic insurance premium payment made life easier for the salesperson, by decreasing the amount of time spent trying to conserve lapsed policies.

DRIPs are even more popular, and those who use this forced-feeding approach are cult-like in their support and enthusiasm for it. People somehow feel less manipulated and abused with this approach because the companies and not the brokerage firms control it. They are really just kidding themselves. The popularity of DRIPs, believe it or not, is occasioned by a nominal reduction in the price per share and the absence of a commission on the purchase. Added to the issues that make this form of dollar-cost averaging so unproductive are these:

1. Participants are saddled with a horrendous record-keeping job. Cost basis determination is nearly impossible, as it is with automatic reinvestment in all mutual funds.
2. Shares are being purchased under demand conditions that are artificially increased.
3. Shares are being purchased at any price at all.

The individual decision-making, averaging-down approach is completely different than these programmed buying methods of systematically becoming over-invested in and falling in love with a particular security. Consequently, when we make our initial purchase of any stock, we allow room to add to our position by buying more of the stock at a lower price, at least once. So if you were making the initial purchase of a stock in a $200,000 investment program, the starting investment would not be $10,000. Right? Right, in practice, its best to keep initial purchases controlled at about 3 percent or even lower. During rallies, make smaller initial commitments than during corrections. Is it clear why?

Accountants love to create work for themselves because most bill by the hour and, thus, they have no reason to recommend things that would cut their billing totals. My understanding, as a non-accountant, is that taxpayers have the option of determining the cost basis of their securities in either of two ways: by individual lots or by average pricing. You have to be consistent in the use of one or the other. The average-pricing method will save you a lot of record-keeping time and keep your accountant's bills in line.

When to Buy More

When to buy more of a stock and just how much more become the key questions. Most of you have probably been told, at some time in your investment life to: sell your losers and let your profits run. That type of thinking will eventually sink your portfolio, particularly when issue breadth runs negative for an extended period of time. It just doesn't make sense with good companies, and absolutely defies the cyclical nature of the financial markets. First you dutifully take a loss in ABC, and buy DEF. When DEF drops, you sell it and are moved into GHI, which then starts to fall. Wait a minute, your XYZ stopped going up so now we have to sell it. Sorry, but this process just has to end at zero eventually. Never forget: no matter how sugar coated or rational the advice sounds, it is motivated by a powerful lust to separate you from some of your dollars. If it were legal for these guys to just take your money all at once, they would.

But the buy-more decision is certainly one of the most difficult to learn to implement confidently. It takes some successful experience and a lot of courage. Take some time to review the historical charts of some of the companies that are listed in the tables in chapter 2, particularly Table 6, which is a study in the profitability of buying those losers and turning them around profitably. All were purchased down 20 percent or more and most went lower before moving back up. Several were added to at lower prices.

Since we are dealing only with investment-grade securities, it is far more reasonable to say, for example, that Best Buy is a better buy at X-25 percent than it was at X (particularly if we've planned ahead and allowed room to buy more within our diversification limits). Well, you might observe, if the market price continues to fall, more and more can be purchased without exceeding the diversification limits. We could wind up investing too much in a company that really is in trouble.

Have no fear: the working capital model is here to protect us from such irrational exuberance. The working capital model, an approach to portfolio design and management that I developed in response to observations such as this, recognizes that market value is just not an acceptable measure to use for questions of diversification. The important number is the amount actually invested in the security or securities under review. The working capital model, covered more completely in chapter 7, uses cost basis for all asset allocation and diversification decision making. Market value is used to determine which securities to buy and sell. Thus, we avoid putting too much money either in a faltering company, an unpopular sector, or a weakening asset classification. Oh yeah, we are also able to keep our portfolio in sync with our investment plan with every decision we make.

How Many Stocks?

A properly diversified equity portfolio would have no fewer than twenty stocks in it, but one with thirty or forty would be every bit as manageable with the right tools. I manage several multi-million dollar portfolios that typically contain between thirty-five and forty-five equity issues, depending on when in the cycle you count them. I've had as many as forty-five in my own program from time to time, and my feeling is that it's foolish to limit yourself unnecessarily. Similarly, the fixed income portion of the portfolio need not contain a huge number of issues, but with increased usage of CEFs, the number of issues per portfolio is growing. Most mutual funds contain much larger numbers of securities than this, making one wonder if the underlying strategy is merely to mirror the market rather than to follow a diversification model of some kind. The management task is to find a comfort level that supports the diversification model.

Now Warming up in the Bull Pen

As you move through your data sources each day, you will notice companies that are moving into your buy range even though they are not currently in the selection universe. You'll find that many of your very best trading experiences will fall into this category, which is one of the reasons I rely on my experience with individual stocks down at least 20 percent, instead of a higher percentage in weaker markets. Every morning I look for this kind of new/old opportunity. The best traders don't get too far below 20 percent before they start back up. One Saturday in July, 2001, I noticed Bank of New York, Colgate Palmolive, Emerson Electric, and Roper. A month later, two of the four were gone. Wow! As you gain experience, you'll develop a list of favorites (and your friendly full-services broker will know which ones to put on his alert screen, too).

Eventually, as you become more experienced, you'll take instant notice of a few stocks that you feel you really should buy ASAP. My personal favorites have changed through the years, but there are dozens that I want all the time. Make sure you remember to control your enthusiasm. The bull pen is (normally) just for your very best traders, and one such item per day should be enough. I'm looking at four or five because I'm managing hundreds of portfolios. Note that no change in the normal purchase guidelines is warranted. As important as buying is, experience will show you that it should not be done in a hurry. Fill up your portfolio slowly. Selling, on the other hand, needs to be done much more quickly. We'll look at that process soon.

Trim Your Hedges with Closed-End Equity Funds

If there were such things as investment enhancement steroids, would you be tempted...of course you would. Equity CEFs are not new, not perfect, and not even close to a substitute for the even more old-fashioned buy-quality-stocks-at-lower-prices approach you're investigating here. What they are is a great way for starting smaller portfolios on the right track. But if you look at what is available out there, you'll see that junk thrives just as well in the closed-end area as elsewhere. Think safety first, and avoid gimmicks and newbies, are hot tips you should pay attention to. Don't be afraid of leverage, in moderation—it makes the world go around.

There is a place for equity CEFs in all portfolios, regardless of size, particularly when the buy list is shrinking. My guidelines are: at least two in all portfolios under $200K, three above $300K, four above $400K, and between five and seven in seven figure portfolios. The diversification potential is obvious, particularly if you have already taken profits in a hot sector, like energy, real estate, or drugs (someday). But the idea is really more of a quality hedge, for lack of a better term, describing this reality: We've taken our profits, and these fund managers will as well. If the sector keeps rising, there's a chance for additional capital gains plus a definite share of banked capital gains when they are distributed. I'm sure that this is legal double dipping; I can't prove it, but I'm sure happy about it.

So we're buying them more during rallies than corrections. Try to avoid buying them at all-time highs, but bite the bullet if you have to. When prices move down, average down more quickly than with individual issues, and going above 5 percent of the portfolio isn't taboo. Don't get near 10 percent, don't fall in love, and keep total exposure below 25 percent of the portfolio. No, they are not selection universe or bull pen candidates. On rare occasions, they convert to open end. It's annoying, but nothing is perfect.

Income Investing: Don't Get Sidetracked by Freebies

If you are looking to add a preferred stock, treasury security, or corporate bond unit trust to the fixed income side of your portfolio, your broker has all the information you need. Make sure he looks at call price and the first-call date too. But it's still up to you to be knowledgeable and careful. You absolutely do not want anything brand new or just coming out tomorrow, with no sales charge and no commission. What, you say, what's wrong with free stuff?

There is no such thing as a freebie on Wall Street. You are paying the underwriting markup and your financial advisor is getting some form of sales credit pat on the back. In addition, contest winners get special points toward a bonus or campaign prize of some kind. Ask about it. The next time he tells you he's going to a conference in Maui at the company's expense, ask him why they aren't sending the clients? The old, "show me the customers' yachts" scenario... Did I mention that there is no such thing as a freebie on Wall Street?

When buying income securities, make sure you avoid paying a premium (more than the face value at maturity), determine current yield (yield right now at the last trade price), yield to maturity (coupon or contract rate), and yield to call (securities may be redeemed early). You should become familiar with these terms, and your broker must be fluent in them! All textbooks on investing will have a section that explains the terms you need to understand when you invest in bonds and preferred stocks. Your best resource is an experienced broker you can trust. The longer a broker has been around, the more honest he is likely to be, for fairly obvious reasons.

Warning Labels

Warning Label 1. Don't be fooled into buying income securities with short-term maturity dates. One of the oldest cons out there is the one where the broker tries to sell you bonds that are maturing in a year or two, even though the yield can be much lower than with longer term bonds. He'll tell you that your portfolio will be more flexible in response to changes in interest rates, and your portfolio values won't be hurt as much by rising rates. What it actually does is:

1. assures you of an unnecessarily lower yield,
2. guarantees the broker a constant 6-percent return on your money, and
3. obtains the broker special bonuses and incentives for selling the firms unwanted odd lot inventory.

That's right, he gets up to a 3-percent markup on each side of the trade. As for cash flow, I'm not quite sure what flexibility is or why it is needed in the income bucket of your portfolio. Unit trusts are cash-flow friendly in rising-interest-rate environments, because they pay back principal regularly, and the monthly income from CEFs is always significantly higher than either long- or short-term bonds. As to the change in market value of income securities because of changing interest rate expectations, it just doesn't really matter to anyone south of the corporate bond trader. More on this later.

Warning Label 2. Don't be fooled into buying anything—equity, income, product, t-shirt—whatever the brokerage firm is just coming out with. It's really common sense. If you have 100,000 brokers selling the same security, what do you think happens to the price? On the flip side, why are these 100,000 brokers focusing on this particular security? Just one more question; what will happen to the price of the security next month, when the 100,000 brokers stop pushing it? Note that the price of a unit trust is fixed by the institutional trustee, and not by an institutional marketing department. I'd like to believe that there is a slight difference there. This may be the reason why the unit trusts aren't pushed quite so hard. Don't forget though, as great as CEFs might be for income, certified pre-owned is absolutely better than new for the very same reasons. Let someone else pay the underwriting and distribution expenses.

Finally, before sticking your toes into those murky income-security waters, make sure you have a feel for what's going on with interest rates. Avoid securities with a current yield significantly higher than normal—the reason is always higher than normal risk. It can be well hidden, but it's in there. The recent trend in interest rates is usually very well publicized: if the trend is downward, prices of rate-sensitive securities will be moving higher. Wait until a week or so after the Federal Reserve makes a move before you shop—never buy on good news. If the move in rates is a disappointment or part of an upward trend, buy just after the announcement—always buy on bad news.

Now I know you must be thinking: if rates are going down, why buy at all? If rates are going up, why not wait? Good questions. Interest rates generally move very slowly and in twenty-five or fifty basis point increments (a basis point is 1/100 of a percent). Wait and see is market-timing jargon with interest-rate-sensitive securities just as it is with equities. Money market rates generally reflect what's going on in the bond market, but there is no profit potential in cash. Remember, if you buy income securities properly, you will have room to buy more if rates increase significantly, thus increasing your average yield. And, the fun part, if rates move downward, a profit-taking opportunity will likely materialize.

One more point should be considered in selecting securities for your fixed-income portfolio. If you are digesting all of this, you will realize the importance of establishing positions in fixed-income securities that are readily added to, such as closed-end municipal bond funds and preferred stocks. Unit trusts and self-liquidating government securities (Ginny Maes, treasury bills, etc.) are difficult to buy more of, but they demand a place in the portfolio because they return principal on a regular basis. These cash-flow machines give you monthly checks that can be used either for new position purchases or for adding to existing holdings. And, don't forget that a portion of this cash flow is destined for equity investments too; our asset allocation model applies to all of our income, regardless of its source. Most recently, the yields on individual income securities and unit trusts have lagged behind those available in the closed-end income funds.

It is unlikely that your professional will ever acknowledge the existence of closed-end income funds. When you ask about them, he or she is likely to avoid the issue or incorrectly suggest that the use of leverage in (some, not all) of them makes them much too risky. The only increased risk is actually to them—you won't be paying through the nose for short-term bonds or new issue preferred stocks ever again. When you compare the individual securities risk and yield picture with what's available in the CEF arena, you'll fire your financial professional for not bringing this to your attention sooner.

Two Important Numbers and Two Important Lists

Wall Street provides great real-time information that you would be foolish not to use to your advantage, and keeping in touch with what is going on in the investment world each day is certainly important. Try to deal with it sanely. There is no need to be at the tape, watching each trade as it goes by on the screen. You really don't need flashing numbers, bells, and whistles to get the job done. Wall Street wants you to believe that everything (buy, sell, panic) has to be done immediately: this deal just won't be available tomorrow. As a trader, you are probably one of their best customers throughout the month, so don't feel at all uncomfortable leaning on them for all the information that you need.

Two or three times a day, when you check in with your broker for prices, talk to him about what's going on in the market and see what he comes up with. After he parrots back the DJIA and/or S&P numbers, dazzle him with your new awareness by asking for issue breadth statistics and the latest market stats. These should be at his fingertips, real-time, but he may never have been asked for them before.

These days you'll be able to find all that online, but if your ambitious professional knows what you are looking for, he or she will be one step ahead of you and can provide impressive service. While I'm writing this, I can't be looking at the most advanced list. But if he or she sees that Harley Davidson shares are up more than two points, interday, and identifies three of my clients who are in that magic 10-percent profit land, she'll earn my respect, her commission, and my clients' gratitude.

Issue Breadth

Issue breadth is the single most accurate barometer of what is going on in the stock market on any given day, end of story. Issue breadth is the single most important number you need to know to understand your portfolio's equity market value performance in the real investment world. Issue breadth frequently undermines the validity of the popular market averages and is, therefore, rarely reported loudly enough from Wall Street. Issue breadth is absolutely the best indicator of what has happened in the stock market in years past. Issue breadth statistics can provide you with valid expectations with respect to the market value of the equity portion of your portfolio. Did I mention that, interestingly enough, this measurement tool was designed to be a stock market indicator; the DJIA and the S&P 500 were not.

Issue breadth compares the number of advancing issues with the number of declining issues on the various stock exchanges. A rational person would expect market rallies to be accompanied by positive breadth, more winners than losers, and market corrections to be evidenced by the opposite. Wall Street really doesn't care.

New Highs vs. New Lows

Another number you have to become fluent in is the differential between stocks achieving new twelve-month highs and those falling to new twelve-month lows. I know it sounds somewhat simplistic, but rallies should be accompanied by a greater number of stocks achieving new twelve-month highs than new lows. Don't you think? During the NASDAQ run up from mid-1998 through early 2000, new lows on the NYSE more than doubled new highs! Question: where did the dot.com gold rush money come from? Who encouraged investors to switch from value investing to no-value speculating? Answer: Wall Street institutions. Remember the revelations about the Wall Street analysts and IPO peddlers. Never forget...

Don't Confuse Me with the Facts

In May 2002, Wall Street was still selling its market correction/bad economy scenario; it had been doing so since the turn of the century. Would you be surprised to learn that:

- On the NYSE, advancing issues had exceeded declining issues by a significant margin, nearly 25,000 ticks (Wall Streeteze for a price change, either up or down).
- Positive breadth days outnumbered negative days by 13.4 percent.
- Positive breadth months exceeded negative months by 63.6 percent.
- Instances of individual stocks achieving new fifty-two-week highs exceeded the occurrence of new fifty-two-week lows by an impressive 62.4 percent.

You just can't make this stuff up! Wall Street's sales ability dwarfs that of the tailor in *The Emperor's New Clothes*. I once had a boss who would say, "Don't confuse me with the facts; I've got to make a decision." He could have made it big on Wall Street.

Numbers and statistics provide information that should add to our minimal understanding of what is going on in the Shock Market. Wall Street collects all the statistics... we've already commented on statisticians, and I just can't help myself from providing you with the rest of the story. During the new economy/dot.com rally, from January 1999 thru February 2000:

- Declining issues exceeded advancing issues by a significant margin, nearly 49,700 ticks.
- Negative issue breadth days outnumbered positive days by 42.5 percent.
- Negative breadth months exceeded positive months by 1,300 percent (there was only one positive month).
- From April 1999 thru March 2000 new fifty-two-week lows exceeded new fifty-two-week highs by an alarming 118.2 percent.

The Wall Street market averages were screaming rally, while the NYSE was experiencing a devastating correction. Manipulation, maybe; fraud, certainly not; greed, of course; brainwashing, oh yeah!

Today's Market Stats
Issue breadth and new high vs. new low numbers give you valuable information that helps you determine both where you have been and where you are. Investing with a quality, diversification, and income

TABLE 8: A partial most-active list, NYSE, June 22, 2007

SYMBOL	DESCRIPTION	LAST	CHANGE	% CHANGE	52 WEEK HIGH	52 WEEK LOW	VOLUME
BX.N	Blacks Tone	35.06	4.06	13.10			76,288,600
TYC.N	Tyco Intl	34.21	0.94	2.83	34.45	24.97	60,942,500
SLB.N	Schlumberger	89.20	3.44	4.01	86.67	54.24	40,145,700
GE.N	Gen Electric	38.24	-0.56	-1.44	39.77	32.06	35,802,100
PFE.N	Pfizer	25.38	-0.54	-2.08	28.6	22.17	30,197,000
F.N	Ford	9.13	0.22	2.47	9.46	6.07	26,704,500
XOM.N	Exxon	82.52	-1.78	2.11	86.58	57.25	21,984,700
ACN.N	Accenture	42.63	0.86	2.06	42.36	26.33	20,177,700
STX.N	Seagate	22.19	-0.04	-0.18	28.51	19.27	19,956,600
T.N	AT&T Inc.	38.85	-0.74	-1.87	41.49	26.36	19,780,900

Use the most-active list several times a day to spot trends, takeovers and hot or cold sectors.

investment plan will keep you out of trouble as you move your portfolio into unknown future.

The daily most-active, most-advanced, and most-declined lists constitute what are normally referred to as market statistics. These five lists (advances and declines are given in both dollar and percent versions) are essential to operating your trading program; don't tell anyone if you've never heard of them.

The most-active list (Table 8) reports on the stocks that are trading with the most volume throughout the day. Some providers (AOL surprisingly, but with a twenty-minute delay) list as many as forty companies. You'll be able to determine trends, isolate popular groups, find takeover possibilities, and get a feel for the general direction of the day's activity. For our purposes, this is the least useful of the lists. This provider uses ".N" to indicate NYSE.

The most-advanced list (Table 11) is the most important of the three in both forms (dollars and percent), but for selling rather than buying. We'll discuss it in chapter 6.

The most-declined list (Table 9) is the one to go to an hour or so after the market opens. It will get you up to speed quickly and provide a clear indication of which individual stocks and groups of stocks are weakest. You will see if any of your buy list items are getting in range, and you may find some of those ol' favorites to set aside in the bull pen for constant scrutiny. Big numbers follow (and often precede) news stories. Most lists will lead you to sources of additional information.

TABLE 9: A partial most-declined list, NYSE, June 22, 2007

SYMBOL	DESCRIPTION	LAST	CHANGE	% CHANGE	52 WEEK HIGH	52 WEEK LOW	VOLUME
CRE.N	CAREINVTRUST	13.50	-1.5	-10.00			6,551,900
ACA.N	ACA CAPITAL	13.00	-1.03	-7.34	16.43	12.6	432,700
FIG.N	FORTRESS INV	24.25	-1.63	-6.30	35.49	23.04	1,832,200
CNK.N	CINEMARKHLDGS	17.42	-1.13	-6.09	19.95	17.75	1,238,100
AVX.N	AVX CORP	16.89	-1.03	-5.75	18.52	13.09	785,400
KB.N	KOOKMIN BK ADS	90.25	-5.31	-5.56	97.58	74.33	395,700
ATV.N	ACORN INTL	25.50	-1.5	-5.56	32.33	18.66	191,600
NWK.N	NETWORK EQUIP	9.13	-0.52	-5.39	11.2	2.73	780,100
KRO.N	KRONOSWRLD-WID	26.37	-1.46	-5.25	42.55	27.41	36,100
FCS.N	FAIRCHILD SEMI	19.38	-1.05	-5.14	20.55	14.94	1,796,800

Use the most-declined list several times every day to find and track buying opportunities.

As a trader, you will be a valued brokerage client—but don't be a bully. It's more pleasant and more profitable to be nice. Over time, a bright account executive will learn your strategy and let you know when something important occurs, particular when he knows you will be able to sell something profitably. Brokers love profit-taking transactions even more than you do...because? Over time, he'll clue you in on downward gap openings in stocks he knows you love to trade. And he will make it a point to always have the statistics you want available.

Be careful, though, I have found that the majority of brokers do not have enough of a spine to support their inflated egos. If you get an outside manager to run your program this way, your insecure broker will make every attempt to undermine his judgment in either buys or sells. Whatever criticism you come up with, right or wrong, he will support, even magnify. Then he'll try to sell you his firm's wrap account managers or mutual funds. Tell your broker that you expect him to support your selection. At the first sign of a problem, keep the manager and let him select the broker. I don't use client-recommended brokers anymore, but this really should be an MBA case study.

I guess it boils down to the tremendous incentives brokers have to sell investment products and to be team players. Here they are handed a lucrative relationship on a platter, with absolutely no responsibility or accountability for the decisions that are being made. They can devote 100 percent of their time to soliciting new business and still be assured of a steady cash flow. It's a mystery why they are not standing in line to

TABLE 10: Statistics that really matter, January 2002 through June 22, 2007

MONTH	NYSE +TICKS	BREADTH -TICKS	NET	CUMM	UP DAYS	DOWN DAYS	NEW HIGHS	NEW LOWS
Jan '99	27,087	31,336	(4,249)	(4,249)	7	12		
Feb '99	25,786	31,947	(6,161)	(10,410)	4	15		
Mar '99	33,812	35,101	(1,289)	(11,699)	9	14		
Apr '99	31,251	26,396	4,855	(6,844)	15	5	1,546	1,099
May '99	29,282	30,561	(1,279)	(8,123)	11	9	1,227	739
June '99	32,172	34,041	(1,869)	(9,992)	12	10	1,439	1,777
July '99	29,377	34,343	(4,966)	(14,958)	7	14	1,783	1,365
Aug '99	301,665	36,455	(6,290)	(21,248)	6	16	1,046	3,247
Sept '99	28,070	35,699	(7,629)	(28,877)	8	13	892	3,820
Oct '99	29,578	33,696	(4,118)	(32,995)	8	13	835	5,176
Nov '99	30,022	34,235	(4,213)	(37,208)	9	12	1,476	3,316
Dec '99	32,592	35,695	(3,103)	(40,311)	9	13	1,882	7,098
Jan '00	28,912	32,956	(4,044)	(4,044)	8	12	1,388	2,224
Feb '00	27,611	32,952	(5,341)	(9,385)	7	13	1,298	3,821
Mar '00	35,558	35,758	(200)	(9,585)	11	12	1,847	2,667
Apr '00	28,225	29,782	(1,557)	(11,142)	10	9	750	1,120
May '00	28,594	33,258	(4,664)	(15,806)	10	12	1,157	1,497
June '00	36,154	29,746	6,408	(9,398)	11	11	1,521	1,185
July '00	29,357	27,996	1,361	(8,037)	12	8	1,478	824
Aug '00	34,738	29,820	4,918	(3,119)	15	8	2,268	818
Sept '00	27,682	28,739	(1,057)	(4,176)	8	12	2,356	1,489
Oct '00	29,698	33,872	(4,174)	(8,350)	8	14	1,172	2,543
Nov '00	27,239	33,744	(6,505)	(14,855)	8	12	1,510	1,611
Dec '00	32,716	25,937	6,779	(8,076)	12	8	3,956	1,840
Jan '01	34,777	27,591	7,186	7,186	17	4	3,626	228
Feb '01	28,670	30,072	(1,402)	5,784	8	11	2,749	386
Mar '01	32,835	32,844	(9)	5,775	11	11	2,139	1,408
Apr '01	32,407	28,969	3,438	9,213	12	8	1,883	849
May '01	35,956	31,848	4,108	13,321	14	8	3,294	357
June '01	31,165	30,555	610	13,931	9	11	2,434	749
July '01	34,565	33,456	1,109	15,040	15	8	2,275	1,019
Aug '01	37,785	35,589	2,196	17,236	14	10	3,570	936
Sept '01	20,141	27,322	(7,181)	10,055	5	10	767	4,258
Oct '01	26,828	34,770	2,058	12,113	12	11	1,167	1,235
Nov '01	34,096	28,175	5,921	18,034	13	7	1,638	656
Dec '01	32,959	28,726	4,233	22,267	12	8	1,986	964

TABLE 10: Statistics that really matter, January 2002 through June 22, 2007 (continued)

MONTH	NYSE +TICKS	BREADTH -TICKS	NET	CUMM	UP DAYS	DOWN DAYS	NEW HIGHS	NEW LOWS
Jan '02	33,925	32,118	1,807	1,807	12	9	1,856	593
Feb '02	30,379	28,668	1,711	3,518	10	9	2,231	936
Mar '02	34,033	29,071	4,962	8,480	15	5	3,706	638
Apr '02	36,073	33,267	2,806	11,286	11	11	3,996	816
May '02	35,230	34,987	243	11,529	11	11	2,709	958
June '02	29,499	33,696	(4,197)	7,332	8	12	1,704	2,015
July '02	30,663	40,695	(10,032)	(2,700)	8	14	735	5,545
Aug '02	37,309	33,586	3723	1,023	13	9	770	1,360
Sept '02	30,202	34,382	(4,180)	(3,157)	9	11	1,146	2,409
Oct '02	36,865	36,554	311	(2,846)	11	12	728	2,747
Nov '02	33,607	27,695	5,912	3,066	12	7	541	541
Dec '02	32,149	32,430	(281)	2,785	10	10	792	537
Jan '03	33,438	34,551	(1,113)	(1,113)	12	9	1,777	767
Feb '03	29,984	31,519	(1,535)	(2,648)	8	11	831	1,662
Mar '03	32,802	32,138	664	(1,984)	11	9	1,099	2,055
Apr '03	39,599	28,413	11,186	9,202	14	7	2,261	414
May '03	40,232	28,004	12,228	21,430	16	5	5,274	126
June '03	36,528	33,254	3,274	24,704	12	9	6,076	98
July '03	35,465	35,834	(369)	24,335	10	12	3,589	349
Aug '03	36,592	30,935	5,657	29,992	15	6	2,766	574
Sept '03	35,724	31,986	3,738	33,730	11	10	4,084	183
Oct '03	41,553	32,373	9,180	42,910	17	6	6,752	140
Nov '03	31,209	26,753	4,456	47,366	13	6	7,486	140
Dec '03	35,158	29,938	5,220	52,586	12	8	6,963	137
Jan '04	35,137	30,444	4,693	4,693	14	6	8,346	68
Feb '04	32,943	29,137	3,806	8,499	12	7	4,380	102
Mar '04	39,043	36,277	2,766	11,265	12	11	4,076	252
Apr '04	29,913	39,255	(9,342)	1,923	6	15	2,821	2,037
May '04	35,215	29,499	5,716	7,639	14	6	644	3,336
June '04	36,817	31,883	4,934	12,573	15	6	2,680	780
July '04	32,403	32,859	(456)	12,117	11	9	1,695	1,133
Aug '04	37,232	31,234	5,998	18,115	11	10	1,286	865
Sept '04	37,541	30,962	6,579	24,694	13	8	3,159	430
Oct '04	36,425	30,273	6,152	30,846	13	9	2,488	770
Nov '04	35,057	26,422	8,635	39,481	15	6	5,931	178
Dec '04	37,673	31,283	6,390	45,871	14	7	5,264	254

TABLE 10: Statistics that really matter, January 2002 through June 22, 2007 (continued)

MONTH	NYSE +TICKS	BREADTH -TICKS	NET	CUMM	UP DAYS	DOWN DAYS	NEW HIGHS	NEW LOWS
Jan '05	29,765	31,761	(1,996)	(1,996)	8	11	1,704	406
Feb '05	32,733	29,664	3,069	1,073	13	6	4,742	348
Mar '05	32,794	39,686	(6,892)	(5,819)	10	13	2,483	662
Apr '05	32,367	33,599	(1,232)	(7,051)	10	11	927	1,687
May '05	38,451	29,657	8794	1,743	13	8	1,514	315
June '05	37,372	32,805	4,567	6,310	14	8	3,904	500
July '05	37,947	29,031	8,916	15,226	13	7	5,639	296
Aug '05	35,750	36,855	(1,105)	14,121	12	11	3,232	683
Sept '05	34,175	35,116	(941)	13,180	9	12	3,501	1,382
Oct '05	29,449	36,350	(6,901)	6,279	8	12	1,062	2,898
Nov '05	35,714	29,889	5,825	12,104	13	7	2,478	3,191
Dec '05	35,790	34,494	1,296	13,400	12	9	2,663	1,826
Jan '06	37,564	28,801	8,763	8,763	14	6	4,663	674
Feb '06	32,427	30,187	2,240	11,003	12	7	3,035	563
Mar '06	36,906	35,647	1,259	12,262	11	12	4,842	780
Apr '06	29,297	31,613	(2,316)	9,946	9	10	4,395	2,061
May '06	32,338	37,914	(5,576)	4,370	9	13	2,642	2,743
June '06	35,298	36,385	(1,087)	3,283	9	13	896	3,333
July '06	32,562	32,221	341	3,624	11	9	1,373	2,084
Aug '06	41,303	33,657	7,646	11,270	15	7	2,605	1,308
Sept '06	34,340	30,778	3,562	14,832	11	8	3,339	830
Oct '06	40,378	31,433	8,945	23,777	16	6	5,301	441
Nov '06	38,239	30,072	8,167	31,944	15	6	5,257	422
Dec '06	34,263	31,352	2,911	34,855	9	11	5,461	331
Jan '07	34,631	30,495	4,136	4,136	15	6	3,996	518
Feb '07	31,129	28,623	2,506	6,642	9	9	5,313	443
Mar '07	38,675	33,922	4,753	11,395	12	10	2,386	711
Apr '07	33,699	30,128	3,571	14,966	10	10	5,807	453
May '07	39,141	31,971	7,170	22,136	15	7	4,750	609
June '07	24,786	28,367	(3,581)	18,555	9	7	3,358	1,282

sign their clients up with independent managers. Can the commissions and benefits from their product sales be that huge? Actually, brokers are compensated best for product sales that benefit the firm the most. Apparently, they've also brainwashed the SEC and NASD into thinking that the clients are benefited equally as well.

TABLE 10: Statistics that really matter, summary

MONTH	NYSE +TICKS	BREADTH -TICKS	NET	UP DAYS	DOWN DAYS	NEW HIGHS	NEW LOWS
From 1/99	3,410,762	3,268,830	141,932	1,144	974	276,265	132,046
1/99-2/00	415,717	465,413	(49,696)	120	171	14,812	33,682
6/00-6/02	779,408	737,882	41,526	275	225	56,287	27,296
6/00-6/03	1,185,757	1,131,545	54,212	407	341	73,945	47,474
1/00-5/02	928,308	902,588	25,720	321	283	62,727	38,625
3/03-3/04	432,942	369,209	63,733	157	91	59,076	4,386
6/00-now	2,902,668	2,704,619	198,049	993	770	257,699	93,080
4/00-now	2,959,487	2,767,659	191,828	1,013	791	259,606	95,697
1999	359,194	399,505	(40,311)	105	146	12,126	27,637
2000	366,484	374,560	(8,076)	120	131	20,701	21,639
2001	392,184	369,917	22,267	142	107	27,528	13,045
2002	399,934	397,149	2,785	130	120	20,914	19,095
2003	428,284	375,698	52,586	151	98	48,958	6,645
2004	425,399	379,528	45,871	150	150	42,770	10,205
2005	412,307	398,907	13,400	135	135	33,849	14,194
2006	424,915	390,060	34,855	141	141	43,809	15,570
2007	202,061	183,506	18,555	70	70	26,610	4,016

NYSE issue breadth numbers and new-high vs. new-low comparisons are critical statistics that Wall Street mostly ignores. It has been years, for example, since the DJIA has reported the inside scoop on the market.

Table 10 shows actual NYSE issue breadth numbers from January 1999 and high-low numbers starting in April 1999. It will be an eye opener if you spend some time looking it over and comparing a few time periods with Wall Street analytical propaganda. A few analyses are provided at the bottom of the table. Here's another interesting observation. The table shows an unprecedented up-trend starting in the first or second quarter of 2000. Why did it take nearly seven years for the averages and your old mutual funds to achieve their 2000 high-water marks? How would the QDI/working capital model have fared? I'm hopeful that after a few more chapters you'll be totally deprogrammed and ready to move forward in the investment world with some knowledge that really will help you succeed, for example: no mutual funds (open end), no NASDAQ. No Problem!

Hot Tips, Trite but True....

Every business, institution, sport, or other popular activity has its trite little phrases that everyone has heard, but that few people really take the time to understand or appreciate. Investing is certainly no exception:

1. Buy on Bad News

The market always overreacts to bad news, causing the prices of otherwise high-quality securities to go down quickly, often after a lengthy trading halt in anticipation of the news. In some instances, if you observe recent activity, you will see that insider trading is alive and well. In most instances, this will prove to be a good time either to establish a new position or to add to an older one. But never violate the rules. In addition to the other statistics we just looked at, every broker has instant access to the most recent news stories on any equity. So after you find out that oils are weak because six of the most declined and eight of the most actives are in that group, get some current prices to see if any of your favorite traders are ready for action. Now this is research that makes sense at the local level.

2. Always Buy Too Soon

Market timing is impossible in the aggregate, extremely unlikely with individual issues, and patently unnecessary to be concerned with at all. Yes, the price of the stock you are buying will probably move lower. That's perfectly OK when you are dealing with quality securities and when you have a game plan. Buying too soon doesn't mean hurry up. It simply means to apply your rules to today's price movements without trying to guess what may or may not happen tomorrow.

3. Don't Be In A Hurry to Buy

Don't allow yourself to get caught up in the hype and fluff of Wall Street gurus and CNBC interviewees. If you don't get what you want at the price you want to pay today, you can buy it or something else tomorrow. It is unlikely that there will ever be a day in which nothing meets your buying requirements, no matter how restrictive they are.

4. Never Buy a Hot Tip

Don't even think about it. Every stock idea someone presents to you has its own special story. It has a new product or technology, a different niche for an old something or other, a new spin, a different twist, or better management. Don't you believe it. First of all, why would anyone share this good poop with you, or with anyone else? Secondly, do you think you are the first one to hear about this special opportunity? Check out your source. How much did he buy? Even if it's an impressive number, don't do it.

5. Just What Is Better Management?
Is it the aggregate dollars paid to executives for their impressive graduate degrees? Or perhaps it's their aggregate salaries. Management involves four things: planning, organizing, controlling, and leading. That's all. Sure we can look at the corporation's long and short-term planning methods, its organizational structure, and control mechanisms. We can be appropriately impressed with the influential superstars that sit on their boards of directors. But how can we predict what any of them will do under fire? Who is the ultimate decision maker?

Some great management organizations include an office of the president, or co-chairmen of the board. We have chief operating officers, chief executive officers, and chief financial officers. If you can't identify the boss, you don't have good management. Most effective organizations are run at the lower levels of management, after a plan is determined above. Isn't this really summed up in the fundamentals?

Break Time: Fixed Income Investing... Why Isn't This Easy?

Most people, including myself, would insist that equity investing is the most difficult to master. After all, that is the venue for: erratic price fluctuations caused by an endless supply of social, economic, and political variables; the standard Wall Street misinformation, corporate malfeasance, self serving financial gurus, and product salespersons; myriad popular and market-moving speculations from IPOs to option and margin strategies; thousands of media talk shows and their financial markets experts. When you think you understand the stock market, brother, you are in serious trouble.

But more devastating than everything that has been done to turn equity investing into a product-shopping mall of some kind, is the bottom line market value brainwashing that has turned the calm, secure, and smiley-faced world of income investing upside-down. I get more phone calls and e-mails from confused fixed-income investors than I ever receive from a simple plunge in equity prices. Admittedly, very few equity investors get to that special place, shouting "Eureka" when they first realize that corrections in the Shock Market are every bit as lovable as rallies. But not recognizing that slowly rising interest rates are as much a boon for fixed-income investors as they may be a temporary setback for a struggling economy...well, that's just another example of irresponsible investor counter-education from our "have I told you lately that I love you" enemies, the financial institutions.

Fixed-income investors must simply learn these simple truths to be comfortable in all interest rate (expectation) environments:

- More interest on your fixed-income dollars is better for you than less income on your fixed-income dollars.
- The amount you have allocated to fixed-income investing should never change because of market factors.
- A change in the market value of the fixed-income securities you own is just not likely to be the result of any change in the credit worthiness of the issuers of the securities.
- A change in the market value of your fixed-income holdings has no negative impact on the regular recurring income that you receive.
- The primary purpose of buying income securities is to generate income.
- Buying fixed income securities in a rising-interest-rate environment has a positive compounding effect on portfolio yields and, at the same time, plants the seeds for future capital gains as interest rates recede.
- The right kind of fixed income securities can be added to as interest rates rise, both to increase the average yield and to decrease the average cost.

Why is this not easy?

It's not easy because financial professionals and pseudo-professionals alike won't let it be. If you have a properly designed investment portfolio, you must view each asset allocation bucket separately and with an understanding of the purpose of each. Avoid advisors who consider the bottom line market value of such a portfolio as anything other than an expectation corroborator. The interest rate cycle is as dependable as the tides and should be enjoyed as much as the Joisey shore. Your portfolio market value should never be a surprise and, more importantly, it should never be looked at as something to be particularly concerned about—at least not immediately. For example, you had to be living in a cave somewhere and smoking something really special to think that your portfolio would be up in market value in March 2005, particularly if it contained fixed-income securities.

You have to learn to love the simplicity of fixed-income investing. Interest-rate sensitivity is a given, and interest-rate expectations are equally sensitive to inflation expectations. Price movements are both predictable and meaning-less. We actually have an investment condition that approaches certainty. This is investment Nirvana, people! Don't let those guys in the pinstriped suits get you confused. Don't panic, don't switch, and don't cry in your beer. Look at the income number on your statement and go "hmmmm" when you see no meaningful change in either direction. Actually, if you're doing this properly, the year-over-year base income figure should have increased.

So the recent bad news, all of it, is really good news for investors (actually, most bad news is) and yes, just as higher interest rates are actually better than lower ones to a certain extent, so should lower stock prices be welcomed with more smiles than tears. Only those speculators who haven't taken their rally profits are unhappy with corrections. Dealing with both events at the same time can make your bottom (line, that is) a bit uncomfortable, but only until you recognize that smaller numbers are better for buying and that their larger cousins are most appreciated with sell orders.

At times like these, some investment professionals will play to your fears, encouraging you to cut your losses in income securities, and to switch to something else. Don't be pushed into stupid decisions by smart arguments. All fixed-income investments (with the exception of open-end mutual funds) are created equally, and switching just doesn't work. An unhappy investor is the broker's best friend, so don't allow interest-rate movements in either direction to affect your investment mood.

Chapter 5
What Your Mother Never Told You about Income Investing

In the beginning, there was money. And the investment gods, in their infinite wisdom, created the corporation and its two forms of capitalization: equity and debt. Corporations raise money by selling shares of ownership called common stock, and by borrowing money through a variety of instruments that range from all forms of bonds, notes, and debentures through a similarly confusing array of preferred stocks. Companies pay investors for the use of this borrowed Capital with interest and dividends, respectively, and such payments are expressed as fixed amounts that are due on specific dates throughout the year, thus, fixed-income securities. Only the income is fixed, market values of all securities do fluctuate, for various reasons.

Although neither type of payment is guaranteed, the corporation generally promises to pay all of its bond interest and preferred stock dividends before any payments can be made to common stock holders. Additionally, corporate debt may be fully or partially insured and/or convertible into the common stock of the issuing company. Fixed-income investing is much safer and significantly more secure than equity investing and, by its very nature, serves to keep the level of overall investment portfolio risk under control. But, income securities may also be callable, fully or partially, at various times, always inconveniently, and usually at face value. Is a corporation more likely to redeem debt in a rising or falling interest rate environment? Arranging to reduce the risk of a call will lead to a lower rate of return.

Well thought-out asset-allocation plans always allow for a portion of the investment portfolio to be invested in fixed-income securities, particularly once the six-figure level has been achieved.

Creators of Even Less Risky Income Securities

The federal government and its agencies are huge issuers of notes and bonds, and government fixed-income securities are the safest and most secure of all the fixed-income vehicles. Both principal, the face amount of the security, and interest are guaranteed by printing presses controlled by the federal government. To compensate for their esteemed position as the safest securities on the planet, they return the lowest possible interest rate available anywhere. Yet, their market value fluctuates with changing interest-rate expectations (IRE, appropriately), just like any other rate sensitive security. They are rarely called, and when held to maturity, there is virtually no risk of loss... in spite of constant market-value changes.

States, municipalities, and their agencies are also significant issuers of income securities. The most important feature of municipal securities is that the interest they pay to investors is totally exempt from federal and home state income taxes. There have been an insignificant number of defaults in United States municipal bond history, and those few have nearly always involved revenue bonds. Municipal general obligation (GO) bonds are considered to be nearly as safe as federally issued securities. As with corporate bonds, investors must look to the bond rating and the current yield of the bond itself to determine the quality of the issue. A suspiciously high yield should be an indicator to the investor of increased risk.

When held to maturity, there is virtually no risk associated with these securities either. Still, many municipal bond issues are insured as to principal, interest, or both, thus assuring an even lower yield to the investor. Investors pay dearly for each level of protection they require, and experience will teach you that insurance and the accompanying AAA rating is pretty much just overkill.

Wall Street is very creative in putting together products and gimmicks that they distribute to the public with an extra markup.

Laddered treasury deals, zero-coupon securities, and various types of unit trusts come to mind, and when rates are high, all but the zeros fit well into the income asset-allocation bucket. But it is difficult to diversify a portfolio properly with individual issues and expensive to work with unit trusts exclusively. All individual issues have liquidity issues, and open-end income mutual funds seem to be incapable of moving in a northerly direction.

Fixed-income investors are fortunate that they can now obtain investment company closed-end income funds (CEFs) that invest in all of the securities mentioned above, plus an endless variety of sector, royalty, real estate, and other specialties. There are right and wrong (high risk vs. lower risk) ways of investing in these types of securities as well, but their liquidity, trading ease, monthly cash flow, and instant diversification make them the security of choice, particularly for traders.

Questions: (1) Why do financial institutions make such a fuss about falling prices in fixed-income securities, when they are aware of these very basic safety characteristics? (2) Why don't financial professionals encourage investors to take profits in these securities when their prices rise during periods of lower IRE?

IRE-Sensitive, Long-Term Hold Securities

All income securities and some high-dividend equities, are IRE sensitive, and as such, their market price will always vary inversely with the expected direction of interest rates. All bond, preferred stock, REIT, and Income CEF prices rise in market value when lower interest rates are expected and fall if higher rates are anticipated. The amount of movement in the price of IRE-sensitive, securities will vary depending on the quality rating of the issuer of the security and the amount of time until maturity, or call date (if applicable) of the issue. Sector-specific CEFs will also react to other variables. All of this makes CEFs much more exciting than the boring stuff inside them. Since the cyclical fluctuations of CEF prices are generally of little long-term consequence, it is critical that investors learn to take advantage of lower prices and higher yields rather than to lose sleep over them. This seems to be a whole lot more difficult than it sounds, and believe it or not, fixed-income investing is the area of investing where the most errors are made.

Since the purpose of income securities is to generate income, it is conceivable that they will be held onto, doing their job, for a long time. Regardless of where you think interest rates are going, your actions should be limited to buying more of one of your holdings when it falls in price and selling the security when you can realize a 10 percent net/net gain. On rare occasions, an income CEF will start paying a smaller dividend; apply patience to the wound, but throw it out the window at the next cyclical down-curve in the road.

Understanding Fixed-Income Securities

The purpose of owning fixed-income securities is quite simply the generation of a secure cash flow that can either be spent or reinvested at prevailing interest rates (i.e., compounded) until it is needed. A plan to spend less than 70 percent of portfolio income can actually produce growth in both working capital and income, thus getting the inflation monkey off our back in retirement. Keeping the IRS away from all forms of retirement income plans, including Social Security, would also be a huge help. Investors are a big enough voting block to get this done but we have never been organized. The classic long-term goal of an investment program is to live off the income produced by the assets, without ever having to invade principal. Therefore, it should be clear that it is not the least bit savvy either to defer the receipt of income or to put off the development of the income stream until the last minute. This is part of what asset allocation is all about, and when done using the working capital model, it assures the constant growth of the income produced by the portfolio.

Investing in income securities is never a hedge against something that may or may not happen in the future, nor is it a place to stash your stash until some other event takes place. It's the key element in your long-range financial plan. The two most common and dependable forms of investment income are dividends and interest. Capital-gains income is a real possibility as well with the type of income generators we've been talking about, but it is not considered part of the base income.

Fixed-income investing will probably remain the orphan of the investment world because it just doesn't generate the type of excitement that equities provide routinely. Still, it is important for investors to understand that there is as much of a need for income in the development of an investment portfolio as there is the obvious need for income in a person's retirement years.

Are All Fixed-Income Securities Created Equally?
Fixed-income yields and security prices generally change much more slowly than stock market prices, and it can actually takes years for interest rates to move in either direction by a few points. At the same time, a trend in interest rates is likely to last longer than a trend in stock prices. There is abundantly more economics than there is emotion involved with interest rate movements, creating a more stable playing field for the investor... at least theoretically.

If you are thinking long term, as you should in this area, the rules become simple and few:

- Rule 1: Always seek out the longest duration, investment-grade only securities with the highest (reasonable) yields.
- Rule 2: So long as you follow Rule 1, Rule 2 is to focus on the cost basis of your fixed-income securities and ignore market value fluctuations.
- Rule 3: Invest in tradable income securities.

All interest-rate sensitive securities are created equally. This means that if your bonds are up or down in price, so are everyone else's. If your fund is down, Johnny's fund couldn't do better unless there are significant quality or duration differences involved.

Investors should almost never switch from one fixed income fund to another, or even worse, take losses on fixed income to move into something else entirely, typically a peaking equity market. Another basic rule is to avoid yields that are a great deal higher than normal. In one sense, fixed-income investing and equity investing are identical...junk is junk. But to really become a successful fixed-income investor you must get to the point where you understand that higher interest rates are a good thing, and so, too, are lower interest rates.

The Delivery System for Fixed-Income Securities
We've seen how stable, predictable, fair, and understandable fixed-income investing really is, in its purist form. The simplicity of the security price-interest rate relationship makes market value fluctuations both expected and easy to cope with. There are a variety of fixed-income investment media that do not share the illiquidity, costs, and complexities of more expensive individual security possibilities.

Unfortunately, some financial professionals have not been properly prepared to deal with the nature of fixed-income securities and are somewhat unfamiliar with alternatives to the standard open-end mutual fund. There are four common forms in which fixed-income securities find their way into investment portfolios: individual securities, open-ended mutual funds, closed-end funds, and unit trusts.

In the stock market, it is decidedly wiser to use individual securities nearly all of the time. But when dealing with most fixed-income securities, there are some other variables in the mix that are impossible to predict or to control efficiently. Call dates and partial redemptions come to mind as the most frequent issues that may have to be addressed with individual securities. Odd-lot bond pricing is another. Using managed programs makes a whole lot of sense in this area, just like REITs and royalty trusts are easier for you and me (normal folk) than owning apartment houses and drilling rigs. But they have to be managed by professionals, not by your fellow 401(k) and IRA participants. Conventional mutual funds are, in reality, not managed; closed-end mutual funds are.

The Final Word on Fixed Income

The word is out. Income investing doesn't have to be scary or boring while it maintains the safety and stability characteristics that we all love. Understanding this will allow us to move on to a discussion of the most fun part of investing with either equity or income securities—profit taking.

Understanding Fixed Income Investing: Expectations

The stock market is generally an easier medium for investors to understand (i.e., to form behavioral expectations about) than the fixed-income market. As unlikely as this sounds, experience proves it irrefutably. Few investors grow to love volatility as I do, but most expect it in the market value of their equity positions. When dealing with fixed-income securities, however, neither they nor their advisors are comfortable with any downward movement at all. Most won't consider taking profits when prices increase but will rush in to accept losses when prices fall.

The Total Return Shell Game

Just what is this "total return" thing that fixed-income investment managers talk about and Wall Street uses as a performance hoop for investment managers to jump through? Why is it mostly smoke and mirrors? Here's the formula:

Total Income (+ or -) Change in Market Value - Expenses = Total Return

So this is supposed to be the ultimate test for any investment portfolio, fixed-income or equity. In reality, it's another Wall Street assault on our pocket-books. Applied to fixed-income or balanced-investment portfolios, it is useless nonsense designed to confuse and to annoy investors.

How many of you remember John Q. Retiree? He was that guy with his chest all puffed up last year, bragging about his 12 percent total return on his bond portfolio, while he secretly wondered why he only had about 3 percent in actual spending money. This year he's scratching his head wondering how he's ever going to make ends meet with a total return that's quickly approaching zero! Do you think he realizes that his actual spending money may be higher? What's wrong with this thinking? How will the media compare mutual fund managers without it? Wall Street doesn't care because investor's have been brainwashed into thinking that fixed-income investing and equity investing can be measured with the same ruler. They just can't, and the "total return" ruler itself would be thrown out with a lot of other investment trash if it were more widely understood.

If you want to use a ruler that applies equally well to both classes of investment security, you have to change just one piece of the formula and give the new concept a name that focuses on what certainly is the most important thing about fixed-income investing... the spending money. We'll identify this new way of looking at things as the working capital model and the new and improved formulae are:

- for fixed-income securities: Total cash income + net realized capital gains - expenses = total spending money
- for equity securities: Total cash income + net realized capital gains – expenses = total spending money

Yes, they are the same. The difference is what the investor elects to do with the spending money after it has become available. So if John Q's investment pro had taken profits on the bonds held last year, he could have sent out some bigger income payments and/or taken advantage of the rise in interest rates that is happening right now.

Better for John Q, sure, but the lowered total return number could have gotten him fired. The working capital approach takes those troublemaking paper profits and losses out of the equation entirely, because of their irrelevance in an investment portfolio that is diversified properly and comprised only of investment-grade, income producing securities.

You may know who Bill Gross is. He's the fixed-income equivalent of Warren Buffet, and he just happens to manage the world's largest open-ended bond mutual fund. How is he investing his own money these days? It has been reported that he has removed it from the total return mutual fund he manages and moved it into...closed-end municipal bond funds1 where he can now get around 7.0 percent tax free! (Interestingly, he doesn't mention the taxable variety of closed-end funds, now yielding a point or two more than the tax frees, but they certainly demand a presence in the fixed-income allocation of qualified portfolios.)

Similarly, Gross advises against the use of the non-investment grade (junk bonds) that many open-end bond managers are sneaking into their portfolios.2 But true to form, and forgive the blasphemy, Gross seems to be as total-return brainwashed as the rest of the institutional community... totally, so he is still giving validity to speculation in commodity futures, foreign currencies, derivatives, and TIPS (Treasury Inflation Protected), which increase in yield with the inflation rate. Safer, yes, but the yields are far too dismal. Inflation is a measure of total buying power, and the only sure way to beat it is with higher income levels, not lower ones. If TIPS rise to 5 percent, REITS will yield 12 percent, and preferred stocks 9 percent, etc. No fixed-income security is an island.

As long as the financial community remains mesmerized with their total return statistical shell game, investors will be the losers. Total returns go down when yields on individual securities go up, and vice versa—this is the way the investment gods designed income securities. Total-return analysis is used to engineer switching decisions between fixed income and equity investment allocations, with statements such as, "the total return on equities is likely to be greater than that on fixed-income securities during this period of rising interest rates."

You have to understand that the primary purpose of fixed-income securities is income production. If you don't agree with the next three sentences, if they don't make complete sense to you, you need to learn more about fixed-income investing:

- Higher interest rates are the fixed-income investor's best friend; they produce higher levels of spending money.
- Lower interest rates are the fixed-income investor's best friend; they provide the opportunity to add capital gains to the total spending money.
- Changes in the market value of investment-grade fixed-income securities are totally and completely irrelevant, 99 percent of the time.

Important characteristics of fixed-income securities include:

- They are securities that generate a predictable stream of interest or dividend income, such as bonds, debentures and preferred shares.
- They normally have specific payment dates and amounts.
- Risk will vary, depending on the type, quality, and maturity of the security, but they are considered far less risky than stocks.
- Fixed-income securities are issued by governments or corporations and have a maturity date when the issuer has to pay the investor the principal or face amount of the security.
- They do fluctuate in market price, but not as a function of investment safety.

Theoretically, fixed-income securities should be the ultimate buy and hold; their primary purpose is income generation, and return of principal is typically a contractual obligation. I like to add some seasoning to this bland diet, through profit taking whenever possible, but losses are almost never an acceptable, or necessary, menu item. Still, Wall Street pumps out products and investment experts rationalize strategies that cloud the simple rules governing the behavior of what should be an investor's retirement blankie. I shake my head in disbelief constantly. The investment gods have spoken, "The market price of fixed-income securities shall vary inversely with interest rates, both actual and anticipated... and it is good."

"It's OK, it's natural, it just doesn't matter," I say to disbelieving audiences everywhere. You have to understand how securities react to interest-rate expectations and learn to take advantage of it. There's no need to hedge against it or to cry about it. It's simply the nature of things.

There are several reasons that investors have invalid expectations about their fixed-income investments:

1. They don't experience this type of investing until retirement-planning time, and they view all securities with an eye on market value, as they have been programmed to do by Wall Street.
2. The combination of increasing age and inexperience creates an inordinate fear of loss that is preyed upon by commissioned salespersons of all shapes and sizes.

3. They have trouble distinguishing between the income-generating purpose of fixed-income securities and the fact that they are negotiable instruments with a market value that is a function of current interest rates.
4. They have been brainwashed into believing that the market value of their portfolio, and not the income that it generates, is their primary weapon against inflation. [Really, Alice, if you held these securities in a safe deposit box instead of a brokerage account and just received the income, the perception of loss, the fear, and the rush to make a change would simply disappear. Think about it.]

Every properly constructed portfolio will contain securities whose primary purpose is to generate income (fixed and/or variable), and every investor must understand some basic and absolute characteristics of interest-rate sensitive securities. These securities include corporate, government, and municipal bonds, preferred stocks, many closed-end funds, unit trusts, REITs, royalty trusts, and treasury securities. Most are legally binding contracts between the owner of the securities (you, or an investment company that you own a piece of) and an entity that promises to pay a fixed rate of interest for the use of the money. They are primary debts of the issuer and must be paid before all other obligations. They are negotiable, meaning that they can be bought and sold, at a price that varies with current interest rates. The longer the duration of the obligation, the more price fluctuation cycles will occur during the holding period. Typically, longer obligations also have higher interest rates. Two things are accomplished by buying shorter-duration securities: you earn less interest and you pay your broker a commission more frequently.

Defaults in interest payments are extremely rare, particularly in investment-grade securities, and it is very likely that you will receive a predictable, constant, and gradually increasing flow of income. (The income will increase gradually only if you manage your asset allocation properly by adding proportionately to your fixed-income holdings.) So, if everything is going according to plan, all you ever need to look at is the amount of income that your fixed income portfolio is generating... period. Dealing with variable income securities is slightly different, as market value will also vary with the nature of the income and the economics of a particular industry. REITs, royalty trusts, unit trusts, and even CEFs may have variable income levels, and portfolio management requires an understanding of the risks involved. A municipal bond CEF, for example will have a much more dependable cash flow and considerably more price stability than an oil and gas royalty trust. Thus, diversification in the income-generating portion of the portfolio is even more important than in the growth portion—income pays the bills. Never lose sight of that fact and you will be able to go fishing more frequently in retirement.

The critical relationship between the two classes of securities in your portfolio is this: the market value of your equity investments and that of your fixed income investments are totally and completely unrelated. Each market dances to its own beat. Stocks are like heavy metal or rap—impossible to predict. Bonds are more like the classics and old-time rock-and-roll—much more predictable. Thus, for the sake of portfolio smile maintenance, you must develop the ability to separate the two classes of securities, mentally, if not physically. For example, if your July 2005 market value fell, it was because of higher interest rates, not lower stock prices. In some years, the combination of higher rates and a weaker stock market will be a double whammy for portfolio market values, and a double bonanza for investment opportunities. Just like at the mall, lower securities prices are a good thing for buyers... and higher prices are a good thing for sellers. You need to act on these things with each cyclical change.

Here's a simple way to deal with fixed-income market values to avoid shocks and surprises. Just visualize the scales of justice, with or without the blindfold. On one side we have a number that represents the current market value of your fixed-income portfolio. On the other side, we have a small "i" for interest rates, and up or down arrows that represent interest rate directional expectations. If the world expects interest rates to rise, or even to stop going down, up arrows are added to the "i" and the market value side moves lower, the 2007 scenario. Absolutely nothing can (or should) be done about it. It has no impact at all on the contracts you hold or the interest that you will receive; neither the maturity value nor cash flow is affected... but your broker just called with an idea.

The mechanics are also simple. These are negotiable securities that carry a fixed interest rate. Buyers are entitled to current rates, and the only way to provide them on an existing security is to sell it at a discount. Fortunately, one rarely has to sell. Over the past few years of falling interest rates, fixed-income securities have risen in price and investors should have realized capital gains as a result... adding to portfolio income and working capital. Now, that trend has reversed itself and you have the opportunity to add to existing holdings or to buy new securities at lower prices and higher interest rates. This cycle will be repeated forever.

So, from a "let's try to be happy with our investment portfolio because it's financially healthier" standpoint, it is critical that you understand changes in market value, anticipate them, and appreciate the opportunities that they provide. Comparing your portfolio market value with some external and unrelated number accomplishes nothing. Actually, owning your fixed-income securities in the most freely negotiable manner possible can put you in a unique position. You have no increased risk from a reduction in security prices, while you gain the ability to add to holdings at higher yields. It's like magic... or is it justice. Both sides of the scales contain good news for the investor... as the investment gods intended.

Income Investing: Selecting the Right Stuff

When is 3 percent better than 6 percent? Yeah, we all know the answer, but only until the prices of the securities we already own begin to fall. Then, logic and mathematical acumen disappear and we become susceptible to all kinds of special cures for the periodic onset of higher interest rates. We'll be told to sit in cash until rates stop rising, or to sell the securities we own now, before they lose even more of their precious market value. Other gurus will suggest the purchase of shorter-term bonds or CDs (ugh) to stem the tide of the perceived erosion in portfolio values. There are two important things that your mother never told you about income investing:

1. Higher interest rates are good for investors, even better than lower rates, and
2. Selecting the right securities to take advantage of the interest rate cycle is not particularly difficult.

Higher interest rates are the result of the government's efforts to slow a growing economy in hopes of preventing an appearance of the three-headed inflation monster. A quick glance over your shoulder might remind you of recent times when the government was trying to heal the wounds of a misguided Wall Street attack on traditional investment principles by lowering interest rates. The strategy worked, the economy rebounded, and Wall Street is trying to scramble back to where it was nearly six years ago. Think about the impact of changing interest rates on your income securities during the past five years. Bonds and preferred stocks, government and municipal securities all moved higher in market value. Sure you felt wealthier, but the increase in your annual spendable income got smaller and smaller. Your total income could well have decreased during the period as higher interest rate holdings were called away (at face value), and reinvestments were made at lower yields.

How many of you have mental bruises from the realization that you could have taken profits during the downward trajectory of the cycle on the very securities that you now lament over. The nerve— falling below the price you paid for them years ago. But the income on these turncoats is the same as it was in 2004, when their prices were 10 or 20 percent higher. This is the work of Mother Nature's financial twin sister. It's like acorns, snowfalls, and crocuses. You need to dress properly for seasonal changes and invest properly for cyclical changes. Remember the days of bearer bonds? There was never a whisper about market value erosion. Was it the IRS or institutional Wall Street that took them away?

Higher rates are good for investors, particularly when retirement is a factor in your investment decisions. The more you receive for your reinvestment dollars, the more likely it is that you won't need a second job to maintain your standard of living. I know of no retail entity, from grocery store to cruise line, that will accept the market value of your portfolio as payment for goods or services. Income pays the bills, more is always better than less, and only increased income levels can protect you from inflation. So, you say, how does a person take advantage of the cyclical nature of interest rates to garner the best possible income on investment-quality securities? You might also ask why Wall Street makes such a fuss about the dismal bond market and offers more of their patented sell low, buy high advisories, but that should be fairly obvious. An unhappy investor is Wall Street's best customer.

Selecting the right securities to take advantage of the interest-rate cycle is not particularly difficult, but it does require a change in focus from the statement bottom line... and the use of a few security types with which you may not be 100-percent comfortable. I'm going to assume that you are familiar with these investments, each of which could be considered (from time to time) for a spot in the well diversified income portion of your asset allocation:

1. Traditional individual municipal and corporate bonds, treasuries, government agency securities, and preferred stocks.
2. The eyebrow-raising unit trust varietals, closed-end funds, royalty trusts, and REITs. (I have purposely excluded CDs and money funds, which are not investments by definition; CMOs and zeros, mutations developed by some sicko MBAs; and open-end mutual funds, which just can't work because they are really "managed by the mob," i.e., investors.)

The market rules that apply to all of these are fairly predictable, but the ability to create a safer, higher yielding, and flexible portfolio varies considerably within the security types. For example, most people who invest in individual bonds wind up with a laundry list of odd-lot positions, with short durations and low yields, designed for the benefit of that smiling guy in the big corner office. There is a better way, but you have to focus on income and be willing to trade occasionally.

The larger the portfolio, the more likely it is that you will be able to buy round lots of a diversified group of bonds, preferred stocks, etc. But regardless of size, individual securities of all kinds have liquidity problems, higher risk levels than are necessary, and lower yields spaced out over inconvenient time periods. Of the traditional types listed above, only preferred stock holdings are easily added to during upward interest rate movements, and cheap to take profits on when rates fall. The downside on all of these is their callability in best-yield-first order. Wall Street loves these securities because they command the highest possible trading costs—costs that need not be disclosed to the consumer, particularly at issue. Unit trusts are traditional securities set to music, a tune that generally assures the investor of a higher yield than is possible through personal portfolio creation. There are several additional advantages: instant diversification, quality, and monthly cash flow that may include principal (better in rising rate markets, ya follow?), and insulation from year-end swap scams. Unfortunately, the unit trusts are not managed, so there are few capital gains distributions to smile about, and once all of the securities are redeemed, the party is over. Trading opportunities—the very heart and soul of successful portfolio management—are practically nonexistent.

What if you could own common stock in companies that manage traditional income securities and other recognized income producers like real estate, energy production, and mortgages? Closed-end funds, REITs, and royalty trusts demand your attention… and don't let the idea of leverage spook you. AAA+ insured corporate bonds, and utility-preferred stocks are forms of leverage. The sacred 30-year treasury bond is leverage. Most corporations, all governments, and most private citizens use leverage. Without leverage, most people would be commuting to work on bicycles. Every CEF can be researched as part of your selection process to determine how much leverage is involved, and the benefits—you're not going to be happy when you realize what you've been talked out of. CEFs and the other investment company securities mentioned are managed by professionals who are not taking their direction from the mob. They provide you the opportunity to have a properly structured portfolio with a significantly higher yield, even after the management fees that are inside.

Certainly, a REIT or royalty trust is more risky than a CEF comprised of preferred stocks or corporate bonds, but here you have a way to participate in the widest variety of fixed and variable income alternatives in a much more manageable form. When prices rise, profit taking is routine in a liquid market; when prices fall, you can add to your position, increasing your yield and reducing your cost basis at the same time. Now don't start to salivate about the prospect of throwing all your money into real estate and gas and oil pipelines. Diversify properly as you would with any other investments and make sure your living expenses are taken care of by the less risky CEFs in the portfolio. In bond CEFs, you can get unleveraged portfolios and state specific and/or insured municipal portfolios. Monthly income (frequently augmented by capital gains distributions) is at a level that is likely to be significantly better than your broker will obtain for you on his or her own. I told you you'd be angry.

Another feature of investment company shares (and please stay away from gimmicky, passively managed, or indexed types) is somewhat surprising and difficult to explain. The price you pay for shares frequently represents a discount from the market value of the securities contained in the managed portfolio. So instead of buying a diversified group of illiquid individual securities at a premium, you are reaping the benefit of a portfolio of (quite possibly the same) securities at a discount. Additionally, CEFs will give you the first shot at any additional shares they intend to distribute to investors.

Stop, put down the phone. Move into these securities calmly, without taking unnecessary losses on good quality holdings, and never buy a new issue. I meant to say, absolutely never buy a new issue, for all of the usual reasons. As with individual securities, there are reasons for unusually high or low yields, like too much risk or poor management. No matter how well managed a junk bond portfolio is, it's still just junk. So do a little research and spread your dollars around the many management companies that are out there. If your advisor tells you that all of this is risky, ill-advised foolishness... well, that's Wall Street, and the baby needs shoes.

Managing the Income Portfolio

The reason people assume the risks of investing in the first place is the prospect of achieving a higher rate of return than is attainable in a risk-free environment. Risk comes in various forms, but the average investor's primary concerns are credit and market risk—particularly when it comes to investing for income. Credit risk involves the ability of corporations, government entities, and even individuals, to make good on their financial commitments. Market risk refers to the certainty that there will be changes in the market value of selected securities. We can minimize the former by selecting only high-quality (investment-grade) securities and the latter by diversifying properly, understanding that market-value changes are normal, and by having a plan of action for dealing with such fluctuations. (What does the bank do to get the amount of interest it guarantees to depositors? What does it do in response to higher or lower market interest rate expectations?)

You don't have to be a professional investment manager to professionally manage your investment portfolio, but you do need to have a long-term plan and know something about asset allocation, a portfolio-organization tool that is often misunderstood and almost always improperly used within the financial community. It's important to recognize, as well, that you do not need a fancy computer program or a glossy presentation with economic scenarios, inflation estimators, and stock market projections to get yourself lined up properly with your target. You need common sense, reasonable expectations, patience, discipline, soft hands, and an oversized driver. The K.I.S.S. principle needs to be at the foundation of your investment plan; an emphasis on Working Capital will help you organize and control your investment portfolio.

Planning for retirement should focus on the additional income needed from the investment portfolio, and the asset allocation formula (relax, 8th grade math is plenty) needed for goal achievement will depend on just three variables:

1. the amount of liquid investment assets you are starting with,
2. the amount of time until retirement, and
3. the range of interest rates currently available from investment-grade securities.

If you don't allow the engineer gene to take control, this can be a fairly simple process. Even if you are young, you need to stop smoking heavily and to develop a growing stream of income. If you keep the income growing, market value growth (that you are expected to worship) will take care of itself. Remember, higher market value may increase hat size, but it doesn't pay the bills.

First deduct any guaranteed pension income from your retirement income goal to estimate the amount needed just from the investment portfolio. Don't worry about inflation at this stage. Next, determine the total market value of your investment portfolios, including company plans, IRAs, H-Bonds—everything, except the house, boat, jewelry, etc. Liquid personal and retirement plan assets only. This total is then multiplied by a range of reasonable interest rates (6 percent, to 8 percent right now), and hopefully, one of the resulting numbers will be close to the target amount you came up with a moment ago. If you are within a few years of retirement age, they better be! For certain, this process will give you a clear idea of where you stand, and that, in and of itself, is worth the effort.

Organizing the portfolio involves deciding upon an appropriate asset allocation, and that requires some discussion. Here are a few basic asset allocation guidelines:

1. All asset allocation decisions are based on the cost basis of the securities involved. The current market value may be more or less and it just doesn't matter.
2. Any investment portfolio with a cost basis of $100,000 or more should have a minimum of 30 percent invested in income securities, either taxable or tax free, depending on the nature of the portfolio. Tax deferred entities (all varieties of retirement programs) should house the bulk of equity investments. This rule applies from birth to five years prior to retirement. Before the age of thirty, it is a mistake to have too much of your portfolio in income securities.
3. There are only two asset allocation categories, and neither is ever described with a decimal point. All cash in the portfolio is destined for one category or the other.
4. From five years prior to and beyond retirement your income allocation needs to be adjusted upward until the "reasonable interest rate test" says that you are on target or at least in range.
5. At retirement, between 60 percent and 100 percent of your portfolio may have to be in income-generating securities.

Controlling or implementing the investment plan will be accomplished best by those who are least emotional, most decisive, naturally calm, patient, generally conservative (not politically), and self actualized. Investing is a long-term, personal, goal orientated, non-competitive, hands-on, decision-making process that does not require advanced degrees or a rocket-scientist IQ. In fact, being too smart can be a problem if you have a tendency to over-analyze things.

For fixed income, focus on investment-grade securities, with above average but not highest-in-class yields. With variable income securities, avoid purchase near fifty-two week highs, and keep individual holdings well below 5 percent. Keep individual preferred stocks and bonds well below 5 percent as well. Closed-end fund positions may be slightly higher than 5 percent, depending on type. Take a reasonable profit (more than one year's interest for starters) as soon as possible. With a 60-percent equity allocation, 60 percent of profits and interest would be allocated to stocks.

Monitoring investment performance the Wall Street way is inappropriate and problematic for goal-orientated investors. It purposely focuses on short-term dislocations and uncontrollable cyclical changes, producing constant disappointment and encouraging inappropriate transactional responses to natural and harmless events. Coupled with a media that thrives on sensationalizing anything outrageously positive or negative (Google and Enron, Peter Lynch and Martha Stewart, for example), it becomes difficult to stay the course with any plan, as environmental conditions change. First greed, then fear, new products replacing old, and always the promise of something better when, in fact, the boring and old-fashioned basic investment principles still get the job done. Remember, your unhappiness is Wall Street's most coveted asset. Don't humor them and protect yourself. Base your performance evaluation efforts on goal achievement—yours, not theirs. Here's how, based on the three basic objectives we've been talking about: growth of base income, profit production from trading, and overall growth in working capital.

Base income includes the dividends and interest produced by your portfolio without the realized capital gains that should actually be the larger number much of the time. No matter how you slice it, your long-range comfort demands regularly increasing income. By using your total portfolio cost basis as the benchmark, it's easy to determine where to invest your accumulating cash. Since a portion of every dollar added to the portfolio is reallocated to income production, you are assured of increasing the total annually. If market value is used for this analysis, you could be pouring too much money into a falling stock market to the detriment of your long-range income objectives.

Profit production is the happy face of the market value volatility that is a natural attribute of all securities. To realize a profit, you must be able to sell the securities that most investment strategists (and accountants) want you to marry up with! Successful investors learn to sell the ones they love, and the more frequently (yes, short term), the better. This is called trading, and it is not a four-letter word. When you can get yourself to the point where you think of the securities you own as high-quality inventory on the shelves of your personal portfolio boutique, you have arrived. You won't see WalMart holding out for higher prices than their standard markup, and neither should you. Reduce the markup on slower movers, and sell damaged goods you've held too long at a loss if you have to, and, in the thick of it all, try to anticipate what your standard, Wall Street account statement is going to show you... a portfolio of equity securities that have not yet achieved their profit goals and are probably in negative market value territory because you've sold the winners and replaced them with new inventory! Similarly, you'll see a diversified group of income earners, chastised for following their natural tendencies at lower prices, which will help you increase your portfolio yield and overall cash flow. If you see big plus signs, you are not managing the portfolio properly.

Working capital growth (total portfolio cost basis) just happens, and at a rate that will be somewhere between the average return on the income securities in the portfolio and the total realized gain on the equity portion of the portfolio. It will actually be higher with larger equity allocations because frequent trading produces a higher rate of return than the more secure positions in the income allocation. But, and this is too big a but to ignore as you approach retirement, trading profits are not guaranteed and the risk of loss (although minimized with a sensible selection process) is greater than it is with income securities. This is why asset allocation moves from a greater to a lesser equity percentage as you approach retirement.

So is there really such a thing as an income portfolio that needs to be managed? Or are we really just dealing with an investment portfolio that needs its asset allocation tweaked occasionally as we approach the time in life when it has to provide the yacht... and the gas money to run it? By using cost basis (working capital) as the number that needs growing, by accepting trading as an acceptable, even conservative, approach to portfolio management, and by focusing on growing income instead of ego, this whole retirement investing thing becomes significantly less scary. So now you can focus on changing the tax code, reducing health care costs, saving Social Security, and spoiling the grandchildren.

Chapter 6
Sell Higher

G rowing up at Lake Hopatcong in northwest Jersey, the most popular entertainment around was the rickety old roller coaster at Bertrand Island Park. The excitement would build as you ascended the first peak, anticipating the breathtaking plunge—eyes wide open, screaming from the thrill with a white-knuckled grip on either the safety bar or your date's hand as she pretended to share your fear... three times through the process, hoarse at the finish, and ready for more. As each peak approached, you could see the downturn approaching; as each plunge accelerated, you knew that you would be saved by the next ascent...

The Shock Market is the Eyes Wide Shut adult version of such childhood thrill rides, with no predictable beginning or end and no way of gauging the size or duration of the relentless peaks and valleys. This is one of the very few things that can actually be known about the market, individual stocks, security groups and sectors, and interest rates. There will be ups and downs, there will be cycles of varying amplitude, altitude, and duration. There will be opportunities to buy at lower prices and to sell at higher ones.

With individual securities, a directional change may occur at any point along the route, with little or no warning. Financial experts squander millions of words attempting daily explanations of the reasons for every movement along the ride. Many insult our intelligence with predictions of future rallies and corrections. For what purpose? None of this microanalysis can provide a reliable answer to the question you ask yourself just as frequently: what's going to happen next? Although each tries to convince you he or she is the best at answering that question, not even the most pompous of Wall Street institutions has shown the audacity to refute the fact that the markets are cyclical in nature; but they all seem to view this natural state of things as a problem to be hedged against. Have none of the Masters of the Universe been to Busch Gardens?

The solution is to operate your investment program within the thrill-ride environment that is the reality of investing—the whys, wherefores, and whens being much less important than the decision-making model you put into place to deal with them. What you do next is always in your hands, and you should be prepared to do something nearly every day. Doing nothing must be a decision to do nothing.

We've spent a good deal of time developing a realistic deci-sion-making model for the important buy decisions made along the downward path of the cars in our selection universe. Our cars have the extended-warranty protection of profitability, dividends, and side-curtain air bags. They are only purchased 20 percent or more below their last peak, but we have no idea where or when the fall will be broken by the next rise, of whatever significance.

Most visitors to the Wall Street Amusement Park aren't thrill-seekers at all. They're not fond of Wildcats, Raptors, and Wicked Twisters, seeking only one-way rides up the track, at least until their stay at the park is finished. That's fine for a trip to Fantasy Land, but the potholes on Wall Street are famous for swallowing up rallies with-out warning. So its time for traders—aka investors capable of mak-ing more than one decision—to take things into their own hands and develop a selling mechanism that works with and through the reality of any type of Mean Streak or Millennium Force that shows up.

The Wizards of Wall Street

The wizards of Wall Street, with no exceptions, think of themselves as infallible stock pickers. Their researchers find companies whose stock prices are likely to rise quickly, to a target that is always signifi-cantly above current prices. Their promotional methods create self-fulfilling prophecies, and the flood of money into the favorites seems to have no end. Financial professionals encourage investors to keep their winners indefinitely, to fall in love with them, and to make them part of a core portfolio that must be held on to for the benefit of the grandchildren. Rarely does anyone point a finger at you and insinuate that you should take your profits and move on. This stops now. We are in the business of growing productive portfolios where the risk is limited by the inherent quality of the companies, a fairly classic diversification model, and an addiction to the thrill of profit taking.

The sell decision, when it comes to individual securities, is the single most important decision that people fail to make most frequently. Be it peer pressure or pure greed, their own ignorance or that of an inexperienced or incompetent advisor, the sell decision is rarely even considered until well after the opportunity for profit has left the portfolio. Why? The reason is simply this: we're supposed to keep things that we love, things that have been good to us, and things that we may still have a use for. Selling is for stuff we want to get rid of because it no longer satisfies or has limited potential or utility. This reasoning, which applies well to family, friends, and possessions, fails miserably when it comes to the scraps of paper that represent financial assets. It boggles the entrepreneurial mind, a mindset you would think that people in a capitalistic society would come to naturally. But selling something when its popular (like your Hula Hoop, Walkman, and Barbie doll) just doesn't compute when it comes to securities. Just as I've had to slap people around to get them to buy when prices are falling, it takes no less than a personality transplant to get the majority of folks interested in or excited about profits.

It's not just Wall Street that has made us so income- and capital gains-averse, although the brokerage community is certainly proficient at playing investors' fear and greed like a fine musical instrument. The tax code tells all of us that investment income isn't nearly as worthwhile as any form of earned income. It must be discouraged and the wealth it creates confiscated and redistributed. Now that 95 percent of the population has an investment portfolio, the myth that only the wealthy invest can be debunked pretty easily. Similarly, the old wives tale about brokerage commissions taking away all the profits when a sale is made can be retired. And the hindsightful lawsuit possibilities when a profit on one sale turns into a loss on a subsequent purchase (while the sold issue continues to rise) should certainly be legislated against. Maybe we can even stop people from taking unnecessary losses, or from putting off profit taking for tax reasons… and maybe there really is a Santa Clause.

The profit-taking discipline I'm suggesting involves a markup on a securities cost basis to a price that the security has already achieved—a reasonable profit number, one that many high quality securities will provide over and over again. Just like the down 20 percent or more from the (fill in the blank) buy target, a 10-percent sell target is reasonable. Actually, there are times when it's perfectly OK, necessary, and even smart to take less. Two key thoughts:

1. Absolutely never allow the greed monster to make you hold out for more than that 10 percent.
2. There's no such thing as a bad profit.

If you can make yourself operate your equity portfolio in this manner, with well defined and disciplined buying and selling rules and procedures, your long-run investment success will become child's play and the Wall Street roller coaster will become your favorite ride.

Dive! Dive! Dive!

The market was just breezing along during that summer of 1987, enjoying one of the broadest rallies ever experienced on Wall Street. From the very start (twelve consecutive up days in the DJIA) equity prices just didn't seem capable of going down. The mystical 2,000 barrier was shattered early in the year and upward the market soared. On through 2,100 it rumbled, then 2,200, and 2,300. "All aboard!" the Street engineers shouted. It seemed like even the comic strip dartboard approach would be successful, and many subscribed to it. The institutional hydra was still young then, with too few heads to be scary and, with only the dark cloud of rapidly rising interest rates in an otherwise clear sky, the small individual investor was once again lured back into the market. A decade earlier, a bear of some kind had attacked the portfolios of small investors and they had had little or no presence in the market for years. Twenty-four hundred on the DJIA by July and on it went. No end in sight.

The institutions introduced hundreds of new mutual funds— their CEOs could remember the glory days when the small investor (suckers) believed in the safety of the markets, the integrity of their stockbrokers, and the sound investment advice emanating from the granite bastions looking out on the Hudson. The institutions pumped up their marketing efforts and pushed the rally onward through August...2,500, 2,600, 2,700, just incredible. Get in there quickly, boys and girls, we're headed for the moon!

Nowhere did you hear even a whisper of the words: take your profits, Sell, lock in these super-high interest rates. How stupid would that sound? How dumb would we look? No one even suggested what would happen in the two months that followed the market's peak that August, although many would claim later on that they had predicted a major break in the market. No written documentation ever appeared, and no Wall Street firm ever uttered the "s" word. The fact that our short-term trading approach was twelve operational years old at the time and had generated mountains of that smart cash we described earlier, may have looked like we knew something was about to hit the fan. Not at all. I didn't have a clue, and truthfully, I didn't even care.

The weakness hit the NYSE on August 18, immediately after the peak at 2,722 the day before. No one on Wall Street today under the age of forty-five or so would be able to describe what I've just related to you. By the way, the average age of a Wall Street portfolio manager is well under thirty. Scary? Nearly everyone has heard of the climactic events of October 19. At the completion of this chapter, you'll understand why it was just another day on Wall Street.

The market had been dropping steadily since mid-August as institutional money managers took profits for their own accounts while continuing to encourage participation in stocks that were still selling near their highest prices in history. The IPO market had enjoyed one of its greatest years. No one suggested to anyone that they sell anything, except those lousy bonds, which had gone down, as they should have in the face of rising interest rates.

The buy-low strategy described here kicked in early in September as the list of opportunities began to grow from two to four and so on. As prices continued to weaken, analysts began to mumble. Most were too young to remember earlier downturns, and the economy certainly didn't look like a doom and gloom scenario was appropriate—just those pesky rising interest rates. And then it happened. Technology bombed the market when those programmed trading sell signals ran fast and furious down the cables, resetting them-

Pop Quiz

1. If you were using the trading disciplines described here, what were you doing during most of the summer of '87?
   - ☐ Using all of my base income to purchase more of my stocks as they continued to rise.
   - ☐ Checking my market value three times a day, and smiling.
   - ☐ Sending my broker champagne for convincing me not to take profits.
   - ☐ Taking a substantial margin position to put a deposit down on a Porsche.

2. If you had an active asset allocation plan at this time, what were you doing in the weeks leading up to the October 19 Crash?
   - ☐ Reinvesting in stocks that had fallen back into buy range.
   - ☐ Checking to ensure that even smaller-than-normal profits were capitalized.
   - ☐ Taking advantage of historically high interest rates by adding to the fixed-income side of my portfolio.
   - ☐ Smiling a lot to see a plan come together in what others perceived as a blood bath.
   - ☐ Waiting to see what Wall Street would blame for the disaster.

Answers to Pop Quiz

If you thought that any of the answers in question (1) were correct, or if you thought any of the answers in question (2) were incorrect, you know the drill. Go back to chapter 1 and pay attention this time through!

selves lower, and lower, and lower. Ironic, isn't it, that technology stocks would have a crash of their own a lucky thirteen years later!

Wall Street panicked, or pretended to for public consumption. Inflation fears, higher interest rates, tension in Europe, foreign oil, war in the Middle East, and so on. All of the usual suspects were paraded in front of the media as the culprits that caused the crash of '87. With all due respect for The Street's ability to analyze and predict (and there should be none), a simple program bug got the whole thing going. It just doesn't take a whole lot of impetus for speculative greed to turn into investment fear. Wall Street had done it again. Those poor unsuspecting individual investors had just gotten pulled back in when the rug was swept out from under them.

Unlike the real economic crash of the '20s none of the institutional biggies fell from their penthouses!

A volatile equity market creates opportunities with every gyration, in either direction, no matter how big or how small the movement. As a trader, you will find that you do best in what Wall Street would describe as either a mixed or wait-and-see market, or one that is directionless and full of uncertainty. For some reason, it's easier to convince people that it is foolish to buy stocks at high prices than it is to convince them that it is foolish not to sell them at high prices. The combination of the tax code, hindsight, the media, friends and relatives, and love of the big winners all combine to make investors feel uncomfortable leaving the party. Surely, nothing that grim can occur that quickly that I won't be able to call a cab and leave when I want to.

The bad news is that bubbles, even smallish ones, always burst, and the worst news is that you won't know what hit you until far too late. The very uncertainty of investing makes disciplined trading the high road to investment success. Uncertainty is the real investment world, so you might just as well learn to work with it and relax; a volatile market will become your dearest friend.

I Love ROK and Roll

Here's a real-world illustration of the power of trading during the twelve months from June 2006 to June 2007. A well known, NYSE dividend payer, rated B+ by Standard & Poor's, was down nearly 10 percent while the market had been moving up in all but one month of the twelve. Possibly on the list of the period's worst performers in Wall Street terms, Rockwell Automation Inc. (ROK) still had potential for profitable trades. Let's see how many could have been pulled off (see Figure 1).

Flying on instruments alone, we buy ROK when it first breaks 59, on its way to an unknown low. Buying continues off and on though early October. The first 10-percent gains occur in mid-October, and the stock can be repurchased during an inter-day dip near the end of the month. The second 10-percent trade occurs before the end of November. Three more inter-day buying opportunities in January turn some profit in mid February...10-percent gain number three. Finally, nearly a month of buying through April produces profit opportunity number four in May and June.

FIGURE 1: Rockwell Automation, Inc. (ROK) daily chart, June 2006-June 2007

Trading opportunities abound even when the market price trends lower.

FIGURE 2: An income closed-end fund (NSL), July '05-July'07

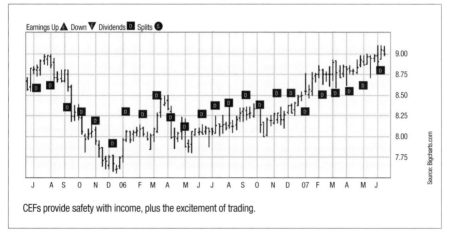

CEFs provide safety with income, plus the excitement of trading.

One stock produced 40 percent in profits during a twelve-month period where the stock itself fell roughly 7 percent. The buy and hold strategy would have produced less than half the uncompounded result...and would still be unrealized for use with new opportunities. As uncertain, certainly, as the outcome was with each purchase, a glance at any number of high quality company charts would show similar experience. Stocks that are trending upward, as the energy sector has been for several years, will also provide trading opportunities that can exceed the net gain for a specific period. In fact, it happens all the time.

CEFs bring trading to the mundane world of income investing (as illustrated in Figure 2), providing traders with additional portfolio safety without totally giving up the prospect of capital gains. In this case, a closed-end income fund produced multiple 10-percent trading opportunities in addition to contributing a monthly cash dividend in excess of 8 percent. Remember, CEF purchases don't require a 20-percent drop in price for buying because:

1. The primary purpose of the investment is, in this case, income generation. If IRE (remember?) work in our favor, the capital gains gravy adds some spicy flavor to this, relatively bland, bucket of the portfolio.
2. The interest-rate cycle is usually much longer than the stock market cycle. We would be passing up too much income by waiting for lower prices.
3. In the case of equity CEFs, we're buying a diversified portfolio of many issues. The relationship to net asset value (NAV) is a better price parameter.

The evidence is in. We don't have to mortgage the farm and find the next Haloid Corporation on which to wager. We can go about the investment process sanely and conservatively and have plenty of thrills and chills along the way, if we can just make a commitment to pull that sell trigger when we planned to. With no greed to cloud the vision, and our fear abated now that we own only higher-quality securities, we can sell our winners proudly and move forward into uncertainty with a happy face sticker on our portfolio.

The Psychology of Selling
I'm sure you'll agree that selling is the most difficult decision for most investors to make. It's strange though, that most investors will sell more readily to take losses than to realize profits. Of course there will be losses using this methodology, but they should be less frequent. A number of emotions are involved in fear-of-profits or FOP but the primary ones are greed, hatred (of both taxes and commissions), pride, fear, and, of course, love. If you don't recognize yourself in one or more of the five paragraphs that follow, you are probably in denial. By the end of this section, it should never happen again. Here's an

interesting fact for you. The vast majority of unrealized gains make it to the Schedule D tax form as realized losses.

Investors won't take profits because they fall head over heels in love with a stock that has gone up in market value. They become complacent, thinking that they know about the company and its management. The strongest love of all is reserved for a company that employed the person for a long time and/or where stock options are involved. Shareholders will actually read the annual and quarterly reports religiously (now there's a waste of time), complete proxy forms (there's another), and honestly believe that the price will continue to rise forever. They add to their holdings in this mother lode by taking advantage of the dividend reinvestment program. Surely they will be rich and famous, having solved the mystery of the stock market. Life is good; love is blind.

Investors won't take profits either because they hate to pay taxes or because some Neanderthal once told them that commissions would somehow make their profits disappear. Why pay now when we can wait until our earned income is lower after we retire? The fallacy becomes clear when these retirees try to construct an income production plan. How much base income (remember, interest and dividends only) is going to be generated annually by $1,000,000 worth of the Magellan Fund? Hate is counterproductive. It clouds the rational mind. Not enough? What's that IRA worth after taxes? It's never enough? Why do we allow the government to tax private retirement plans, IRAs, and Social Security... how dumb is that?

Can I Be This Smart Twice?
Investors won't take profits because they love to have a winner that they can brag about to their buddies. They need to talk about the home run they just made on Conglomeration Suspender Co. They've done better, they think, than Cousin Bill who insists on clipping those boring municipal bond coupons.

Investors won't take profits because they have no clue about what they will do for an encore. These buy and holders are smart enough to realize that they have just been lucky, but their limited experience keeps them from appreciating the fact that there are no guarantees in the investment world. That stock price could tumble.

It could tumble quickly and wipe out their retirement plans in one fell swoop. "But I don't know if I can do this again, or if I can trust anyone else to help me", they cry. Fear conquers all. Or was that love? No matter. Investors won't take profits because they don't want to miss out on additional paper profits. Basically, they're greedy, Enough said.

The take-your-profits recommendation is not something that the average financial advisor is comfortable with, but more for defensive reasons than professional ones. They understand investor love and hate, greed and fear, and have learned how to deal with it. Suggesting a profitable sale can be dangerous in a hindsightful and litigious world. What if the price of the sold stock continues to go up? Worse yet, what if the price of a new purchase goes down? Sounds like churning to a lot of attorneys.

So most professionals, and most brokerage firms, have chosen the product path to avoid such problems. They sell the firm-recommended mutual funds, pocket the big initial commission, and settle for residuals on the reinvested dividends. If the fund doesn't perform, it's just not their fault at all, and the firms, or the fund companies, have big legal departments. Brokers learn to take the path of least resistance early, and with individual securities, it's much easier to convince a client to sell a loser than it is to get him to dispose of a winner. Greed runs the keep-a-winner mindset; fear causes loss taking. Brokers learn early to go with the flow. Strangely enough, the Wall Street conventional wisdom booklet supports this approach.

Rags to Riches to Rags

I bumped into an old college friend while vacationing in New England in the early '80s. It seems that Bill had done extremely well with an up and coming software company, even before the technology blitz of the '90s. He had become a millionaire practically overnight. After learning that I had become an investment manager, he asked me to review his portfolio and give whatever advice I could.

The company he worked for had been increasing its sales 30 percent or more per quarter for eleven consecutive quarters. It paid no dividend whatsoever and was rated a below investment grade B by Standard & Poor's. Some would define this as a growth company, as Bill did, under the premise that all operating profit was reinvested in the company to produce unlimited future growth. (To a limited extent this could be true, but under closer examination, you are likely to find more growth in executive salaries than anywhere else.) Bill's portfolio was invested 100 percent in the company's stock, with options for much more at about 25 percent of the current market price. The investment portfolio was worth a little over one million dollars.

The family home had a substantial mortgage and nothing had been put away for the two children's educations.

What is wrong with this picture? How many of those negative emotions are involved here? What would you advise Bill to do, and when?

Stop: Answer the questions yourself first, then proceed.

Don't think for a minute that this is an uncommon scenario. I've encountered it quite frequently and it is nearly impossible to convince people that they are in serious danger. Did I just hit a chord with you? If so, pay attention and don't even think anything that begins with, "but my company..."

My advice to Bill was to sell 50 percent of the portfolio first thing in the morning and then to unload at least another 40 percent of the shares after January 1 of the following year. He should have a mental stop loss order in mind at a price about 10 percent below current market, just in case the price began to come under selling pressure sooner, rather than later. (A mental stop loss order is the same as tying a string around your finger as a reminder to do something.) Ten percent of the final portfolio would still be in his company's stock, and he could create a well diversified and productive portfolio with the proceeds. At the time, his portfolio could have generated nearly $75,000 a year in tax-exempt income. He was young and so were his children. He could be set for life if he took the proper steps.

Greed, Fear, Pride, Love, and Hate

Bill was one of the company's most productive salesmen, and he was certain that sales would continue to grow at a good clip (his personal production was up.) He knew senior management and they were confident that the stock price was going to continue to rise. (Sounds like love to me.)

Bill was not happy with the suggestion that he should take his profits and secure his future income. He concluded that I was jealous, thinking that I had never had such a big winner. I pointed out that my (larger than his) portfolio had been produced safely, if not quickly, in the manner I described for him. "My company will re-place IBM as the industry leader and I will be very rich indeed." Bill bragged. Watch out, Bill, your greed and (foolish) pride are showing.

Bill was finally convinced to sell some shares to put money away for his children's education, but he wasn't going to pay the taxes that would be incurred if he were to sell a large block of stock. A friend had convinced him to wait for a wonderful oil and gas tax shelter that he and his associates were putting together. Then he could sell the stock, buy the shelter, pay no taxes at all, and make even more money. And besides, he was genuinely afraid of investing. He didn't understand it, and he thought it was risky. Could I find him a finan-cial planner that would review his situation and come up with alter-natives? And by the way Steve, "I've got some company stock options that I have to take advantage of right away..." (Hey, is ignorance an emotion? I guess not.)

No Happy Ending This Time

Five days later his company reported a disappointing 20-percent gain in quarterly earnings and the stock's price fell more than 30 percent. It never recovered. Bill's employer was eventually taken over at a fraction of its former value. The new company was ab-sorbed by Computer Associates, which became one of my favorite trading stocks until it fell from grace with S&P a few years ago (and changed its name to CA, Inc.). Bill left the table with about 10 per-cent of his original wealth.

I had a securities attorney friend check out the oil well deal, and he cautioned Bill that it should be avoided because he could not find any information on it. More well intended advice that Bill failed to take. The friend who took his money for the tax shelter left the country, never to be heard from again. The wells never even existed.

The financial planner did well also, pocketing commissions on two real estate tax shelters. These were the ones that led to a bunch of embarrassing class action suits for the brokerage firms. It seems that Congress changed some tax rules, and the sheltered income was sheltered no more. There's more, but you get the point!

Here's that old voice of experience again. There's an important lesson within Bill's story that I'm sure you noticed. Bill's company had reported a 20-percent gain in quarterly earnings and the stock

price tanked. They were a profitable company before the announcement, and they remained profitable afterward, but never again did the
stock perform as it had earlier in its existence. Earnings disappoint-
ments like this one happen all the time, really, so don't be lured into
the old growth of earnings, buy-at-any-price trap. In its infinite marketing wisdom, Wall Street knows how to push those greed buttons. It
will do the same thing with an earnings surprise to the upside. Take
the profit you targeted and move on to the next opportunity.

Do the math using a 30 percent per-quarter growth rate. How
long before the numbers become unsustainable? Is there such a
thing as an infinite market for a product or a service?

Establishing Reasonable Targets

If you intend to make money in the stock market you have to protect
yourself not only from your own emotions, but also those of your
friends, family, and associates. Although Wall Street and others in
the financial products industry would like you to believe differently,
one size does not fit all! You have to establish a selling discipline
that works for you, based on your goals and asset allocation model.
You should learn to fear the prospect of leaving any profits on the
table. You must learn to sell out of love, not hate. You can continue
to hate to pay taxes, but not to the extent that you will consider losing $1,000 to save $300. Greed cannot be allowed to overpower good
judgment. As far as pride... you just have to grow up a bit if you
want to be successful in the investment world.

On Wall Street, there are hundreds of thousands of MBAs being
paid hundreds of millions of dollars to convince you that their employers and their wonderful analysts can predict the future. In the
process, they assign target prices to securities that are usually significantly higher than the stock price has ever been. These educated
guesses are often good news for the stock's price in the short run
but they do little to dampen the speculative tone of equity investing.
In many instances, the target prices set by Wall Street analysts have
nothing to do with a company's profit potential, just with the price of
its common stock. This is a very real distinction of which you need to
be aware. We've addressed a few of the reasons why Wall Street firms
rarely go public with sell recommendations. Can you imagine what it
would be like out there if speculators reacted as negatively to sells as

they react positively to buys? (Actually, they do. A downward earnings surprise is every bit as potent a sell signal on Wall Street as a sell recommendation would be, but it's politically correct.)

If you still salivate when you listen to Wall Street propaganda; if you still start to sweat before each Federal Reserve meeting; if you still twitch when you hear that the DJIA is falling; if you still believe your twenty-three-year-old financial advisor as he confidently tells you what "we think" the prospects are for anything; then you still need to be seriously desensitized.

Targets must be both reasonable and quickly attainable for a stock to be a good trading vehicle. The 10-percent sell target is reasonable in three important ways:

- It is a price that has been achieved within the past twelve months. Since you bought the stock at least 20 percent below its high of the past twelve months, it can obviously increase by 10 percent above your cost basis without breaking through into any new price territory.
- If we can average a six-month turn-around per trade, our annualized rate of return will be excellent. If you can accomplish this twice in a twelve month period, after reinvesting the total sale proceeds, your gain on the money stream for the period will be 21 percent without including dividends received. You should be able to live with that.
- It is not uncommon for 10-percent moves to occur very quickly, even in the high quality companies that are rated investment grade. Have another look at Table 6, where the average holding period was less than four months. If you are fortunate enough to get an instant winner, you can experience even better yields on a given money stream, but I really don't recommend that you spend your time with this type of research or analysis. You will see the results after just a few trades.

A target is simply a goal, an objective that may be totally or partially achieved, even exceeded with some regularity. But it is by no means a number chiseled in stone, and it is never something that should be translated into a stop loss order. First-edition readers take note.

Over the past few years a great technological improvement has allowed me to change my procedures to place them more in line with the KISS Principle. Approximately 90 percent of my stock selection routine has been automated. Specifically, all stocks that qualify to be considered in the first place are screened. Then, those that meet my criteria and are approaching buying range are developed into a daily watch list spreadsheet, from which it is easy to create both a buy list and a bull pen. As a result, the supply of potential buys has increased substantially.

- Profit targets are managed as part of the daily worksheet routine. You will see a stock price approaching its target, and you simply check up on it periodically. When the goal is within range, a half a point or so below target, make a notation on your daily order log. Try to keep your buy and sell order notations separated in some fashion to avoid errors.
- When you have potential sell orders, you may want to check in with your broker more frequently for real-time quotes, or ask him or her to alert you when the target has been reached. If the price refuses to attain the target today, keep it on the order log as long as it's within a point of the target, and be patient. With larger portfolios, there may be several stocks in the "ready room" every day.
- When a stock price reaches the 10-percent target, pull the trigger and sell the stocks ASAP. Say "I love you" and move on to the next order.

Fire when You See the Whites of Their Eyes

When I take a moment to reflect on the act of profit taking, a lot of thoughts swirl around in my head. First of all, I really get a kick out of it. I mean is this crazy or what. I just sold some ACO for six or seven of my clients, because a quick peek at the AOL most-advanced list showed nearly a two-point gain. Wham-bam-thank-you ma'am! Ten percent in just a month or so, but why? I don't have a clue, and frankly, Scarlet, I couldn't care less. But I'll share something with you that may not be clear from the amount of time I've spent hounding you to learn the selection principles and buying rules outlined in the preceding chapters. There is no greater thrill in this business than a quick profit.

Secondly, profit-taking opportunities happen at the least predictable moments and you need to be ready for them, but if I were to generalize about just how itchy your trigger-finger should be, I would have to answer cyclically, and in terms of statistics that matter...page back if you have to. The market flows through a time sequence that includes corrections and rallies of all proportions. Directional changes are totally unpredictable, but breadth and high-low stats help to tell you where you are at the moment. The calendar year is of no significance whatsoever. Tactically, then, and this is just a general plan:

- During extended periods of negative breadth, sell below target because the number of buying opportunities should be increasing and you'll be able to put the money back to work quickly. The longer the correction lasts, the more that it makes sense to take profits too soon.
- As your equity bucket fills up with a continuing correction, you'll have fewer chances for gains of any kind and should be spending time averaging down on your best trading positions.
- When the cycle starts back upward, your buying opportunities will slowly decrease and more stocks will approach their selling targets. This is normal mode, and holding out for the 10 percent becomes the proper game plan.
- As the rally continues, expect breadth to turn positive first, then new highs will start to exceed the new lows, and finally the buy list will begin to shrink. The longer the rally, the more important it is to take the money and run. There will be signs that sentiment is changing or that things are weakening, but the clearest indicator is not enough buys on the buy list. At this point, be willing to take less than 10 percent again, and don't forget to take your losses on your weakest, downgraded positions.

So, when buying opportunities are either abundant or scarce, fire when you see the whites of their eyes. A growing buy list is evidence of weakness in the type of stocks we invest in, so it is likely that your unrealized profits will evaporate. If this assumption proves to be wrong, you will probably be able to take profits in the new purchases relatively quickly anyway.

Don't Ever Look Back
Looking back is something you have to wean yourself from, if you intend to be a successful trader. The principle should be relatively

easy to follow. Simply, what difference is there between a $10,000 profit made from one 60-percent gain and the same $10,000 made from several trades averaging around 10 percent?

"No difference," is the correct answer (and yes, I am always talking about profits after those variable cost commissions). But which of the two is easier to attain? Wall Street labeled the years 2000 and 2001 just plain lousy because, with a buy and hold mentality, there just weren't too many stocks sitting in portfolios with big gains. The 10-percent target approach, however, enabled profit taking on over one hundred different stocks in both years.

Takeovers and Stock Splits

Takeovers and stock splits will cause the price of a stock to rise rapidly, most of the time. Many investors have great difficulty dealing with the good fortune of a takeover, and many don't quite understand what's involved in a stock split. Most often, the stock price will be strong prior to any announcement, and it doesn't matter in the least what the perceived or actual reason for a price run up happens to be. Fast or gradual, based on rumor or fact, sell on the good news. No exceptions, no buts, no what-ifs. Sell. Sell, be happy with yourself even if the amount is less than target, and move on to the next opportunity.

Just because a takeover is announced, there is no assurance that it will actually happen. Many companies have been the subject of takeover rumors periodically for years. The price runs up. (Sell it.) Nothing actually happens. The price goes down. (Buy it again.) One client didn't want to sell so that he wouldn't have to pay a commission and reduce his profit on this sure thing, which was to settle in six or seven months, if the government approved the merger. Let's just let this $25,000 sit around doing nothing for up to a year to save $100. What was he thinking?

Another client was outraged that I had sold a stock just a day or two after a split had been announced. The profit was about 17 percent. "Didn't you know about the two-for-one split?" he whined. "What difference does it make if I sell one hundred shares at $50 per share or two hundred shares at $25 each? We'll probably be able to buy the stock back again some time in the future anyway, below $25.00 per share." I explained. "Why will the stock price go to $25? How could that

happen so quickly?" By the way, as stocks proceed out of a safe buying range below $80 per share, those with a stock split history are quite
likely to do so again. Just as likely is a post-split slide in the stock price.

Profit taking on good news is smart investing. Actually, it's
the primary purpose of investing, unless you are an arbitrageur.
They're the ones who helped push the price up for you in the first
place. Say thank you and move along.

What dictates how quickly or how slowly you will sell? You
have a managed trading program that is logical and based on sound
principles. It is a methodology that has produced millionaires and,
more importantly, maintained them at that level. It is an autonomous
system. Run with it. In other words, you must absolutely stick with
the rules when the profit level is at or above your target. Above your
target should never happen, unless the current day's trading has
lifted the price above target, and you know how to deal with that.

Accepting less than a ten-percent profit makes entirely good sense
in situations where the buy list has grown, and where there are a lot of
stocks on it that you would really like to get back into. The profit potential of some of these issues may make them a better idea than waiting
for an older position to mature. Remember that faster turnover of the
hamburgers and french fries accelerates aggregate profits.

Here's an illustration that may help you: if my $10,000 investment
generates two 10-percent trades in a twelve-month period, my total
gain is 21 percent. If I make four trades of 5 or 6 percent, I actually
generate more total profit. Three sevens beats two tens every time.

$10,000 x 1.10 x 1.10 = $12,100 or 21 percent
$10,000 x 1.05 x 1.06 x 1.06 x 1.05 = $12,388 or 23.8 percent
$10,000 x 1.07 x 1.07 x 1.07 = $12,250.43 or 22.5 percent

You need to be an optimist to succeed as a trader, but be careful not
to let your easy success turn into arrogance. Believe it, there are
humiliating losses out there in your future. It's unavoidable. So no
matter how invincible you think you are after a hot trading streak,
don't tinker with the program. Absolutely never:

• Borrow on margin or from anywhere else to buy securities, no
  matter how many there are that have piqued your interest.

• Take a loss on a perfectly acceptable holding in order to switch to an old favorite that has come into range.

As you go through your daily routine, you will become totally aware of what has been happening in your territory. Today's plan is ready for implementation. You can't wait for the opening bell. But where are "they"? What do "they" recommend? What do "they" see happening? How do "they" explain what has been happening? Just who are "they" anyway?

You don't need them anymore. You have become a they. No other opinion is relevant, considering how well trained you are in a discipline that just makes sense. Upon completion of your daily buy list, you are aware of the opportunities that may be out there today. The more buys there are, the better a 6-to-9-percent profit looks. This is it, profit-taking time. Time to pull the trigger.

At first you may want a second opinion. You may have heard a good report or seen a favorable write-up. Merrill Lynch says it's a $60 stock, and here you are thinking of selling at $52. Don't be confused by Wall Street greed food. There are no facts, remember, only speculation and opinion. You really do know, however, that if you sell your XYZ Widget Ltd. at $52, not only will you have made money, but you already have identified several new opportunities for reinvestment of the proceeds. Pull the trigger and move on to the next opportunity.

Your Accountant Will Not Be Happy

First of all, if your accountant has obtained his license to sell securities, you have a problem. The conflict of interest is unacceptable. Here's another one for an investigative reporter to get into...heads would roll.

This is something you are going to have to deal with, though. As I'm sure you are aware, accountants, attorneys, even some doctors know all there is to know about all subjects, including investing. Keep in mind that it is our expectations of them that have turned them into what they are. Investing may not be as demanding intellectually as some other professions, but accountancy is just naturally hindsightful. Most accountants are so caught up in the "tail" (lowering the tax-paid number) that they allow it to wag the "dog" (making as much money as possible). The focus is on the financial transactions of the past. At your next meeting with your accountant, count the times he says coulda, woulda, or shoulda.

Keep in mind that it is the accountant's job to make you happy and not vice versa. It is his or her job to find a better way to classify or protect your earnings, not to reduce or to delay them. Would he be as quick to tell you to cut your salary as he is to suggest that you not take short-term profits? Would you be as willing to consider it? Will he guarantee the long-term profits he says you should be waiting for? Would he let you become a bad debt write-off instead of a paid account?

Never sell a stock at a loss just to offset profits, never. I have nearly two hundred clients with as many different accountants. Only one recommends indiscriminate loss taking just to reduce taxes. (Maybe they know by now that I wouldn't consider it!) If the accountant insists, try this out. Tell him that you will accept his advice if he will. Offer to help him reduce his taxes by not paying his fee.

Finally, as a last resort, if you can't get over your hatred of taxes, just send me a check for the amount of your gains as a consulting fee, and I'll pay the dreaded taxes for you.

What To Do about the Real Losers?

There are going to be some losers, but because of the nature of the trading strategy, it is vitally important to define what we mean by a loser. We are buying stocks during a down-trend in market price in anticipation of an eventual turnaround. We even buy more of them from time to time to reduce our average cost so we can exit profitably sooner. A loser is a stock that no longer fits within our basic, qualitative, fundamental, selection criteria. (Which are?) A loser is also a fundamentally sound stock that we have been unable to trade within a reasonable amount of time. We're built to trade, not to hold.

A Matter of Quality

A reduction in the S&P quality rating or a cut in the dividend is a clear indication of problems ahead. This is why you want to focus on such things in the selection process. Unrated securities don't become "unrated minus" and nonexistent dividends can't be cut. You must depend on fresh information from a company spokesperson, from a report in the media, or from your financial advisor; I'm sure that they all have your pager number with them at all times!

When fundamentals deteriorate, any profit becomes acceptable and small losses become tolerable. We do not want to hold on to companies once their quality becomes suspect. Still, it may not be necessary to take a huge loss immediately. Judgment again. A small loss under these circumstances is acceptable, but there is no need to rush into a major loss. Be patient. More often than not, there will be a rebound.

A case in point is Merck (see Figure 3), which fell from an elite A+ to a mere, better-than-90-percent-of-all-other-rated-companies A-. I don't believe the dividend was ever cut, but you just don't take losses on companies of this stature. Positions were added to during the two-year decline, and by early 2006, Merck was my biggest single holding loser. Today, with no losses realized, only two hundred shares remain. Years ago, IBM went from A+ to B+, and then to B, and the price went from one hundred something to forty dollars per share. Panic selling just never seemed necessary. The same process took place before the price and then the rating rebounded. So use your judgment, but always avoid averaging down on a stock once the quality rating has fallen below investment grade, even on Big Blue.

A Matter of Time

We are looking to trade stocks frequently. Therefore, a stock that we have been unable to sell profitably after a reasonable period of time is one that we should be looking to sell, even if we do so at a minor loss. Twelve months is about the limit. Ironic isn't it? The time period that most people want to wait before they'll consider taking a profit should be the trader's bailing out point. Even though our socialistic tax code encourages short-term loss taking, you just can't run this trading program effectively if you allow that to be a factor in your decision making. Help us all by speaking out against taxation of all investment and retirement income.

You've probably noticed that I say twelve-month period more often than I say one year. I'm not trying to add to the number of pages. The distinction between the two is very real and important. The institutional hydra's hypnotic stare has created a calendar-year worship that is totally inappropriate. As a trader, an investor who thrives on and prays for volatility and movement, the last thing you want to compare yourself with is some easily manipulated index of what happened between January 1 and December 31. It is entirely

FIGURE 3: Merck (MRK) weekly chart 2003-2007

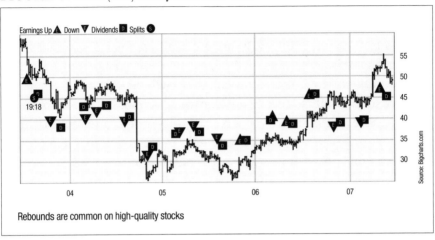

Rebounds are common on high-quality stocks

possible that the entire equity portion of your portfolio was just purchased in the last quarter of the year. (Remember the November syndrome?) I refuse to do calendar-year analysis either for my clients or for any of the analytical tools that feed performance fodder of this kind to the data mills.

Again, given sound fundamentals, there is no rush to take a major loss. But any profit or a small loss should be taken without a second thought. And of course, the "poip" (how's your Brooklynese?) should be removed from the selection universe with a disdainful click. Individual stocks should have a volatility index all their own. I'm surprised that no one has thought to come up with one similar to the beta index, which compares stocks' price movements to the market.

This new index will change periodically. Stocks that have dutifully provided a 10-percent-plus trading range for years get lazy. Others that were once stable start to gyrate. It's interesting to see a stock's personality change, and you have to be able to change as well. That may mean getting back into a stock that you tossed out of the selection universe in the past.

The "ATH" Profit Level Decision

Traders look at trading statistics to determine how they're doing, just as buy and holders watch their market value close enough to develop chronic migraines. From time to time, however, a trading portfolio will sport all-time-high (ATH) market value numbers. An

ATH in market value alone can simply be the result of new cash being added to the portfolio; an all-time-high profit level is different. A portfolio is at an all-time-high profit level when the difference between the market value and the amount invested (i.e., the total lifetime profit) is at a new ATH.

Generally, an ATH profit level will happen within a market environment featuring positive breadth and more twelve-month highs than lows...or, the working capital model definition of rally. You may experience situations where the market value of all the individual securities in the portfolio were below their purchase cost but the overall portfolio value was still at an all-time-high profit level. Ah, trading!

Here's a great analogy to use on your friends at the club when they are skeptical about your new investment strategy, particularly in such a volatile market. The waves of the markets are similar to those at sea. The ocean can go from dead calm to raging storm in a matter of minutes. The trading strategy you are learning smoothes the waves and allows you to surf the crests like a Hobie Cat buzzing by a Day Sailer. Trading gets you to your objective more quickly and with less (financial, not nautical) risk.

Any time a portfolio achieves a new ATH profit level the worst performing security in the portfolio should be looked at for elimination. I said security instead of stock purposely because an income security may occasionally be the worst performer because it no longer pays out an acceptable amount of income. You should be able to tell when an ATH occurs without putting your hands on a monthly statement. Your equity-buy list will be shriveling up. You will be taking profits on more things than you are buying, maybe even on a preferred stock or two or a municipal CEF. This is hard evidence. The rally is in full swing, and it's time for market value worshipers to expand their hat size while you increase your working capital.

Selling a loser at any time is a painful but necessary experience. Selling a loser at a time of strength is good for the portfolio in the long run but it most certainly is not a strategy that must be applied blindly every month that your account market value goes up. Look at everything carefully; you'll know which positions you want to unload. If there aren't any, that's a good thing. Always dispose of downgraded issues first.

And no matter how much better you may feel because you were able to write off the loss for tax purposes, you are merely rationalizing. There is no such thing as a good loss.

Major Losses

Major losses absolutely will happen too, no matter what strategy you employ, but they happen infrequently when you manage the amount of risk you accept during the security selection process. You can realistically expect to be successful nearly 95 percent of the time if you follow the rules that we have talked about. It is generally safe to average down until a stock falls below $10 a share, assuming that the quality remains intact and that diversification rules are not seriously violated. Strange, isn't it, that a stock rated investment grade can be reduced to a single-digit price, while others rated far below that level can be at lofty valuations. That's the stock market. At that point, you have to be prepared to cut your potential loss by selling before it becomes $4, $3, or less. I try to make an exit from $7 to $4, but that last tragic drop often comes all at once and without notice. Below $4, I suggest prayer.

I hate taking losses (and you should too) even more than most people hate taxes and commissions, but I recognize their inevitability, cry a lot and move on. Somehow it's easier for me to rationalize a loss at a time when everything else seems to be moving forward according to the plan.

Two Important Lists

Market statistics must be looked at periodically during the day, not only to see if it is time to implement your planned sell decisions, but also to identify new selling opportunities. Unlike buying opportunities (which are abundant more often than not) profit-taking opportunities are precious and must not be squandered.

The most active list (Table 8) and the most advanced list (Table 11) will help you identify important intra-day movements. If your broker can't provide this information real-time, switch. You can get it online yourself for free, and even a twenty-minute delay is better than no numbers at all. With the advent of the Internet, you are now in a position to get relatively current quotes from practically anywhere. When you hear that there is a big move to the up-side, login or call up your broker to check all of your positions. You may discover a profit-taking opportunity that could disappear if those institutional profit takers get there before you do.

You've heard all of these little witticisms before, but now you should be well beyond familiarity. You should be leaving appreciation and heading toward understanding.

There's No Such Thing as a Bad Profit

You will be using two types of computers to manage your investment portfolio. The one that requires a keyboard is used to provide information to be analyzed by the one that resides between your ears. You will be making your decisions in the world of uncertainty (the only one available to mortals), so try to avoid looking over your shoulder or second-guessing yourself when something you've sold continues to rise in price...remember instead all those times in the past that you forgot to sell and watched your profits vanish into thin air. Hindsight is a sure killer of an otherwise productive investment strategy.

There are people out there (mostly accountants and financial planners) who will review the past year's transactions and point out how you could have done better here or there if you had waited or, better still, if you had purchased one of their products. Always compliment them on their creative use of hindsight. Then ask them why they didn't call you before you did whatever it was they criticized, to advise you about their idea. Naturally they were willing to guarantee the results in advance! Sure.

The only decisions that should even be subject to discussion are those that blatantly disregarded or circumvented the rules you established for yourself. Tape a reminder on your monitor: "I will not violate the rules."

Never Count Your Winnings while You're Sitting at the Table

Not only is it rude in poker, it's pointless in investing. Even the IRS knows that a profit doesn't count until it is realized. They are not your winnings, profits, or values until you take the action necessary to remove them from the threat of loss (i.e., the table). You will always have many positions out there at some acceptable level of risk, measured by S&P quality ratings. It takes disciplined decision making to move them from the table to the pocketbook.

TABLE 11: A partial most-advanced list, NYSE, June 22, 2007

SYMBOL	DESCRIPTION	LAST	CHANGE	% CHANGE	52 WEEK HIGH	52 WEEK LOW	VOLUME
BX.N	BLACKSTONE	35.06	4.06	13.10			76,288,600
MA.N	MASTERCARD	168.43	3.74	2.27	169.4	43.67	2,234,700
TPL.N	TEXAS PACIFIC	283.50	3.5	1.25	282	140	3,300
SLB.N	SCHLUM-BERGER	89.20	3.44	4.01	86.67	54.24	40,145,700
GHL.N	GREENHILL	68.48	3.08	4.71	77	51.02	712,200
MWA.N	MUELLER WTER	19.35	2.98	18.20	18.45	13.02	1,996,000
AMN.N	AMERON INC	92.84	2.89	3.21	95.38	52.49	179,500
RIG.N	TRANSOCEAN	109.20	2.59	2.43	106.85	64.52	10,888,900
M.N	MACYS INC	41.43	2.56	6.59	46.7	32.57	12,661,000
HOG.N	HARLY DAVIDSN	62.55	2.43	4.04	75.87	50.74	3,844,800

This is where you look for profit taking opportunities, particularly when you know you have stocks approaching sell targets. Take several looks at this every day, for sure.

I like to think of the fixed-income portion of my portfolio as the bank, not that I would ever buy CDs or have a savings account in a bank. But, the idea that is comforting to me is that I've taken a portion of my newly created capital, my profits, and placed it in a safer place for compounding.

Have you ever seen the game show, *The Weakest Link*? Its one redeeming feature is the requirement that contestants bank their winnings if they want them to go forward to the next round. Not a bad way to look at the profits you should be taking on your equities.

Sell on the Good News

The market always overreacts to news, good or bad. In the previous chapter, we talked about buying on bad news for that very reason. Take advantage of an upward spike in a stock's price when it provides a quick profit on a new purchase, a small profit on an old holding, or a significant reduction in loss on a position that was targeted for an eventual ATH sale. If you find it necessary to determine what The Street thinks it knows, get the current skinny from your broker, take your profits anyway and don't ever look back.

Sell Out of Love, Not Hate

Here's a classic story about how a combination of ignorance and brilliance can lead an otherwise sophisticated investor to panic in response to what he perceived to be happening in his political and social environment. In a sense, he was blinded by the light of his own background, intellect, and experience.

He had made a killing in the first eight months of 1987, and at the market peak was about 75 percent in cash ready to pounce on the many excellent opportunities that appeared daily from mid-September on. On the fatal October 19, his portfolio was invested in twenty-five of the very best companies in the world by nearly any measure. His working capital was ahead by nearly 20 percent for the year, but current market value had suffered under the weight of the correction. He was perfectly positioned for another round of impressive gains as the market rebounded, as the quality sector always has from corrections of all shapes, causes, and sizes.

He appreciated all of the facts and he understood that this would normally be the correct scenario. He knew, though, that this time it was different. The government was in a shambles, crooks and thieves ran the country, hyperinflation was just over the horizon, staggering unemployment was imminent, and political/economic chaos were in sight. The sky really was falling, this time. He was absolutely certain that this would play out from conversations he had had with well-placed, knowledgeable people around the country.

Everything in the portfolio was liquidated and the rest is history. He had been selling out of love willingly and fruitfully for years. But an overdose of "know" and "certain" created a hate for the system that could not be dealt with rationally.

Fortunately, there has never been a correction that has not succumbed to the next rally.

You Can't Make Too Much Money

This is what you want to be complaining about every year of your life. The next gripe is that you're getting too thin or too healthy. Never lose sight of the fact that the very object of the investment exercise is to make as much money as you possibly can, legally, and in a manner that minimizes the inherent risks involved in the process.

Mid-Term Exam Time

Management involves about the same number of principles as investing, and we've dealt with each of them to a certain extent. You should know

194

by now that the trading approach described here is a synthesis of basic investment principles with management's planning, organizing, controlling, and directing (decision making). Before you move on to the final chapters, make sure that you have the answers to these important questions:

- What are the three basic principles of investing?
- How many classes of investment securities are there?
- Of what investment significance is the calendar year?
- What is more important, current income or current market value?
- What is analysis paralysis?
- What is an investment product?
- What differentiates an investment manager from other financial professionals?
- There is no such thing as a bad _____!
- Why aren't CDs or money market funds investments?
- Wall Street is _____ driven?
- What "tails" often wag the investment dog?
- What is a WRAP account?
- Consumers buy products, investors buy _____?
- Name three levels of diversification.
- Who should be broken up: The Yankees? Wall Street?
- What is the purpose of a fixed-income security?
- Why are dividends important?
- What is issue breadth?
- What human emotions have to be controlled most rigorously?
- What is a day-limit order?
- What is the gist of the investor's creed?
- What's a DRIP?
- Of what importance are market stats?
- Why does Wall Street hate volatility? Do you?
- Why are investors reluctant to take profits?

Chapter 7
Performance Evaluation

C ontrary to popular belief and media propaganda, investing
is not a competitive event. Rather, it is a uniquely personal
and goal directed activity that individuals must organize and
control for themselves. By definition, investing is a long-term enterprise; from experience, it is best dealt with by using the fundamental principles of two disciplines: investment and management.

As much as you love to hear quarterly growth numbers and comparisons with this or that average and index over short-term blinks of the
investment eye, you will not be accommodated here. Analysis of quarterly and other calendar-year numbers accomplishes little while generating transactions that often damage the health and long-term viability
of the portfolio. Performance statistics need to be apples-to-apples
comparisons, and no index alive will ever look like a properly diversified portfolio of investment-grade, income-generating equities combined
with an equally well diversified group of fixed income securities.

This methodology for trading stocks and bonds differs markedly
from one defined by conventional investment wisdom. We've emphasized the importance of QDI until it has practically been branded on your
forehead. We have established rules, procedures, and guidelines; defined
reasonable targets for profit taking; and fit it all into a cozy little asset
allocation package. Finally, we've introduced you to the working capital
model, which provides both the framework for the operating strategy
and a brand new approach to asset allocation and diversification decision
making. In this chapter, we're simply going to use the working capital

model to exorcise the market value and calendar-year performance evaluation demons from your body of investment knowledge.

Exorcizing the Wall Street Performance Demons

Come on, admit it, even though you've made it through all of this new strategy information, the two most important things on your mind are the market value of your portfolio and how that number relates to the market value last December 31. You are not alone. The vast majority of investors are fixated on the bottom line number, regardless of the makeup of their portfolios, and irrespective of what is going on in the investment markets. Inappropriate performance expectations beget unhappy investors and cause errors in judgment. Few investors are willing to admit that they don't understand fixed-income investing, even fewer know how to evaluate the performance of an equity-trading strategy, and no one seems to have the courage to look at performance in a non-calendar-year context. Wall Street's best friend, of course, is? Right, the unhappy investor.

Before there can be performance evaluation, there have to be performance expectations; and before there can be valid performance expectations, there must be a basic understanding of the securities in the portfolio. The stock market is and always will be a volatile place, where even the best and most profitable companies can be expected to rise and fall in market value. Similarly, income securities will always rise and fall in price as IRE change. The factors that affect these normal and harmless fluctuations are many and mostly unpredictable, so the investment task is to understand this and to work within it. For, as much as we may try, we just can't change Mother Nature... yeah, she's everywhere.

Demon # 1: Calendar Year Analysis

It's not just The Street that has you all charged up to achieve better than some benchmark between January 1 and December 31. The tax code encourages you to lose some races quickly to offset other races that you just might win, but then it's better if you win those more slowly. What nonsense.

Here's a three-step approach that will at least personalize calendar-year analysis enough to make it more useful:
1. If prevailing interest rates are higher than they were last December, it's likely that your income bucket has declined in market value

and risen slightly in current income production. If the opposite is true, you've realized capital gains, the income bucket has risen in market value, and your current income has not risen quite as much.

2. If your buy list has been short most of the year and you have abundant smart cash ready to invest in equities, your market value is likely to be higher as well, but it can't be compared with any index that I'm familiar with. A long buy list and minimal smart cash means that there is a correction going on and your market value expectations should be lowered.

3. Combine your income bucket expectations with your equity bucket expectations and you'll have a good feel for what your market value should have done over the course of the year.

Generally, your portfolio should do better than the NYSE index (the only one even close to comparable) in a down market and not quite as well in a strong upward market. Always keep in mind that there is no frequent position change within averages and indices; they are stable portfolios. Yours is not, and theoretically, the average age of positions in your portfolio is going to be about six months. Also, if you are going to compare yourself with one of these annual performance gizmos, does it make sense to purchase any securities after August? One other point bears some attention. In a strong market, with greed bubbling around you, a good portion of your portfolio is going to be in...? Cash.

Peak-to-Peak Is Not a Game Show

Way back before the word "pentium" existed and computers were both huge and slow, the investment world was much less complicated. Money managers looked at investment portfolio performance over the course of market cycles using peak-to-peak and trough-to-trough analysis. Somewhere, this very logical, sane, and realistic approach has gone tar pit in favor of the frantic short-term analysis that Wall Street cultivates today. Call me cynical, but I don't think that this was by chance. These boys are smart, and they clearly get more action with quarterly frenzy than they would with logic and system. And don't you find it comical how they can pompously lecture us about the risks of being impatient and the importance of viewing investing as a long-term endeavor, while they constantly

FIGURE 4: The S&P 500 Index (June '04-June '07)

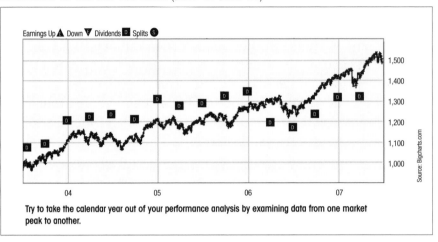

Earnings Up ▲ Down ▼ Dividends D Splits S

Source: Bigcharts.com

Try to take the calendar year out of your performance analysis by examining data from one market peak to another.

focus on short-term numbers. Media hype has some people analyzing their performance on a day-to-day basis.

The objective of peak-to-peak analysis is to look at equity portfolio performance from one significant peak to the next with a reasonable amount of time between, but at least twelve months. Figure 4 shows such an analysis period between February 2004 and March or April 2005, and another between March 2005 and April 2006, but many analytical possibilities present themselves. Trough-to-trough analysis, also popular in years past, measured a portfolio management strategy against a falling market.

Not only were the analytical periods more consistent with the cyclical nature of the market, the purpose was not to compare oneself with anything in particular. The objective was to see if the strategy being used was keeping pace with the market itself. Thus, investors weren't changing strategies as frequently, they were happier with themselves as masters of their own destinies, and they were not nearly as dependent on Wall Street as they are today. Not the type of scenario that sells mutual funds or other products. And voilà, this is why we have no software packages for peak-to-peak analysis, and why most of you are likely never to have thought about it.

But think about how much better it is. Here I am, running my portfolio calmly, in a goal-directed manner starting in February 2004, an interim peak in the S&P 500. Thirteen months later, after uninterrupted volatility, the average peaks again, up roughly 5 percent. How did my stock and bond trading methodology do during that time frame? Isn't that more civilized than a quarter-to-quarter bobsled ride?

Demon # 2: Market Value Focus

Certainly more diabolical than the four-lap competition associated with calendar-year analysis is the market value myopia that has replaced even a rudimentary understanding of the securities markets. All stocks and bonds are not created equal; in fact, they are not even close. Few investment professionals would deny that different kinds of stocks (by quality, sector, capitalization, geographic location, IRE sensitivity) have their own cycles within the overall market cycle. Even fewer, I hope, would expect income securities to be impervious to IRE, specific industry economics, and the tax code. Similarly, I would expect the majority of investors (even those who use short-term gain-friendly trading approaches like mine) to recognize that investing itself is a long-term proposition with goals and objectives that may mature decades into an unknown future. Finally, they all seem to recognize the importance of asset allocation and, possibly even diversification.

But in spite of all this understanding, knowledge, and experienced wisdom, every last one insists on comparing the monthly, quarterly, or annual change in portfolio market value with the change in some totally unrelated index or average. Somehow, Wall Street has managed to brainwash investors and investment advisors alike into thinking that market value is a measure of quality, utility, and productivity when, in reality, it is merely a measure of the relationship between supply and demand. That relationship is much more volatile than the viability or fundamental quality of the securities in a portfolio. Pshew, that's much too cerebral for me.

If I own guaranteed or insured bonds with a maturity value less than market value: (1) Does it affect the income I receive? (2) Will it change the amount I receive at maturity? Apparently, Wall Street wants you to think it does. Similarly, if my investment-grade equity portfolio has fallen in market value, either with a general decline in equity values or not, does this mean that the companies I own are in trouble? Again, Wall Street would like you to think so. But why? Because an unhappy investor is Wall Street's best friend.

Rethinking Performance Evaluation

At the end of every calendar year, investors and investment professionals alike rush around to determine how they performed. Bottom
line growth is expected to be better than the gain in the DJIA or the
S&P, no matter what, end of discussion. You need to try to avoid all
the hype and concentrate on the more important things: (1) Recognize the importance of income, particularly that which is generated
by profits. (2) Have realistic expectations for each individual security owned. Income investments are asked only to produce cash flow,
not growth in market value. For growth, buy under-valued stocks
and wait patiently for profits to happen.

To make money trading stocks and bonds, you are committed to taking advantage of the natural and expected fluctuations in their market
values. You know it will happen, and you will be ready to deal with it as it
does. It will be extremely helpful to you if you do these three things:

1. Think of the securities you still own as inventory or work in progress and focus your evaluation exclusively on the QDI.
2. Take reasonable profits as often as you can, stocks or CEFs. Find
   another high-quality security that fits in the portfolio.
3. Measure equity performance in terms of completed trades, not in
   terms of market value at the end of some meaningless time interval. In a trading environment, only completed (bought and sold)
   transactions can be compared with the averages.

A non-Wall Street, working definition of performance would
read something like this: the functional effectiveness of efforts to
produce a desired effect, expressed either as objectives or goals. An
objective is something that is aimed at and a goal is an end result
that you are striving to attain. None of this speaks of indices or averages, calendar quarters or years, or even of competition. Let's take a
stab at deprogramming ourselves so that we are looking at performance in a manner that is somewhat more consistent with this new
approach to portfolio management that we're studying.

A New Wall Street Line Dance

When your focus is on high quality/low risk securities in a balanced
portfolio which seeks annual increases in base income plus regular

contributions from capital gains, a simplistic look at the change in market value from point A to point B is simply inappropriate. But what replaces the Wall Street demons to which you've become addicted? If we reconcile in our minds that we can't predict the future (or change the past), we can move through the uncertainty more productively. It's easier to evaluate portfolio performance when we can use information that we don't have to speculate about, that is related to our own personal investment programs.

You should start to develop an "all you need to know" performance chart that will help you manage your way to investment success (goal achievement) in a low failure rate, less emotional environment. The chart will have four data lines, and your portfolio management objective will be to keep three of them moving upward over time. Note that a separate register of deposits and withdrawals should be maintained. We'll call this fifth line the pat-on-the-back line. If you are paying fees or commissions separately from your transactions, consider them withdrawals of working capital. If you don't use the specific selection criteria and profit-taking guidelines we've been talking about, your chart will not produce the smiley face you're after. One of these lines is known as the inflation-buster line.

Line 1: Working Capital

As you know, working capital is the total cost basis of the securities and cash in the portfolio. Deposits and withdrawals, capital gains and losses, and base income all directly affect the working capital number and indirectly affect future base income growth. Securities become nonproductive when they fall below investment-grade quality (fundamentals only, please) and/or no longer produce income. Good sense management can minimize these unpleasant experiences.

An average annual working capital growth rate between 7 and 12 percent would be a reasonable target, depending on asset allocation. The larger the income allocation, the lower the anticipated growth. Right? An average cannot be determined until after the end of the second year, and a longer period is recommended to allow for compounding. This should be an upward-only line, since only withdrawals and realized capital losses will reduce the total. A new look at some widely accepted year-end behaviors might be helpful at this point. Offsetting capital gains with losses on good-quality companies becomes suspect because it always results in a larger deduction from working capital than the tax payment itself would have been. Similarly, avoiding securities that pay dividends or deferring profits for tax reasons foolishly reduce the growth rate of working capital. There are two basic truths at the bottom of this:

1. You just can't make too much money.
2. There's no such thing as a bad profit. Don't pay anyone who recommends loss taking on high-quality securities; tell them that you are helping to reduce their tax burden, and put your votes behind tax-reform candidates.

If you are withdrawing more money from your portfolio than you are depositing, you will not be able to grow working capital. If you have more capital losses than capital gains, you need to review the procedures for selecting, buying, and selling securities. In the absence of excessive withdrawals, the amount invested in the portfolio's assets must increase at an annual "beat the bank" rate. No exceptions are acceptable, and you should understand why.

Line 1 will move steadily upward from left to right, because market value changes have no direct impact on working capital.

Line 2: Base Income

Line 2 records the accumulated base income produced by the portfolio, and it too will always move upward from left to right if you are managing your asset allocation properly. The only exception would be a 100-percent equity allocation, where the emphasis is on a more variable source of base income...the dividends on a constantly changing stock portfolio. In that case, the rate of growth in base income would not be increasing regularly. The reason for isolating this number, as opposed to total income, is that income from trading cannot be counted on with as much confidence as routine dividend and interest payments from profitable companies and well managed closed-end funds. Base income will become retirement income much sooner than you anticipate, and it needs to be paid attention to regularly to assure that it is growing.

Base income can also be looked at as disposable income, or spending money. As a retirement planning spot check, you can simply compare it with your projected expenditures and see if is adequate to fill the gap between what you will need and that which will be provided by Social Security and retirement plans. As you grow older, the need to develop a steady stream of base income becomes more obvious. But don't discount the value of starting right away. I don't care what your total income is, any six-figure portfolio must have an income component. The base income line should also move steadily upward, but not quite as steeply as working capital.

Line 3: Trading Results
Line 3 reflects historic trading results and is labeled net realized capital gains. This total is most important during the early years of portfolio building, and it will directly reflect both the security selection criteria you use and the profit-taking rules you employ. If you build a portfolio of investment-grade securities and apply a 5-percent diversification rule (always using cost basis, of course), you will rarely have a downturn in this monitor of both your selection criteria and your profit-taking discipline. Any profit is always better than any loss and, unless your selection criteria is really too conservative, there will always be something worth buying with the proceeds.

The 10-percent target is a guideline, remember, and three 8-percent singles will produce a larger number than one 25-percent home run. Obviously, the growth in line 3 should accelerate in rising markets (measured only by issue breadth or new high/new low numbers). The base income line will also benefit from the increased capital gains production because some percentage of every income dollar is allocated to income securities. Note that an unrealized gain or loss is as meaningless as the quarter-to-quarter movement of a market index. This is a decision model, and good decisions should produce net realized income.

One other important detail, no matter how conservative your selection criteria, a security or two is bound to become a loser. Don't judge this by Wall Street popularity indicators, news stories, your horoscope, or analyst opinions. Let the fundamentals (profits, S&P rating, dividend action, etc.) be your guide. Market value just can't be trusted for a bite-the-bullet decision...but it can help.

When you first start using this trading approach, you'll find it useful to calculate the profit percent on each trade, and the length of time the security was held. You should expect an average yield of around 10 percent in a generally rising market and a one to two point lower average in a declining market. The average holding period will work out between four and seven months—the quicker, the better. For CEFs and other securities, the holding period isn't nearly as important as it is with equities. With income securities, every profitable trade should be greatly appreciated.

Line 4: Market Value
This brings us to line 4, the one that you are no longer manic about, total portfolio market value. This line will follow an erratic path, almost always staying below the working capital line. If you observe the chart after a market cycle or two, you will see that lines 1 through 3 move steadily upward regardless of what line 4 is doing. But, you will also notice that the lows of line 4 begin to occur above earlier highs. It's a nice feeling since market value movements are not, themselves, controllable.

Line 4 will rarely be above line 1, but when it begins to close the cap, a greater movement upward in the net realized capital gains line should be expected. In 100-percent income portfolios, it is possible for market value to exceed working capital by a slight margin, but it is more likely that you have allowed some greed into the portfolio and that profit-taking opportunities are being ignored. Even if that closed-end royalty trust of yours is paying 12 percent right now, a 10-percent profit should be taken. Both it and the 12-percent yield will change. Don't ever let this kind of gift from the investment gods elude you. Studies show rather clearly that the vast majority of unrealized gains are brought to the Schedule D as realized losses...and this includes potential profits on income securities. And, when your portfolio hits a new high-water mark, look around for a security that has fallen from grace with the S&P rating system and bite that bullet. This is the ATH decision that was discussed in chapter 6.

You will be surprised to find that, over significant time periods, your line 4 may track above most market averages on a peak-to-peak basis...even with 30 percent invested for income.

The Fifth Line
What's different about this approach, and why is it so low tech? There is no mention of an index, an average, or a comparison with

anything at all. Yet, this method of looking at performance will get you where you want to be without the hype that Wall Street uses to create incurable dissatisfaction. It provides a valid use for portfolio market value, but far from the judgmental nature Wall Street would like. Its use in this model, as both an expectation clarifier and an action indicator for the portfolio manager, on a personal level, should illuminate your lightbulb. Most investors will focus on line 4 out of habit, or because they have been brainwashed by Wall Street into thinking that a lower market value is always bad and a higher one always good. You need to get outside of the market-value box if you hope to achieve your goals. Cycles rarely fit the January to December mold, and they are only visible in rearview mirrors anyway. But their impact on your new line dance is totally your tune to name.

The market value line is still a valuable tool, but no more so than the other three we've examined. If it rises above working capital, you are missing profit opportunities. If it falls, start looking for buying opportunities. If base income falls, either the quality of your holdings has also fallen, or you have changed your asset allocation for some (possibly inappropriate) reason. A falling line 3 means you are using some other selling or loss-taking discipline. If you are following all the rules, a falling working capital line can only result from incredibly bad luck in a relatively small portfolio.

Now for the fifth and last line to place on your chart—and if you are retired or nearly retired, this one can be viewed as a financial cardiogram. This is the line where you track your total investment in the portfolio. No, not the cost basis of the investments, which is the working capital, this line reflects the net result of all deposits to and withdrawals from the portfolio... whatever the source or reason. The only non-cash item that becomes a deduction is a loss of capital brought about by a tax-loss transaction on a fundamentally solid investment. Typically, this line will slope upward for younger people and won't start to move lower until retirement age. So long as lines 1 through 3 continue to move higher, it really doesn't matter if this one moves into negative territory.

Now remember when we said that the classic retirement scenario is to live off of the income generated by your investment portfolio? Well, it's the job of line 5 to track that relationship, in coordination with line 1, the working capital line. If you are spending less than your portfolio is generating, lines 1 to 3 will continue to report a growing estate for your grandchildren. However, if the working capital line moves lower, it is likely that you've crossed into negative cash-flow territory and some tighter expenditure controls could be necessary. But it's all right there in front of you. You will know exactly where you are, where you've been, and what you need to do without even once bothering to raise the question, how's the stock market doing?

Your goal should be to make line 5 your personal pat-on-the-back line. This happens when it turns negative while your working capital line keeps rising, a very realistic scenario if you keep your withdrawal rate below 75 percent of annual base income.

By the way, regarding the inflation buster line I mentioned earlier. You got it—it's the base income line, which we'll get back to later in this chapter. But first let's have a look at a hypothetical chart of the first ten years of a $100,000 portfolio and see what it has to tell us. Note that the three upward-only lines (working capital, base income, and capital gains) have not been severely hampered by the 20 percent that has been withdrawn from the original deposit. The wide spread between accumulated base income and accumulated net gains and losses tells me that this is a 70- to 80-percent equity portfolio during a pretty good rally in the stock market. As this investor moves closer to retirement, the base income producers would have to make up a larger portion of the portfolio. Think how much easier it would be to grow a portfolio if regular deposits were made in amounts large enough to offset portfolio expenses.

If It's Broken, Fix It

I have been unable to find any one average, index, or model that even comes close to reflecting what is or should be going on within a diversified portfolio built on the conservative principles discussed here. But, the transaction-driven Wall Street institutions want us to believe that the popular averages are so sophisticated they can be used for performance evaluation by anyone at all...irrespective of goals, objectives, whatever. Additionally, there are hundreds of mutual fund houses selling tens of thousands of mutual funds. One would hope that there have to be at least a hundred unique fund types, either by general direction, focus, geography, asset allocation, managerial style, income level, degree of aggressiveness, etc. Why else would so many even exist? It stands to reason that there are significant and distinct differences between funds or our financial advisors would all be selling the same one. It should be obvious that they all need to have their performance analyzed by somewhat different measures. And perhaps much more importantly, the performance of the thousands of individual fund managers needs to be evaluated differently.

The first problem is really related to compensation. Financial advisors are encouraged to sell the products that are must lucrative to their employers. Even independent advisors quickly learn which of the securities and products they can sell will produce the best rate of return and the most perks for them, not for you. Certainly,

FIGURE 5: The working capital line dance

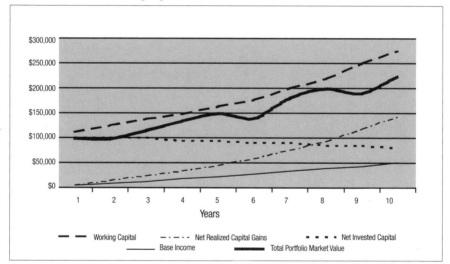

Keeping the working capital, cumulative base income, and cumulative capital gains lines moving up is both the result and the goal of the strategies presented in this book. Follow the rules and market value will be pulled up as well.

they expect that the investment managers running the funds are investing according to the fund descriptions they are provided, and therefore, the client's interests are being properly tended to. And in the event of a less-than-expected performance, they can find a better fund to try next year.

But the second problem, the one concerning the very different type of performance evaluation that fund investment managers must contend with, often sinks the best efforts of the front line financial professional. Fund managers are compared only with other fund managers—not with the market. Sometimes, the interests of the client can get lost in the shuffle. Wall Street is no longer paved with individual security portfolios and individually orchestrated investment plans. Wall Street has become a suburban mall filled with products and life-simplifying services for everyone, and no attempt has been made to revamp the performance-monitoring methodology to make it applicable to the new, one-size-fits-all mentality.

The Objective Function

We've seen that the objectives of the portfolio are the key to determining just what measurement tools need to be used, and we've described a fairly routine way to monitor all of the important numbers. And just as the working capital model does not list beating the S&P 500 as an objective, it is doubtful that any legitimate financial or investment plan will have "beat something" as an objective. Typical objectives would be:

1. to prepare an education fund for my children;
2. to have an investment portfolio that generates $60,000 per year in disposable income by the time I retire;
3. to take diction lessons and make enough money to afford a Jaguar; or perhaps;
4. to preserve the capital I have accumulated so far, and make it grow at approximately 10 percent per year.

A 1-percent annual growth rate, incidentally, would have beaten the market from 2000 through most of 2006, assuming the DJIA is your favorite. The 1 percent would have beaten the others by even more, in the face of statistics that point to a huge rally going on in the same period of time. Every portfolio will (and should) have somewhat different objectives, but safety of principal, growth of capital, and generation of retirement income certainly should be among them.

If you are ever sitting with your financial advisor or planner, and the information you provide is being recorded as check marks on a form of some kind, ask the person to stop. Your personal data is going to be plugged into a computer program that will regurgitate a sophisticated personal financial plan, just for you. The package, with all its bells and whistles, is meant to impress you and to gain your trust. Even though I don't recommend that you do so, you can get the same software and run the program yourself.

What you want from a knowledgeable professional is: his or her professional analysis of your circumstances with a resultant plan that is simple, practical, manageable, and based on assumptions that you understand and agree are appropriate. Don't expect a financial planner to obtain the investment performance that you require if he or she can't put together a basic plan, including asset allocation and income projections, right there at the kitchen table. Commissioned financial professionals get paid for product sales only. Some also get paid for the time spent in planning. The presentation of the plan is not nearly as important as the plan that is presented.

So once your financial plan is created and you've been guided through the mall to get the products that will fulfill your needs, the next step is to set up a methodology for performance evaluation that works regardless of the popular averages, especially since those averages have recently parted company with the realities of the marketplace. You'll find that most financial professionals won't have a clue.

The Annual Trading Summary
OK, convinced? If you look hard enough, you will be able to find financial professionals who are willing to go backwards in time to move their business and their clients forward in a goal-directed manner. So if you want to try the methodology presented here but don't have the time, you probably know someone who will be able to help. But let's get back to more of what's involved with analyzing performance using the working capital model.

Line 3 of our all-in-one performance chart was a record of cumulative trading results, and this number needs to be looked at fairly frequently to get a feel for how the trading is going. The first step is to construct an annual trading summary. This is an extremely easy and functional tool to put together—easy because it is simply a process of matching each sell transaction with the appropriate buy transactions and assessing the amount of dollar gain, the percentage gain, and the holding period. Any decent spreadsheet program will do this for you, including all the calculations necessary for the preparation of your IRS Schedule D Form. You can get this information online. (Have you noticed that the IRS only recognizes realized gains and losses? Interesting, don't you think?) Here are some guidelines for evaluating trading performance.

More than 90 percent of your sell tickets should involve profit taking, and you should make money on better than 90 percent of the securities you select. These are not the same thing, and you should be able to achieve both if you stick to the rules. Additionally, your trading activity should include all of the equities in your portfolio (except, perhaps, utility stocks) over an eighteen to twenty-four month period. (Actually these are conservative expectations, unless your selection criteria are inherently speculative.) If you haven't been able to take a profit on a twenty-four month holding, start looking for the first minor loss opportunity, at the next portfolio ATH.

The average net/net gain should be well above the one-year CD rate that was in effect at the beginning of the year, but at least 10 percent. The average holding period should be less than eight months, but it will more than likely be less than six months. The one-year CD rate is used as a benchmark because it represents what you could achieve with an absolutely risk-free (for lack of a better word) product.

If you take another look at the data presented in Table 6, you will see the type of information you need to record and the types of calculations that are to be made. In that illustration there were about fifty-five sell transactions for an average (after commission) gain of a bit more than 10 percent and an average holding period of less than four months. There was just one loss transaction. You would be extremely pleased with those results, particularly if you remember what happened to the quality sector of the stock market that year.

Obviously, a conservative trading discipline can work even in the worst of times, but how many of your holdings didn't pan out? A process called "portfolio aging" examines that important point. Trading is the key to the portfolio's ultimate success, so don't waste time kidding yourself. Some stocks are going to get sold at a loss eventually. Accurate aging information is a must, though; otherwise the proper amount of patience won't be applied.

Portfolio Aging
In a trading environment, reasonably rapid turnover is very important for long-term success. Setting up a portfolio inventory

sheet that lists the purchase dates of each of your equity holdings is an easy way to monitor your performance in this important area. As issues are sold they are removed and replaced with
new purchases. Older holdings should be identified and watched
closely, twice:

1. The first thing to keep an eye out for is the time to reduce the average cost of the holding. This process allows for an earlier profitable exit point for the entire position.
2. The second look at the stock is one of frustration. It has now become your worst performer, other than the occasional down-graded
   issue that is always dealt with first and needs to be tossed. However, any stock with an "A" in its name, profitability in its quarterly
   reports, and a sustainable high dividend deserves some respect.

The age of the stocks in the portfolio should reflect the desire
to trade frequently. The better (less greedy) you become, the more
likely it is that the average age will be less than six months, which
is an achievable and reasonable target. The fact that a stock fails to
become tradable quickly enough doesn't detract from either its value
or its ability to produce income. It's just quite likely that you can
replace it with a more volatile one.

Do We Really Need Tax Lots?

Once you have taken the average-down step, or added to an income
CEF, you will own what our ridiculous tax code refers to as differing tax
lots… a concept that I'm sure your accountant is in love with because of
the hundreds of extra billing hours it represents. I have one client, and
I'm thankful that it is only one, who has been hypnotized into following the annual loss-taking ritual that I caution you to avoid. In this very
large portfolio, adding to positions is a fairly routine occurrence, particularly in the income bucket. Last year the accountant decided that my
client should take losses on the higher-priced portions of a half a dozen
or so of these holdings, which my investment management software
keeps track of on an average cost basis. Hmmm, wouldn't you think that
the accountant's software would be more in tune with what the investment industry's software is doing? So this guy has gotten his client to
lose money on perfectly good tax-exempt income providing municipal

bonds to save thirty-five cents in taxes per dollar of loss. And then there's the carnage to my cost basis records. Go figure!

Portfolio Performance and the Red-Eyed Inflation Monster

As far back as I can remember, investing in the stock market has always been touted as the ultimate hedge against inflation. It wouldn't surprise me if this were one of the arguments used by the insurance industry back in the '80s to get regulators to endorse the sale of variable insurance and annuity products. Certainly we're all afraid of the inflation monster, but how can an increase in the market value of my stock portfolio, my mutual funds, or my real estate protect me from the beast? Frankly I'd rather be protected from the Wall Street beasts that are spreading such counter-productive fabrications. Hey guys, we've got money and we want to invest it. Cut the baloney. We can handle the truth.

Inflation is, straight from Webster's New World Dictionary: "an increase in the amount of money and credit in relation to the supply of goods and services, an excessive or persistent increase in the general price level as a result, causing a decline in purchasing power." Wikipedia chimes in with: "cash inflation is measured by comparing two sets of identical non-monetary items at two points in time, and computing the increase in nominal cost not reflected by an increase in quality." (Dismal science indeed, this is exciting stuff.) In any case, we are talking about purchasing power, and I'm sure your experience is the same as mine. Bill collectors couldn't care less either about the market value of your inflated index funds or how much gold you have buried in the basement. They want cash, on time, or they'll be taking your ranch for cheap.

So once again we see that Wall Street has created a self-serving piece of conventional wisdom that is really just another financial fantasy. The only way to beat down the inflation monster, boys and girls, is with ever-increasing annual income levels. Now let's pretend that the masters of the universe, smart as they constantly remind us they are, just missed the point of the econ 101 discussion which was gathered in pretty well by the future labor union leaders in the room. These guys look for bigger salaries, more benefits, and cost-of-living escalator clauses. They could care less about their market values when a fat wallet feels so much better up against the hip.

This brings us back to that constantly rising base income line, and a renewed emphasis on the rule-of-income... he who has the income, rules. If your portfolio deals with inflation every day, you won't be bothered by it when you hang up your wing tips. Follow these simple rules:

- Never invest in a security that does not pay income. Any security (or product) that does not pay income should be considered speculative.
- When your total portfolio reaches six figures, or you reach age thirty, at least 30 percent of your portfolio should be invested specifically for income.
- Using each security's cost basis in asset allocation decisions will assure an ever-increasing level of portfolio income.

Here we have a simple, easy-to-manage solution to a very real (but not nearly as scary as we've been led to believe by the financial community) problem. Maybe those index funds, gold futures, IPOs and NASDAQ-filled mutual funds, and all those other forms of inflation hedges will look a bit less attractive to you. Now I personally think that the impact of inflation is significantly less for some people than it is for others due to countless personal lifestyle variables, but it exists. And as much as I live and breathe stock market every day of my life, I've got to tell you that there is absolutely no cure for inflation in just being there. You have to trade, and you have to reinvest according to a simple asset allocation model for it to work.

Always keep in mind that Wall Street is the great manipulator of our time, and its lifeblood is product sales. If a myth keeps the public buying mutual funds, then a myth they will create, teach, sell and promote until it becomes part of their package of goodies that move investors where they want them to be. So long as the places you go to eat, play, view, party, vacation, ride, and so on, only accept money, the increased value of your mutual funds just increases the management fees you pay to Wall Street. That's all. Similarly, if demand drives up the value of my home, it increases my real estate taxes, my insurance premiums, and what service people feel they should charge me; thus, it actually reduces my disposable income.

One final thought about the stock-market-beating-inflation mythology, when it gets mingled with the equally tainted buy 'n hold fantasy, and the (incredibly insensitive to the needs of just about everyone) Internal Revenue Code. Let's say our growth in market value has actually beaten the inflation rate. We still don't have a whole lot of income, because income payers generally don't grow as fast or because mutual funds are pretty much always reinvested to increase the income of the salesman. Now, here comes retirement: The IRS is going to tax our Social Security, our pension benefits, and even all that money in our 401(k) and deferred comp plan. Our IRA is totally taxable and so are the capital gains on all of the other securities we've owned since puberty.

Now, we've got to sell to restructure the portfolio to produce the income that we were never encouraged to think about by financial planners, accountants, stockbrokers, or even the media. So we enter retirement not quite as flush with cash as we hoped, and we can't even blame corporate America for the dilemma... except for the financial institutions. Oh well, maybe interest rates will be up when we retire. What's wrong with this picture? Base income management keeps you safer.

Shark Attack! (Not a Golf Story)

In retailing, there is an unethical marketing strategy called bait and switch, which works something like this: an advertisement is placed for a popular product at a special sale price. When the shopper gets to the store, the advertised product is always just sold out and sales people try to switch the consumer's interest to other products.

In the financial world, certain professionals will use an approach that I call a "shark attack and switch." Here, the sales person, leading either with his lofty designation (CPA, CFP, RIA) or his firm's big name and solid reputation, goes straight for the portfolio jugular vein: Boy did your portfolio perform badly, ours were in the top 10 percent. You shoulda done better compared with the Dow. Why don't you own an annuity? We've got a lot of work to do here. My poor dad can beat up your rich dad.

Remember all that work that went into your investment plan. Well, the attacker is usually unfamiliar with what you were trying to accomplish. This will be apparent from the type of criticisms he throws in your face. A portfolio needs to be analyzed in light of the plan and objectives that were used in its development. Proper observations, after a brief review, might sound like this: Did you mean to construct an aggressive (conservative) portfolio? What was your fixed/equity allocation model, your income target? Are you planning on retiring soon? Watch out for land sharks whose entire pitch is a criticism of what was in place when they arrived. Something you own (maybe everything) should be just fine. Always aggressively question major changes within the same asset class.

After a while, you will recognize all the stories you've read about here, and you should be able to scare him away with your own questioning. What's his or her plan? What do they think your asset allocation should be? How does he rate portfolio performance? How much importance does she give to income generation and trading?

The Working Capital Model: A Line You Can Follow

If we score good marks in trading, income building, and aging, it is reasonable to assume that our bottom-line portfolio value will increase. And although this is entirely true, the timing of the increase may be out of line with more conventional measures. This is because we are constantly seeking out new opportunities that are moving in what direction? You should have thought "down" immediately.

The year 1987 provides an excellent illustration again. Wheelbarrows full of profits were made that year and reinvested in equities that were dragged down in market value during the last few months. Working capital grew by 15 percent or more, but market value told another story. There were no bankruptcies and no dividend cuts. Unless you followed the typical Wall Street sell-low hysteria, your market value rebounded nicely and working capital just kept right on truckin' into the new year. And then, of course, after the normal ride back up the hill, the wizards suggested that you come back to the party...right before the next correction, as many of you will remember.

The working capital model methodology just doesn't let this scenario become your scenario, and not because of some mystical capabilities or because of some super-effective computer program. It's really just a matter of greed control and discipline. Since we are buying the best companies when they are down in price and selling other good companies that have moved ahead in price by 10 percent or more, what is left in the portfolio at the end of any day of the year? You are absolutely right. Stocks that are not quite camera-ready, because they are in cyclical downturns or they have temporarily fallen out of favor with Wall Street for some other reason. If you are trading properly, you will develop the patience and fortitude

TABLE 12: A working capital view of two portfolios

PORTFOLIO TYPE	TRADING	BUY AND HOLD
AMOUNT INVESTED	$100,000	$100,000
TRADING RESULTS	$15,000	-
DIVIDENDS	$3,000	$800
YEAR-END WORKING CAPITAL	$118,000	$100,800
YEAR-END MARKET VALUE	$115,640	$98,784
HIGHEST 1987 MARKET VALUE	$130,000	$144,800

The buy and hold, or let your profits run, strategy satisfies the ego. The working capital, profit-taking approach grows the portfolio.

to deal with this and to adopt a totally different and more useful method of examining your performance.

In one sense, all rallies and corrections are the same. They all come to an end. More people remember the crash of '87 than relish the memory of the rally of '87. The same is true of the rallies and corrections that followed. The same scenario has repeated itself as long as anyone alive today can remember. Pity that most investors, as fixated as they are on charts, tables, graphs, and statistics, never quite get in sync with the market. The working capital model does it automatically.

The trading portfolio in Table 12 (above) is the equity portion of a program developed according to the guidelines described in this book. The other is the classic buy and hold equity portfolio with no trading targets or income discipline. So long as the focus on working capital is maintained, illusory paper increases and decreases in value will not influence the asset allocation model or your decision making.

Now, I realize that this approach is different than anything you've dealt with before, but in one fell swoop it eliminates all of those nagging ifs, ands, or buts, that make standard bottom-line market value analysis totally useless to a trader. Just like in the game of Monopoly, the winner is always the person with the most money invested in income-producing assets.

The working capital model was developed many years ago when it became evident that a trading strategy was quite different from other styles of investment management. In years of rapidly rising interest rates and, more recently, with the divergence of the popular averages from the realities of the broad market, this method sorts things out clearly. It shows you where you are and allows for meaningful comparisons with where you've been. As a kicker it allows for an instant and accurate appraisal of asset allocation!

I can't overemphasize the importance of monitoring the age of the securities in the portfolio to avoid hanging on too long to non-productive assets. Use the ATH selling decision throughout the year to keep your portfolio a lean and mean growth and income machine. Here's a hypothetical conversation from the midst of the 2000 to 2001 Wall Street debacle

Good Year, Bad Year

"How are you doing in this market, Steve?"

"Pretty well so far. Trading has been really good because of the volatility. I've taken lots of quick, short-term profits that I've put back into new fixed income and equity positions. Most of my older hold-ings have come back well enough to escape gracefully. My base income hasn't been growing as quickly as I'd like lately because of lower inter-est rates, but I've been able to sell some fixed-income securities profit-ably as well. I expect to increase working capital by about 10 percent again this year. It's been another great year!"

With a blank stare and an open mouth, then: "What are you talking about? The market averages have been down for nearly two years!"

"Really, I don't pay much attention to those figures; they have no correlation to the design and structure of my portfolio."

Smiling at his next attempt: "Oh, I see, when did you get out of the market? You sure were lucky."

"Actually, it doesn't ever make any sense to be out of the market. My equity allocation has always been around 70 percent and it will stay there until I'm a bit closer to retirement. I consider myself an investor, not a speculator."

We are always replacing sold inventory with new bargains, ones that have potential for future profit. When the new buying opportunities dry up, smart cash from base income and capital gains builds up while the profit taking continues...the investor's creed in operation.

Investment Time

If I were to buy an existing portfolio of securities (a mutual fund) on January 1 of any given year, it might be important to look at its value on December 31. I could then compare my performance with other, similar entities as a form of managerial control. Is this practical or productive? It certainly is not if there have been any changes made to the portfolio during the time period. Even for the majority of mutual funds, just comparing the simple year-to-year unit value (net asset value) change with the change in an average or index just doesn't compute. If the manager of a mutual fund is not trading, just what are you paying him for? And, believe me, you are paying.

Investment time is a concept that you're just going to have to understand and appreciate. It involves the application of patience and reasonableness to a living entity that has no start or end date, although Wall Street has created funds and unit trusts with ending dates... because they know they can sell anything. But most portfolios are dynamic. Their changes, all of their changes, cannot be quantified, catalogued, or crammed into some arbitrary time period for analysis.

Every investment program requires time to produce the desired long-term effect. A shortsighted analysis, made too soon, inevitably causes errors, sometimes portfolio killers. Individual investments require time to produce trading gains. A calendar-year racetrack allows an average of just six months for each investment to produce. Some will, but the others won't be given a chance. Think in cycles instead of years...don't forget.

Which Bottom Line?

At a small seminar a few years ago, we were debating whether the working capital model form of analysis was really the breakthrough it appears to be on the surface. One person accepted the value of profits and of income and he could see how frequent trading should lead to excellent growth in values, long-term. But he couldn't help but focus on the year-to-year value changes in the bottom line. Any business, he pointed out, must focus on the bottom line.

Absolutely. But businesses focus on bottom lines with names such as: profits, total sales, return on invested capital, inventory turnover, and the like. They even compare such numbers with results in other years. This practice makes abundant sense, since growth in these important areas produces growth in the enterprise as a whole and benefits all concerned. Never do you hear them crow about how the value of their inventory has grown 20 or 30 percent. If it did, the business would be in serious trouble, and management derrieres would be on the pavement. In fact, growth in the value of inventory by a company or within an industry is often mentioned in the media as the reason for falling stock prices. And who spoon-feeds that information to the media? You got it, the wizards of Wall Street.

Break Time: Missing the Boat, A Study In Discipline
Managers learn quickly that they have limited resources to help them achieve the interim goals and long-term objectives of their organization or business. Most find that a well thought-out plan, with a consistently applied set of operational procedures, helps to move the company forward through an ever-changing economic environment. There are no clear charts to follow and no certainty about the future to guide decision making. Decisions, therefore, have to remain focused and cannot commit the organization to directional changes that could threaten the company's long-term viability.

Managing an investment portfolio is no different. The parallels are overwhelming. The message is clear: adopt a sensible program and stay with it. If change appears necessary, move slowly and without risking the health of the portfolio. Never let emotions take a leadership role in the enterprise.

I can't help but think of an ex-client who, early in 2000 faxed me his conclusion that I had missed the boat on the market by sticking stubbornly to my high-quality, profitable, and dividend-paying company selection criteria. Another "ex" determined that the conservative investment style that we had used so successfully together for nearly twenty years was simply broken and useless. To the scrap heap it went, in favor of a new age guru with connections in the media. The future of investing, he called it. The first guy sold a large equity portfolio and announced that he had put it all in CSCO, along with the rest of his portfolio. The stock is just now getting to about half of its price at that time and is yet to pay a dividend. The other guy, now deceased, liquidated a six-figure municipal bond portfolio and gave it to his new age NASDAQ Guru.

No one is happy with single-digit gains when their buddies and their accountants have become expert in producing exponential growth. Income is for fools. By this time next year I'll be rich. Goodbye. As in many other life situations, though, some temporary and foolish pleasure can cause a lifetime of pain.

At the end of every stock market rainbow is a black hole, in which you will find the charred remains of many a Wall Street speculator but, sadly, no evidence at all of the people who led the pigs into the pit. I can't emphasize strongly enough how even treading water in quality investments and a balanced portfolio always comes out ahead in the long run. Bubbles always burst. Splat! The carnage is always devastating. Missing a speculative ride on a hydroplane is far better than going down with the ship. Boring investment portfolios may not get the media attention, but they always seem to come out of hard times undamaged, whole, and strangely more attractive than those flashy speculative upstarts.

Institutional Wall Street, the financial press, and each new iteration of Guru thrive on delivering their snake oil to the savvy investor. They always have. Nothing ever changes. Savvy investors seem to always have the ego and the appetite for everything the Street chefs place on the table before them.

Why would anyone be surprised at the demise of the NASDAQ? So many tales could be told to re-emphasize lessons that are only temporarily learned, like: greed rules, and the pigs always lose. Will you be caught in the next speculative bubble? There absolutely will be one, you know.

Administrations will change, and so will the direction of interest rates. Stock prices will move up and down forever, I hope and fully expect. The magnitude of the opportunity for profit is directly proportional to the magnitude of the change in either direction. You just have to understand the rules. It's depressing when you appreciate just how many people either don't know that there are rules or think that they can make up their own as they go along.

The NASDAQ is the only index yet to make a comeback of any magnitude, but only because the new bubble is a sector thing, multiple speculations in indices of speculations. Junk squared. Yet another, stroke of Wall Street genius, with a whole new group of lazier, but equally savvy... pigs. Nope. Nothing ever changes.

The aftermath of greed is so much fun for the value trader to observe. Ahhh, human nature, it never disappoints. Constant entertainment. Remember Red Auerbach? I have this image of myself, sitting on a chaise at the beach, feet up, puffing on a victory cigar, sipping a mint julep (I'm in the South now), just watching those speculative boats slipping beneath the waves. Join me. It's so fun!

But let's press on and learn some more about the playing field of the investment game. Can you guess what it is?

Chapter 8
The Investment Dashboard

I s it clear to you now that there isn't a whole lot of hard, scientific, fact-based investing knowledge out there? Wall Street doesn't want you to know it, but ignorance is the playing field for the investment game. One of the keys to success in the markets is to be aware of this. Instantly you will realize that 99 percent of what you hear and read about investing is, itself, just speculation (this book being the other 1 percent). No amount of past, no matter how creatively analyzed, equals future.

To invest profitably, you must be able to distinguish between what is and is not knowable; you must stubbornly limit the number of inputs you allow into your decision making process; you must avoid any form of hindsightful analysis; you must never think in terms such as coulda, woulda, and shoulda; and lastly, you should watch the tape on CNBC with the volume turned off.

Once you have established a plan and a set of rules, strategies and procedures with which to implement that plan, you are ready to move forward into management and operations. But recognize that the investment playing field contains hazards, pitfalls, and static that has to be avoided and filtered constantly. Here are some basic avoidance guidelines:

- Avoid taking unsolicited advice and/or that offered by commissioned salespersons.
- Avoid taking investment advice from people who have not made their money investing.

• Avoid drastic directional changes.
• Avoid direct-from-Wall-Street advice like the plague.

The purpose of an investment program is to grow and preserve wealth. The plan is to follow a prescribed set of actions that can reasonably be expected to accomplish a reasonable set of predefined goals. It makes no sense at all to compare the results of such a program with the movement of anything, particularly things that are not constructed in a similar manner. It is also foolish to assign arbitrary time constraints to something that, by definition, has no beginning or end.

Somewhere along the narrow streets of lower Manhattan, the purpose of the investment program has been lost. It has been relegated to cardboard and pallet shanties while, many stories up, financial institutions prosper. And the foundation of their prosperity is a complex web of conflicts of interest just begging to become scandal fodder...all the more reason for investors to be on their toes, trading regularly, and trusting Wall Street not at all.

Boeing, Boeing, Stage 1 Window Dressing

Way back in the dark ages of my investment career, I had the opportunity to spend some time with one of my employer's separate account (mutual fund) managers, a person responsible for billions of client investment dollars.

"Why do you hold so much Boeing stock?" I asked. "The value is about three times cost: why not take profits and diversify or add to income?"

"Because Steve, Boeing is one of our largest insurance customers and they like us to hold a large position in their stock."

So what do you think would happen to Boeing's market price if they switched insurance companies? And what lesson is to be learned here? This isn't price to earnings or current ratios; nor is it sales projections, profitability or even buy-out rumors. This is politics, greed, and manipulation. And who has more influence on market prices than major institutional money managers? Those of us who go out there and buy a few hundred shares of McDonalds for our IRA have no clue what is motivating the buy-and-sell strategies of these huge investors. Do they make major decisions, buying millions of shares of stock, just because their clients think it would be a nice idea? No, manipulation and influence peddling is not a new thing, it's just gotten bigger and more dangerous.

Stage 2 window dressing takes over quarterly, as the media blithely reports how their institutional bedfellows are rushing in to buy large quantities of the most popular issues while separating themselves from groups that have performed poorly. This business-as-usual scenario has been a fact of life in the market since the first pension fund was given to an outside money manager. Let's show our clients how smart we are in our quarterly reports. They'll see that we owned the hot issues and had nothing to do with the losers. Fund managers pay too much for some stocks and take losses on others just to fool their major squeezes.

The sad thing is that it works so well. Employee benefits executives would rather defraud plan participants than go through the expense and embarrassment of changing investment managers. They too have to look smart to bosses and board members. The con job flies well with a media that rarely has the guts to doubt conventional wisdom, and with millions of unsuspecting individual investment hopefuls, who are mesmerized by whatever information they receive from people who are, after all, the experts. Wall Street has created a new art form. No matter what the cost, they will appear to be smart, and someone else will always be at fault when it hits the fan.

This is the environment of the individual investor, but there is no reason to be scared, be a Boy Scout instead. Ninety percent of equity price movement is the result of institutional trading, and these guys are a whole lot more into politics and marketing than they are into investing. This is how they feed their families and no one in their organizations seems to care how they earn those million-dollar bonuses. It becomes your job to protect yourself, so trade, take profits. Be prepared.

Through the Looking Glass with Aunt Alice
Now that you know all about the opportunities for gain in IRE sensitive securities, have a headshake with this true story.

Years ago, when interest rates moved into double digits, my elderly Aunt Alice accumulated a portfolio of Ginnie Maes that delivered income at a rate of about 13 percent. As interest rates rose, the market value of these federally guaranteed securities fell, as one would have expected them to—but not Alice.

This was a problem. Even though her income was more than she needed to meet expenses, she couldn't cope with the decline in market value reflected on her monthly account statements. And she just knew that interest rates would keep going up forever—happy with the income, unhappy with the force of interest-rate gravity. What a dilemma. Some people should keep their rate-sensitive, registered securities stashed in a safe deposit box for perpetual smiles... they won't be able to observe the fluctuations.

Incidentally, I've observed over the years that people become increasingly pessimistic as they age, and that they worry much more about the future than one would think. Watch out for this in your own thought processes and behavior. Reach out for a younger person's perspective if you sense a negative change in your attitude.

So Alice went to her local bank and traded in her absolutely government guaranteed securities for some shiny new 8.5-percent CDs. "No more erosion of my nest egg," she boasted proudly. At least not until her income shortfall forced her to liquidate some of those wonderful CDs to meet expenses. Now why do you think that her bank financial advisor didn't suggest that safe deposit box? Conflict of interest...you think? Wouldn't it be ironic if the bank took Alice's money and used it to invest in some wonderful 15-percent Ginny Maes? Let's do the math. They had to earn 8.5 percent to pay Alice and another few points to cover overhead. With these self-liquidating government securities, they walk away with a guaranteed profit of 3.5 percent. The only problem would be the banker's inability to sleep nights afterward. Yeah, right.

Conflict of Interest (no pun intended)

Margin borrowing, leveraging, writing uncovered options, and the like are flawed investment strategies because they are based on a presumption of knowledge of the future. If I can borrow on my portfolio at 8 percent and invest the proceeds at 15 percent, why wouldn't I do so? Because there are no guarantees out there, period. Options and shorting strategies bring a second level of speculation into the picture...timing.

But, do the Masters of the Universe advise against these speculative addictions? Please, "let them take drugs" would be more like it. Equities and fixed-income securities investors are encouraged to pre-sign margin agreements in case of emergencies, which is not really a bad thing. But many monthly account statements highlight "available borrowing power," a popular euphemism for margin borrowing. So even if you think you've found a sure thing in something you've been reading recently, you haven't and you shouldn't ever use margin as a growth strategy. Remember, borrowing power is based on market value, and the rate you are charged is based on the highest possible current benchmark. No fixed-rate margin loans exist. Margin borrowing is for emergencies only, and with a limit below 20 percent of the portfolio value, if possible. Only the most well disciplined people should consider its use at all, and the margin balance must be cleaned up ASAP.

Why do they let you borrow as much as you wish? Well, the firm sets the rates, higher for the smallest (and less likely to pay it back) clients, and they share none of the income with your investment advisor. It's easy money, and nothing is done to discourage you. Shouldn't there be a "WARNING: The SEC has determined that margin borrowing is addictive and is dangerous to your financial health" label on your account statement? Wall Street must be better connected (politically) than the tobacco companies ever were...but I suppose both are still subsidized in one way or the other. Shouldn't we expect better from financial institutions? You should, but you can't. If you are on a fixed income from your portfolio, and you tell your financial advisor to buy securities for you on margin, ten bucks says that he won't say no.

We humans are as creative on the dark side of commercial activity as we are in developing beneficial new products and services, so it should come as no surprise when a new scandal or scam makes the nightly news. In the face of huge financial benefits, some corporate executives can't resist taking an extra dessert even before their shareholders have finished dinner. Some scandals have more of an impact on investors than others, and most produce unwarranted layers of government regulation and control that stifle honest creativity.

Plain vanilla fraud and theft are less worrisome to me than situations where the general acceptance of misinformation or business-as-usual practices allows inherently bad product ideas and blatant mismanagement to become accepted by regulatory authorities, financial professionals, and myopically gullible consumers. Just so you and yours don't get financially blown away by some of the more serious candidates for blockbuster scandal awards (BS awards, if you will), I'm going to devote some serious time to them here.

The Real Scoop on Annuities

Securities firms, banks, and insurance companies have always been the big three Wall Street financial institutions. At one time, it wasn't too difficult to distinguish between them. Securities firms sold stocks and bonds; banks provided check clearing and financing services; insurance companies sold life insurance policies and annuity contracts. It was a simpler world and one less prone to the conflicts of interest that exist in and about the modern Wall Street.

Today, securities firms own banks, banks sell insurance, insurance companies sell securities. Actually, it's difficult to distinguish one financial institution from another as they compete for the growing pool of investment dollars...and, of course, they all nickel and dime you to death with nuisance fees.

Serious problems occur when mutual funds are packaged with insurance and annuity products and the critical differences between them are either overlooked or undisclosed—perhaps innocently, perhaps not. The founding fathers of the annuity contract would not be pleased. The time-honored distinction of the annuity contract was the guaranteed retirement benefit it contained. "You will never outlive your income," boasted the insurance companies. They were able to make good on the promise by coupling a return of principal plus interest with the annuitant's life expectancy. Those who died earlier than expected helped to pay for those who did not. This was no investment product, although the disciplined savings of the deferred variety was certainly emphasized. The guarantee was the unique and sacred element. Like bank savings accounts and federal government securities, risk of loss was not a factor. The guarantee was a benefit well worth the lower than market yield. Over a hundred years, the concept became generic. Annuity = Guarantee. This product is safe. Equities were nowhere to be seen.

Enter the modern day variable annuity, sold by an industry that has lost touch with its noble roots, if not the realities of the stock market. (How much did it cost to get this one past the state insurance departments?) The sales pitch emphasizes the prospect of gains in the stock market rather than the safety and security of the contract. Hundreds of annuity companies rushed in to sell their mutual funds to unsuspecting retirees. In its zeal to claim its share of the investment dollar, the industry has rationalized away the risk of equity investments. Financial planning computer models were programmed to include variable annuities in their asset allocations. And it's such an easy sell because this is what the customer hears: a guaranteed retirement income + stock market appreciation.

Let's back up a century. Just who needs an annuity anyway? Annuities were developed for the protection of the indigent, not as an investment vehicle for the wealthy, or anyone else. An annuity is simply a series of identical payments made over a specific period of time. Any departure from a plain vanilla life annuity reduces the payout because of additional time or life contingencies. A fixed amount is paid to an annuitant until his or her death. Any leftover funds belong to the insurance company, and the insurance company pays any shortfall... a simple concept, actuarially pure, easy to deal with, no surprises. (At least not until the government decreed that men are required to live as long as women. I feel so much better now that I'm protected from sexist actuarial tables.) Annuitants would never outlive their income, but absolutely nothing would be passed on to their heirs, a dismal prospect for the kids, but a valuable benefit for the retiree. Certainly, the annuity was a last resort financial alternative... but a perfect solution for the Social Security disaster.

A Last Resort Alternative

Forget all the sales talk, there is no such thing as a guaranteed variable annuity. The words just don't fit well together, an oxymoron, and we've already learned about the role of equities in planning for retirement income. If the portfolio can't do it, a fixed annuity may be the right thing, but equity investing just doesn't belong in the picture. Retirement is an income problem; growth, the primary purpose of equities, should not be an issue.

It is irresponsible to rely on equity mutual funds to provide retirement income. If the portfolio numbers are just short, and (a) a windfall (inheritance) is anticipated within a few years, or (b) the retiree is in poor health, an annuity should not be considered at all. You should be able to invest the money conservatively, generate adequate income and have an estate left over for the heirs. Remember to satisfy the income need before looking at equities. There are no exceptions!

So here we have a last resort product, designed for the poor, that the industry has chrome-plated, spit-polished, and supercharged for snob appeal marketing to people who should be ineligible. Why? There are three obvious reasons:

1. They are a captive audience for the company's high-fee mutual funds.
2. They are an easy way to hold customers' money hostage for eight years or more.
3. Financial professionals themselves have been brainwashed into thinking that the product is suitable and safe for everyone.

The industry uses ridiculously high commissions to influence their own representatives' judgment. The needs of the retirement program are hardly a consideration, and sadly, the majority of annuity salespersons actually believe the speak. As far as they are concerned, RISK is just a board game they played in college.

Responsible managers need to say no to greed and speculation, particularly when it comes to retirement portfolio design. There is no reason to sell inappropriate products when proper ones are still available. Let's create income annuities for people who can afford to generate their own cash flow from a securities portfolio and provide good old-fashioned life annuities to those who can't. Keep equity mutual funds away from the retirement plan; it's just not what they are meant for.

The Annuity Product and Social Security... Please
The opportunity for tinkering with annuity formulas makes today's providers of the product suspect as well. There is room for manipu-

lation in two of the three elements of the formula. The exception is mortality rates, which are scientifically calculated and maintained by professional actuaries. Unisex humans have an anticipated life expectancy, and all companies use the same tables in their calculations. Males will get a lower payment than they should, and women will get more than they would have in years past. Not much room for manipulation here. (Question: if non-smokers pay lower life insurance premiums, shouldn't smokers get higher annuity payments? Maybe if they sue...)

The guaranteed interest rate that the company is absolutely sure it can earn is a judgment call that will depend on how aggressive the company is going to pursue the business. But the expense assumption is the big one, hot for manipulation. The actuary has to create an expense number for the product, based on input from the executive suite. Lower numbers produce more competitive, higher annuity payments. Failures happen when earnings are less than assumed or expenses are higher than anticipated, but the Ponzi scheme can go on for a long time. So what do you think the addition of the stock market does to the risk factor for the consumer? For the time being, only the company is safe. They have the money to take care of their executives and, if the assumptions prove erroneous, it's not their retirement that is in jeopardy. Professionals must know what they are selling, and knowledge goes way beyond blind faith in the corporate party line. Even AARP has come out with warnings about variable annuities. Purge them from your portfolio. And for that old-fashioned guaranteed life annuity, the highest payout rate is a danger signal. Caveat emptor, still and forever.

But what if we made a trade. In exchange for eliminating all variable products, let's give the industry Social Security to run with. After all, it is supposed to be a fixed life annuity, isn't it?

Who's in Your Wallet?

The working capital model stresses the importance of dividends as an indication of the financial strength of those companies that fit best within this trading methodology. And although we may be short-term owners of many corporations, we have a long-term interest in making these companies perpetual investment-grade entities—the more of them the better. Corporate executive compensation affects all of us. Please don't misunderstand—I strongly believe that everyone has the right to become filthy rich, legally, of course. I respect anyone who gets there honestly because their success creates jobs, opportunities, wealth, and a higher standard of living for everyone. But, once they sell shares of their successful enterprises to the public, they have a responsibility to share future profits and growth. That's what those common share certificates we never see anymore are all about. These are our companies and obscene executive compensation, in all its forms, deferred or otherwise, is simply stealing from shareholders. All bonuses, incentives, perks, and club memberships should be in the form of dividends, as should salaries over a number like four or five million per year. Abolish stock options totally...you get the point, but do you really?

With every new scandal, a voracious media and a hypocritical Congress exacerbate the fear of shocked investors and call for more regulation of the very entities whose success, freedom, viability, and competitiveness they should be nurturing. Ironically, politicians are always the most outspoken critics...probably because of their familiarity with cover-ups and improprieties. But no one ever questions the integrity of the financial institutions that invent, produce, price, and promote products and services that do far more long-term harm than the few incidents of corporate malfeasance. For example, here's a recent Wall Street triple play that's attracted much less attention than it should.

Early in 2003, a major New York newspaper reported on a service that the Masters of the Universe were providing to the poor unfortunates that lost most of their 401(k) nest eggs in the bursting dot.com bubble. Basically, mutual fund salespersons are now allowed to advise plan participants how to select from the funds offered by their employers...for an additional fee of up to 1.5 percent. A Labor Department ruling lifted the ban on this previously barred practice. It's like non-lawyers giving legal advice legally. And as the innocent chicks line up to be plucked, the same financial institutions who brought on the last disaster are granted a new license to steal. These same folk fired their value fund managers, shunned asset allocation, and tossed value investing aside as they force fed high-risk mutual funds down these very same throats.

The triple dip:

1. fees and expenses inside the mutual fund,
2. commissions to the salesperson, both initial and residual, and
3. an exceptionally high investment management fee for electronically choosing which of these very same products uniquely meets the participants' retirement goals.

It's kind of like protection money to the mafia. How can a company that sells only their own proprietary products charge a fee to select investments from these very same products AND claim to be objective? These are the same people, using the same selection techniques as before. There are more personal, self-directed ways to invest 401(k) dollars using individual securities. Make sure your employer considers the lower-cost possibilities, and make sure that you understand this, with regard to the rest of your growing nest egg.

Caveat Investor: The "Hypocritic" Oath

Every investment house, mutual fund marketer, and brokerage firm touts its unique ability to put together the correct mix of funds, annuities, and indices to assure your investment success. And the billions that the institutions spend on advertising is the primary tool they use to brainwash you. One would think that full-service firms make the bulk of their profits from the obscene commissions that they charge for securities transactions. If they charged less, you would be less likely to nibble at the bait and commit your fortune to their products and special fee arrangements. They don't want the commissions and they don't want your broker to want them either. Do they know human nature, or what?

Over the years, the propaganda machine has managed to reinvent the investment wheel, adding a collection of spokes and ball bearings that didn't exist thirty years ago. Most savvy investors would agree that mutual funds are safer and cheaper than individual stocks and bonds, that commissions and taxes are the highest priority considerations in an investment program, and that investment professionals are advisors first and salespersons second. Brainwashing, anyone?

But the reality of the financial institutions is a reality of blatant hypocrisy. They make a whole lot more inside their products than they do with those pesky commissions... and with fewer lawsuits. Your future is just not their main concern. The proof is in the way the institutions whip their stockbrokers into shape. Account executives are paid more for selling products than they are for designing portfolios of individual securities. Lucrative commissions are paid on mutual fund and annuity products, particularly the proprietary variety. Fixed fee and managed money arrangements are encouraged. The brokers' portion of individual security commissions has been reduced to a pittance and now stockbrokers are actually being assessed a ticket charge when they have the audacity to purchase stocks the old-fashioned way. If you don't sell products, baby, there won't be any prizes and rewards for you.

So what percent of financial professionals do you think can afford to lead their clients down the path to an individual security portfolio, especially now that they have two new generations of index funds to pitch?

The Manhattan Triangle: Enhanced Index Funds

The Bermuda Triangle is no longer numero uno in mysterious losses. The Manhattan Triangle has taken over the coveted top spot, sucking billions of unsuspecting franklins into the Charybdis of investment products... many never to be seen again. The Wall Street institutional brain(washing) trust is truly amazing... intelligent, foresighted, resilient, and creative.

First there was the development of the mutual fund into the medium of choice for transferring millions of innocent retirement dollars into the pockets of investment bankers and venture capitalists. Professional managers are at our disposal to protect our portfolios with proper asset allocation, quality, discipline, diversification, and knowledge. "Our Managers are always in the first performance quartile," the firms all boast. Then, out of the other side of the oracle of Wall Street's mouth, came the index fund trial balloon. After all, who really needs management? What! Isn't management the key element of the 650,000 mutual funds they've been cramming down people's throats for thirty years? Wasn't this an outright admission of the failure of all the other funds?

But the plain vanilla index fund just didn't work out very well, at least not for investors. So the wizard reached inside his rib cage and produced the new and improved enhanced index fund. And what do you think it was enhanced with? Why management, of course. Back to square one, again. These funds juice up the index by weeding out laggard stocks while adding faster-growing ones. Some even buy options and futures to hedge their positions in the hope of making more money, while protecting themselves if the market turns against them. You would think this investing system would work. But statistics showed that only one out of five enhanced index funds beat the S&P 500. These funds have the same drawbacks as any actively managed fund: poor stock selection (buying low quality at high prices), poor timing (selling low, always), and poor judgment.

But what else has changed? The safety that is supposed to dwell in mutual funds automatically is now being jeopardized with hedging strategies, leverage, and market timing… go figure, and we haven't gotten to the good stuff yet. The third generation of index funds has hit the Street and is a tremendous success, reminiscent of too many earlier bubbles. When quality stocks crash after being pumped up in price by speculation, there are no bankruptcies, dividend cuts, or layoffs (except, justifiably, on Wall Street). The companies may lose a cap category, but they function, and business proceeds as usual. But when an illusion comes unraveled, how much value remains for shareholders?

Indexed Investment Illusions: iShares and ETFs

How many of you remember the immortal words of P.T. Barnum? Of Yogi Berra? On Wall Street, the incubation period for new product scams may be measured in years instead of minutes, but the end result is always a lopsided, greed-driven, gold rush toward financial disaster. The dot.com melt down spawned the index mutual funds, and their dismal failure gave life to enhanced index funds, a wide variety of speculative hedge funds, and finally, a rapidly growing number of index ETFs. Déjà vu all over again, with the popular iShare variety of ETF leading the lemmings to the cliffs. How far will we allow Wall Street to move us away from the basic building blocks of investing? What ever happened to stocks and bonds? The investment gods are not happy.

A market or sector index is a statistical measuring device that tracks the movement of price changes in a portfolio of securities that are selected to represent a portion of the overall market. Index ETF creators:

1. select a sampling of the market or market sector they expect to be representative of the whole,
2. purchase the selected securities, and then
3. issue securities that you can trade on the normal exchanges just like ordinary stocks.

Unlike ordinary index funds, however, ETF shares are not handled directly by the fund, and as a result, they can move either up or down from the value of the securities in the fund, which, in turn, may or may not mirror the movements of the index they were selected to track. Confused? There's more...these things are designed for manipulation.

Unlike managed closed-end funds (CEFs), index ETF shares can be created or redeemed by market specialists, and institutional investors can redeem 50,000-share lots (in kind) if there is a gap between the net-asset-value and the market price of the fund. These activities create demand in order to minimize the gap between the fund net-asset-value and the fund price. Clearly, these arbitrage activities provide profit-making opportunities to the fund sponsors that are not available to the shareholders. Perhaps that is why the fund expenses are so low... and why there are now hundreds of the products from which to choose.

Two other iShare/ETF idiosyncracies need to be appreciated:

1. Performance return statistics for index funds typically do not include fund expenses.
2. Some index funds, iShares in particular, publish P/E numbers that only include the profitable companies in the portfolio.

So, in addition to the normal risks associated with investing in general, we add: speculating in narrowly focused sectors, guessing on the prospects of unproven small cap companies, experimenting with securities in single countries, rolling the dice on commodities, and hoping for the eventual success of new technologies. We then call this hodgepodge of speculations a diversified, passively managed, inexpensive approach to twenty-first century asset management. How this differs from the beginnings of the dot.com mess is a mystery to me. The fact remains that the share prices of the companies included in the indices are being pumped up by demand for the indices and not by their own fundamentals or basic economic prospects. High-priced iShares and ETFs give holders a false sense of security that will eventually lead to disaster.

But let's not dwell upon the three or more levels of speculation that exist in all index funds. Let's move on to the two basic ideas that led to the development of plain vanilla mutual funds in the first place: diversification and professional management. Mutual funds were a monumental breakthrough that changed the investment world. Hands-on investing (without the self-centered assistance of the banks and insurance companies) became possible for absolutely everyone. Self-directed retirement programs and cheap-to-administer employee benefit programs became doable. The investment markets, once the domain of an elite group of wealthy entrepreneurs, became the savings accounts of choice for the employed masses. ETFs are just not the answer to the problems we've experienced lately with traditional mutual funds: (1) fund manager compensation undermines manager's focus on stated fund objectives, and (2) self-directed retirement programs themselves place buy-sell decision making in the hands of participants. In fact, they add to the problem by over-pricing large numbers of securities with artificial demand.

Sure, you might find some smiles in an iShare or two, particularly if you have the courage to take your profits, and there may be times when it makes good business sense to use these products as a hedge against a specific risk. But please, stop kidding yourself every time Wall Street comes up with a new short-cut to investment success. Don't underestimate the value of experienced management, even if you have to pay a little extra for it. Actually, there is no reason why you (and I mean every one of you) can't learn either to run your own investment portfolio, or to instruct someone how you want it done. Every guess, every estimate, every hedge, and every shortcut increases risk, because none of the crystal balls used by those creative product hucksters works very well over the long haul. Products and gimmicks are never the answer. ETFs, a combination of the two, don't even address the question properly.

A Landfill of Investment Propaganda

There's a new form of propaganda out there and it isn't emanating from Wall Street. Every day, thousands of radio talk show hosts interview hundreds of authors, columnists, financial experts, and economists in an effort to entertain growing audiences throughout the nation. Financial news and talk radio programs attract millions of advertising dollars from sales reps creatively barkering a wide variety of investment snake oil. Radio listeners and guests have the pleasure of listening to an endless stream of ads containing economic predictions, chaos hypotheses, doomsday messages, financial panaceas, and other landfill quality scenarios. The problem is that these sideshow fringe products and Barnumesque speculations are being given credibility by talk show hosts and listeners alike.

A client recently told me not to buy fixed-income securities because the long bond interest rate was rising, and it was better to sit on cash until rates started to go down again. He had heard about it on talk radio. Listeners to radio shows where I host Q&A's have called in to ask me questions like, "How much of your clients' portfolios are you placing in gold?," "How do I go about finding investments denominated in euros?," and "How much should I be paying for investment diamonds?"

In one interview, I was asked to comment on the fact that the United States had become a debtor nation and, therefore, how will we be able to compete with the European economy, with a GNP larger than our own? One of the commercials predicted that the dollar would become totally valueless in just a few years. Another suggested that it was a fairly simple matter to make a fortune in currency futures.

In the late 1990s, a Wall Street selling a new economy turned investors into speculators. Today, a splinter group of speculation peddlers is painting the strongest economy on the planet as failing in their effort to sell sideshow products as safe alternatives to more conventional investment mediums...and not an economics Ph.D. among them. Even those awful mutual funds are safer than precious metals, currency trading, and options. The euro is the yen of twenty years ago… same scenario, same hype, nothing happened. Twenty-five percent of $100 is $25; 5 percent of $1,000,000 is $50,000. Which is bigger and better? And China has surpassed Europe as the chic economy?

I'm no international economist, but I've put in enough classroom hours to understand that these things are cyclical as well as statistical, with three basic elements:

1. There has always been a natural migration of funds (and attention) to hot economies anywhere in the world. China is no different from Europe, Japan, and Indonesia. Smart U.S. companies participate.
2. Politics of the moment. The United States has made some rather unpopular moves recently and remains a target of extremists. Other countries can't afford to align themselves with us publicly. Again, smart companies diversify their interests throughout the growing world economy.
3. Our interest rates and inflation rate are among the lowest in the world. Smart foreign companies would rather invest at a short-term 7 percent in Germany, for example, than at 3 percent in government bonds here, another piece of the weak dollar puzzle.

The experienced perspective sees opportunity in everything, and what we have in our economy today is nothing more than a financial circle of life scenario without the animated characters. Despite all the hype and criticism, the U.S. dollar, the U.S. economy, and the United States standard-of-living are still king. Find the profitable international companies and let them make you money… you can't do it yourself, and you can't carry your bouillon with you on vacation.

How many of you would have dealt with those talk radio questions like this:

1. I've never purchased the long bond, nor have I ever been victimized by higher interest rates, which, for the most part, are good for investors.
2. The fixed income portion of a portfolio should always be added to. It's called compounding.
3. A debtor nation owes money to the government of some other nation. It has nothing to do with securities or the balance of payments. The United States is the biggest net creditor nation in the world.
4. No gold, no euros, no diamonds.

5. We have individual companies with gross revenues higher than the GNPs of most of the world's countries. The bigger the GNP of other nations, the better it is for all nations.

This is not a competitive sport. The dollar may purchase fewer quiches in France, but that has no bearing on the number of burgers you can buy here. I guess we could fix everything by raising interest rates and increasing inflation to bolster the dollar...hmm.

The Economic Cycle

Now that you have a feel both for the cyclical nature of the markets and for the new information that you can use to determine where you are within each portion of a cycle, it should be much easier to deal rationally and patiently with the barrage of financial information that crosses your path. Wall Street likes to use technical analysis to identify stock market rallies and corrections, an arbitrary up or down 10 percent in the weighted DJIA. I think there's a better way, but "more winners than losers" just isn't the kind of explanation a knowledgeable chief economist is going to come up with. The financial community is expected to give reasons for what's going on out there. Historically, the same reasons have always been used, with appropriate spin for the correction or rally at hand. Standards are energy prices, the situation in the Middle East, the over-heated economy, recession, and employment numbers. Recently, weather events and terrorist activity have become explanation staples.

Economic movements between recession and expansion are measured in a technical manner, just like rallies and corrections, but with enormous numbers that are probably a lot less knowable. Just how important to the average guy do you think a quarter or two of declining GNP really is? Not very, I would guess. And why isn't it reported more clearly that some areas can be booming while others are suffering. Sometimes, simplicity is easier to deal with, and wherever you are, here's a sure-fire way to identify the next meaningful recession.

- Unemployment goes up month after month.
- Prices actually go down.
- A parking place can be found at the Mall within a hundred yards of the entrance you really wanted to use.

- You can walk into any restaurant in town, particularly the most expensive ones, on a Friday or Saturday night and get immediate seating.
- There are no rush hour traffic jams on weekdays or volume-only problems on Sunday afternoons.
- Professional sports events are being played with a growing percentage of empty seats.
- And the acid test, when you can walk onto any public golf course on a weekend without a tee time and wait less than two hours to play.

The media wants you to love rallies and to hate corrections, but you know better now. Hopefully, you find them equally attractive now, as I do. Wall Street is powerful enough (and greedy enough) to cause both rallies and corrections, but the economic and interest-rate cycles are not quite as easy to manipulate. Actually, short-term interest rate manipulations are the government's favorite tool for dealing with the economy. Pity they don't use the tax code instead. Wall Street and the financial media combine to spin the economic news to meet their current needs.

Good News, Bad News
"The market went down today because there are just too many people employed. The strength of the economy is someday going to cause prices to go up. When that happens, inflation could become a problem and the Fed will have to raise interest rates to slow things down." Sound familiar? How about this one: "The market jumped up today, rejoicing over the increase in first-time jobless claims during the latest reporting month."

This topsy-turvy kind of thinking is not going away anytime soon, and by now, I'm sure that you don't want it to. It produces the day-to-day, month-to-month, directional changes that make for successful trading. An irrational market that moves unpredictably and quickly in both directions is the easiest market environment to manage.

Enlightened Self Interest
Every worthwhile project should come to the point where you can lean back, view your accomplishments, and say with conviction, "Done." And then there's investing: at the same time a body of knowledge and experience, and a mysterious unsolvable puzzle;

an exciting environment that changes daily, but manageable with the right tools and concepts; a straightforward by-the-book business that can be managed unemotionally, while the basic product or inventory being controlled is the most emotion packed of all...your money. A book like this can't be done. Five years from now, I suspect that I'll be itching to document fine tuning adjustments like those that have been made here, and there's no doubt that Wall Street will have created new topics for discussion.

But I firmly believe that you have the information, the methodology and, hopefully, the optimistic, positive, mindset to move forward productively. The methods and procedures described here are easy to use, logical, and founded on basic, and sound principles of at least two disciplines: management and investing. Don't toss it aside just because it isn't mainstream, recognized, or put forth by the normal media or financial institution gurus. The approach has stood the test of time, and is operating well for many people... but not so many that it flattens the curves. Take three things with you into your active investment life and your chances for success will increase significantly:

1. The working capital model and its application of cost basis analysis to asset allocation, diversification, and portfolio performance evaluation;
2. The investor's creed; and
3. QDI.

Investors don't operate in a vacuum. Economic, political, and social factors are constantly changing, and it's in your best interest to keep your eye on those beyond Wall Street who have their hands in your pocketbook. They come in all shapes and sizes, but they have a common denominator...they just can't connect the dots. They dwell in the fantasy of a black and white, rich and poor world, and somehow blame the business world for their problems instead of applauding them for bringing them employment and the goods and services that give them the lifestyle envied around the world. There is more danger to investors (and to our attackers) in big government and special interest lobbyists than there is in big business. So protect yourself with your vote as well as with your investment strategy.

Several important, albeit peripheral, subjects just didn't fit the flow of the working capital model methodology or the basic concepts that have now been thoroughly explained—not the least of these being a section on how to go about changing your portfolio from what it is to what you now know it should be. We haven't discussed no-load funds, bond swaps, zero coupon deals, penny stocks, the core portfolio, socially conscious investing, and more. By now, you should have a good idea of what fits and what doesn't, so pick the topics you want to explore and dive in. Another hour or so and you'll be ready to get out there and make the doughnuts.

Changing Strategies the Right Way

Years ago I had a wealthy client who enjoyed traveling to exotic places around the world attending investment seminars. Every few months, I would receive a call asking if I was familiar with the incredible success one guru or another had had with his new approach to investing. "I want you to go to Dallas and speak with this guy so that you can redesign my portfolio to be more in step with this new strategy," Al would say. For years, I was able to poke enough holes in each new miracle cure to avoid what I knew was eventually going to happen.

One year, I was invited to Florida to play golf with Al, his broker, and the latest investment guru. I had just figured out that my travel expenses to manage Al's portfolio exceeded the income that his account generated, so I attempted to stop the wheel spinning for both us. I explained the finances of our relationship, and suggested that he come to New Jersey with his entourage to meet at my office. I didn't expect him to come and he didn't disappoint me. His new manager would only accept cash deposits...

Major changes in a securities portfolio should be evolutionary, not revolutionary. Some of what you've learned here just might be interesting enough for you to consider altering your direction or asset allocation in any number of ways. Make certain you are making an intellectual and not an emotional adjustment. In other words, don't sell your present holdings out of hate for their current lack of performance. High-quality companies get beat up just like the no-quality variety. Be patient.

A shift in strategy must be given both implementation time and development time. In most instances, there is plenty of time to get things coordinated, unless you are already in or near retirement. In that case, take two aspirin and call a portfolio doctor in the morning. Implementation is the process of changing the asset allocation and/or the securities within the portfolio. Development involves managing the transitional (and changed) portfolio in accordance with the new rules and guidelines. Here are some first-step ideas, assuming that you have established a reasonable plan:

1. Organize your portfolios in one easy-to-access brokerage firm that provides detailed and comprehensible statements and annual summary information. Combine IRAs, SEP IRAs, etc. to minimize the number of separate pieces of paper you have to deal with. I've taken over portfolios that contained nearly one hundred different mutual funds. Simplify your life and your record keeping.
2. Cease all automatic reinvestment programs of any kind whatsoever, including the repurchase of additional mutual fund shares. All income should be directed to your primary personal or IRA brokerage account. Then you will be able to use the cash flow to implement change.
3. Identify securities where reasonable profits can be realized. If some are securities you've owned since puberty, sell a portion each year unless the value is more than 50 percent of the total portfolio. Then reduce it to that level immediately. Determine the cost bases of all securities.
4. Get ready to sell all securities that don't fit your quality guidelines, at or near break-even. The ATH decision can be used later with any major losers. This would include all zero coupon adventures, CMOs (if you don't know what they are, good), metals, and other exotics.
5. Inappropriate annuity holdings should be looked at closely. Treat any mutual fund element like you would any other fund, looking for a profitable exit point. You should be able to exit the variable portion without penalty. If not, use the annual no-penalty withdrawal provision in that area first; most annuities will have such a provision. Cash out the balance of the annuity as soon as the penalty falls into the 1- or 2-percent range, depending on the abundance or scarcity of new equity opportunities. If the equity bucket is full, pull the trigger...I know that you know why.

Breaking The Code of Silence—No Load Mutual Funds

The automobile industry has always been one of the most important in America. Millions of new and used cars are sold (and leased)
every year. In the old days, "What's good for General Motors is good
for the country" was an economic axiom. What I could never understand though, was how car dealerships managed to make a buck
when they were selling cars below invoice. How many cars do you
have to sell at cost or below before you make a profit? Why are all
these dealers beating the doors down to obtain additional franchises? I guess they make it up in volume. I've known many car dealers,
but none of them would spill the beans, as my friend in low places,
Deep Pockets, does below:

> *Mutual Funds are one of the most confusing areas investors
> have to deal with. The interesting part is that people believe
> what they want to believe and it is often difficult to help them.
> Let's start with the most important concept: free doesn't exist on
> Wall Street. When you truly understand this you are on your way
> to avoiding disappointments on the street of dreams.*
>
> *OK, you're thinking: he's wrong, he's wrong, what about no-
> load funds? Wanna buy a bridge? Read the prospectus. The
> managers of the most popular no-load funds are paid millions.
> The companies that sponsor them make millions. The office
> buildings that headquarter these funds are marble-covered pal-
> aces. Where does all the money come from? Believing that no-
> load funds are cost-free is like buying an EZ-Pass tag and telling
> your friends that the Governor lets you use the New Jersey Turn-
> pike and Garden State Parkway for free. You know it's not true
> but it makes you feel better if they believe it.*
>
> *No-load funds have many ways to charge investors—12-b(1)
> marketing fees, fund expenses, and trading costs to mention a
> few. These don't include the hidden costs of the trip to Europe
> that the management team made on the Concord to uncover
> investment opportunities in France. The 12-b(1) fees and fund
> expenses are stated in the prospectus. Trading expenses (com-
> missions) are generally hidden toward the back, but they are in
> there. It is not uncommon for a no-load fund to have nearly 3.5
> percent in hidden fees. So much for freebies.*

Mandatory Mailings to Shareholders, Who Pays the Freight?
Publicly traded corporations, mutual funds, REITS, and any other
entity that issues securities are required to provide prospectus
material to investors when they first go public. The idea is a good
one but, as I'm sure you've noticed, most prospectus material is
totally incomprehensible. Without advanced degrees in securities
law, mathematics, and Greek, the real costs and risks of a security
remain buried under an impenetrable cloak of legalese. The reason
is simple—if you knew all the risks and appreciated all of the costs,
you just wouldn't go there. But the media pumps up the prospects
for all new issues, and most speculators rely on wire house advisors
to get them a piece of the action.

But the prospectus is just the beginning. Our government recognizes that the average investor hasn't a clue about what he or she
is doing, so it requires that corporations send quarterly and annual
reports to all shareholders, even to traders like us. Similarly we get
notified about meetings and are asked to vote on minor changes
in by-laws and takeovers in either direction. Wrap account mutual
funds have multiplied the number of recipients of these notices, and
then, of course, there is the deluge of class action suit announce-
ments every time the ambulance chasers get wind of a major corporate failure or bankruptcy. If you own one share, you get to vote…
don't be impressed. The costs don't come out of executive benefit
packages. It's your money and the world's trees being wasted.

And that's not the end of it either. All brokerage firms must send
paper statements and trade confirmations to all interested parties as
well. They, of course, take every opportunity to sell their products
with pamphlets and enclosures, and unless the account holder elects
to get their information online, the flow continues. Additionally, financial advisors are required to receive and retain yet another copy
of all of these account-related papers, and just being able to obtain
them online isn't at all good enough. Level upon level of redundancy
is the mandated expense of corporations, financial institutions, and
independent advisors. Rainforests, what rainforests?

Brokerage Account Statements
If you've ever scratched your head about the content, layout, or
meaning of brokerage firm account statements, you are not nearly

alone. Is there any reason why the basic, no-extra-charge statement can't be standardized? Don't expect it anytime soon, although some progress has been made. I'm relatively sure that account statements are designed by staff who have no contact with clients and not a whole lot of knowledge about investment products, securities, or even the financial markets. Statements are subtly designed to create transactions—particularly the more sophisticated ones. They may also contain inaccuracies that can cause you to make poor decisions.

I remember one firm that created a new form of income that it called "return of capital income." My clients who owned unit trusts and GNMAs got excited at first and angry not much later. How basic was this, and it made it through how many levels of management? Several brokerage firms used to cut off statement transactions on the last Friday of the month, and the oddities go on and on. One of my clients with yet another broker had a seven-figure municipal bond portfolio that we were both very happy about. Over the years, municipal unit trusts and closed-end municipal funds began to yield much more than individual bonds and the portfolio was adjusted to reflect this change. The brokerage firm's statements included the closed-end funds under the equities category and the unit trusts were listed as mutual funds. "What have you done to my portfolio?" was the message on my answering machine one Saturday morning. All was explained to the client's satisfaction, but from that point on I was forced to accept lower yields in individual bonds to the detriment of the long-term growth of the portfolio. The client didn't want to have to think about it.

And where are we today, with our modern technology, online access, real-time quotes, and high-speed downloads? One of the biggest and most well respected of all the financial institutions lists all closed-end funds, equity, municipal, real estate as, you guessed it, equities. Yes, one of their best features is that they trade like equities, but a client statement should allow for an assessment of asset allocation, don't you think? How difficult can it be? What level of incompetence, Peter, is allowable?

Unit Trusts

Somewhere between the diversification, liquidity, and yield problems of individual bonds and the outstanding features of income

CEFs lies the unit trust. Unit trusts are put together by Wall Street brokerage firms and assigned to a trustee for supervision. They are not managed in the manner we have described here, nor are they hedged in any impossible way against the vagaries of interest-rate movements. The securities within the trust are not even traded. Instead, nearly all are held to maturity and principal payments are directed to unit holders. The trustee does collect a smallish fee and it goes without saying that the trustee and the brokerage firm are part of the same institution.

Unit holders receive interest and a portion of principal every month, plus the proceeds of positions that are closed out entirely. Thus, a regular monthly cash flow from a high-quality, diversified portfolio is assured. There are a few minor annoyances to contend with (monthly adjustments to your cost basis for example), but unit trusts are an easy way to get a large portion of the fixed income job done, with various types of income and at yields that really are very competitive. Don't lose sight of this important fact: it is the yield that is important, only the yield. Generally, investors should plan on holding unit trusts to the very end, but profits should certainly be taken if the opportunity presents itself. Markups are not a factor (see below) as they are with individual bonds because the trustee fixes the NAV per unit each evening.

Your Government Loves You: But Not as Much as You Thought
There has always been a great deal of speculation concerning the rationale for the government's gift of the IRA (Individual Retirement Account) to the American taxpayer. Without even attempting to explain the history of IRAs—the variations, confusing rules, requirements, and fine points, let's just focus on why it should be taken advantage of by absolutely everyone.

Don't let the diminutive size of the annual contribution turn you off to the concept: you are allowed to put away a sum of money, every year, to accumulate on a tax-deferred basis if you deduct it from your current taxable income, or on a tax-free basis if you don't. In a relatively short period of time, the total annual income generated by a well-constructed IRA portfolio will certainly exceed the annual contribution by a wide margin. Don't bother to waste time whining about the prospect of paying taxes upon withdrawal. Sure it's coun-

The Shell Game called "Bond Swaps"

by Wall Street broker, "Deep Pockets"

The bond swap is as old as Wall Street and the U.S. tax code. What a scam this one is. People desperately try to avoid taxes, losing thousands as Wall Street con artists literally steal their money.

A bond is an IOU from the issuer to an investor, a contract to pay interest for a given period, at a stated rate, until a certain date in the future. Then, at maturity, the principle is returned. The contractual interest rate is fixed, but it is adjusted to current rates by selling at a premium or a discount to its face value. A bond's credit worthiness and the number of years until maturity are the primary forces influencing the adjusted, or current rate. Agencies like Moody's and Standard and Poor's determine the rating, or risk level, of the bond.

At tax time, the scam goes like this: Harry the broker knows that Mr. Jones hates to pay taxes, especially capital gains taxes on his stock portfolio. Mr. Jones is encouraged to sell his bonds at a loss, and to buy similar bonds to replace them. This way he will maintain the income stream even though he lost capital on the bond sale. On bond trades, the amount of markup is not disclosed to the customer.

The broker finds a replacement bond to complete the swap. So, without knowing it, Mr. Jones has given the brokerage firm a total of between 3 and 4 percent, per bond, twice, while he gets to deduct about thirty-five cents for each dollar he has lost. Not a bad deal for the broker, but to cover the trading costs, the replacement bonds just have to be of a lower quality.

Every year, every financial institution's research department provides advisors with lists of potential bond swap pairs. Brokers are encouraged to push their clients into these high-expense loss transactions. Why don't the institutions provide lists of swaps for profit? They are, after all, required by law to know their customers. Soon, they may also be required to act in the customer's best interest...

terproductive to tax retirement income, but you're going to become part of the movement to change that, right? In the overall scheme of things, the contribution boils down to less than $100 a week, which I believe can be made up by claiming one more dependent.

Keep in mind though, that tax free is always better than tax deferred, particularly at retirement. Don't avoid the construction of a personal portfolio just because you have self-directed savings plans working for you. The underlying assumption in all self-directed retirement plans is that the average person can invest wisely enough to make contributions grow nicely over time. This may or may not prove to be true, although you should be able to do it better now. But Uncle Sam will take his share and the amount may be larger than you expect. Here are some very important don'ts:

1. Don't ever speculate with this money. Many people make the mistake of thinking of each annual contribution as an opportunity to make a killing to get things rolling. This rarely works and results in a portfolio filled with mistakes, generating no income and unlikely to ever fulfill its potential. Speculating is always a waste of time and money.

2. Construct the IRA as you would any other portfolio, starting with an equity CEF. Continue to add more of these funds until the portfolio working capital reaches $30,000. Then begin to move into individual equities. If this is the only portfolio, normal diversification rules apply. If it's part of a larger investment plan, it becomes the perfect arena for trading high-quality equities.

3. Don't spread the money around. The larger the pot becomes, the easier it is to manage. Take every opportunity to roll over other qualified money into one primary IRA portfolio. (Qualified is a term used to identify money that is not subject to the income tax, yet.) Some newer IRA types (Roth, education, and health care) must be maintained separately. Refer back to #1.

4. Don't wait until April 15 to make last year's contribution. Why would you defer the moment when you start to earn tax-deferred income? To obtain the maximum benefit, try to get the money working on January 2 every year.

5. Don't think of the IRA itself as an investment, or as something you need to go out and buy. It is not an investment. IRAs are special accounts into which one places money that will be used to purchase various securities. Securities are investments. Financial institutions, particularly banks, will try to sell you an IRA. It's just their way of fooling you into a CD, a money market fund, or a mutual fund.

Zero Coupon Bonds

Zero coupon bonds are investment products created and marketed by the financial community in all different shapes and sizes, and with a slew of fancy acronyms like STRIPS or TIGERS. One Wall Street insider once referred to them as "certificates of confiscation". First the financial institution purchases large quantities of the treasury, municipal, or corporate security in the marketplace, staking their claim to the stream of interest payments that they will receive from the issuer. Then, they flip through an interest rate projection table, or use a simple computer program to calculate how long it would take to double or triple the value of the securities at various rates that are somewhat below the rate they will guarantee in the product they sell to consumers. The sales pitch sounds wonderful: "Our new series of ZAPPP zero coupon education assurance bonds will triple in value in eighteen years, just in time for little Johnny's first college tuition payment."

So in eighteen years, your $15,000 investment has become $45,000. Very impressive, until you flip through the present value tables and calculate the actual rate of return. For example, at 7 percent, a dollar triples in about sixteen years, not eighteen. The higher the rate, the less time it takes. Additionally, Uncle Sam is not willing to wait eighteen years to collect his share of the interest, so you will actually experience negative cash flow during the holding period of the product. Finally, an inflation rate of just one percent per year has reduced the purchasing power of the forty-five grand by an additional 20 percent or so.

The plot thickens when you realize that your financial advisor controls the actual rate of return. The lower the internal rate he gets you to accept, the higher his commission. Gotcha! Furthermore, the vendor of the ZAPPP Zeros has either bought the bonds cheap or is underwriting them in-house for a really exciting double dip. You don't think that they are taking advantage of their customer's love of family, do you? Not our trusted friends on Wall Street. I guess the ultimate "Shame on You" award, though, would go to the financial professional that would place one of these things in portfolios of people who are at or near retirement and in need of income. And then there's the utter idiocy of zero coupon municipal bonds. I can't bring myself to comment on those, which I understand have become the most popular variety today.

Psstt! If you purchased any zeros in the distant past, when interest rates were higher, you have a chance to redeem yourself by selling them at a profit. Just Do It. If you bought them to lock in low rates, return to "Go" immediately.

The Ransom Concept: Mutual Funds and Annuities

We've discussed the inside of no-visible-load funds and the problems with associating any equity mutual funds with annuities. But let's not let loaded funds or fixed annuities off the hook too easily. Mutual fund salespersons get their commissions in one of three ways and always in addition to the annual fees and charges inside the no-load variety. It gets complicated quickly, but there are three types:

Life insurance people like to get paid their 4 percent or more up front, probably because the wash-out rate among them is so high and they don't expect to be around to collect on the back-end variety. The net effect is that the commission is deducted from the amount invested in the fund. There are two types of back-end load funds, the first of which is most popular with stockbrokers. They get their up-front money from the firm, plus residuals on new deposits, but customers are held for ransom for up to six years by slowly declining penalties for leaving the fund group. You'll only hear about the second type from salaried people. The buyer gets tied in for only one year and there is no up-front sales charge. The broker's commission is only 1 percent.

In all cases the funds share a portion of the performance with the selling firms. This arrangement kicks back up to 1 percent of your money to the brokerage firm for as long as you hold the fund. Annuities are less complex. They pay huge commissions, up to 8 percent or more, to the salesperson, which you pay back to them in the form of a penalty if you decide to break the contract. Penalties have an effect on people that is quite similar to taxation. I've seen people refuse to take significant fund profits because they didn't want to pay the remaining penalties and, as we all know, profits and tides have much in common.

A Core Portfolio

I'm guessing that the financial community developed the core portfolio concept when it became fairly obvious that the buy-and-hold strategy had outlived its usefulness. It's pretty much the same thing, except that it names specific stocks that you absolutely must own if you expect to keep up with inflation, the market, the Joneses. Pick a reason. Naturally, it too has evolved into uselessness as you now can obtain various types of magical sector core index funds, small cap, and socially responsible core funds and so on.

Whatever is most popular at the moment moves to the core of your portfolio...they probably even have one that uses—get this radical idea—individual stocks and bonds. Core portfolio just sounds so much more knowledgeable than "buy and hold a diversified group of solid blue chips, reinvest the dividends, and grow with the pace of the economy" did in the middle of the last century.

How often have we listened to financial commentary and come away from it with conclusions like this: An up market is good. A down market is bad. Sideways, mixed, and lackluster markets are boring and increase the level of uncertainty in the minds of investors. Similar observations are often made with regard to interest rates, and the vast majority of investors/speculators would certainly agree. Volumes have been written either on what to do or not to do in response to these observations, but most are clearly wrong. Let's erase a century of Wall Street's conventional wisdom in one fell swoop. The market is neither good nor bad... it just is!

An up market is really only good if you purchased securities when the market was branded bad by the media. Then you have the opportunity to profit from your brilliance by selling securities that have risen in price. It is totally normal that not all securities rise at the same rate, or at all, during an up market, but most high-quality securities will move up eventually. The fact that your portfolio market value has risen is meaningless unless it becomes a call to action; profit-taking action is always good.

A down market is never bad in a properly designed portfolio. The doom and gloom spewed out by Wall Street and the financial media when the market averages fall, even for as short a period as a few months, is comical at best. This is the model year clearance sale of the financial markets, and an opportunity to fill up those shopping carts. But as the cash dries up, what then? A properly designed portfolio includes cash flow. The fact that your brokerage statement reflects a smaller value than in months before is meaningless unless it becomes a call to action; bargain-hunting action is always good.

Sideways, mixed, and lackluster markets certainly can be boring, but all they require is the patience and discipline to wait for the opportunities that will be created by either of the other market types. As to the level of uncertainty, there is no such thing as certainty in the financial markets, so why bother with that thinking at all. The stock market will never stay boring for long, nor will it stay bad or good forever...that's just the way it is.

Advice for the Next Correction

Yes, Virginia, there will always be another correction. And when it happens, you won't believe how quickly attitudes, interpretations, and expectations will change. "How low can it go?" will become the operative question as the street of dreams becomes characterized in the media as one paved with nightmares, and stained with the blood of CEOs and board members. You may hear comparisons with crashes of the not so distant past. Is it a new recession threat, higher oil prices, the upcoming election, hurricane season, more Olympic terrorism fears? For every 100 points the bar moves lower, the more fearful investors get and the more susceptible they are to the incredibly poor advice that spews forth from Wall Street and from investment professionals in general. Stuff like, sell, wait and see, move to cash.

A cynic would explain it away as the general inability of humans to learn from their mistakes, and I would have to go along with that as a reasonable explanation. Please don't be insulted, but don't take comfort in knowing that you are not alone, either. Most people don't appreciate this simple relationship: for every seller there is a buyer. That's right (a light bulb should start to flicker), and those buyers intend to make profits on the stuff that the wizard's mutual fund managers are tossing out of their growth fund windows.

In all corrections, regardless of the combinations of factors that get it started, two additional negative forces start to make things worse. Institutional money managers don't want to look stupid by owning stocks that may continue to go down. The media will interpret even semi-positive news negatively for pretty much the same, go-with-the-flow, reasons. Part of this is the market mentality that most professionals can't seem to shake throughout their mutual funds-only careers. The myth of market timing and the total disdain for profit taking are powerful forces as well. Is it possible that investors, like crap shooters, don't really expect to succeed?

So here is some advice that you just won't hear on CNBC or read in The Journal, but it is based on one incredibly simple market fact: there has never been a market correction that has not succumbed to yet another rally. How's that lightbulb? So when the doom and gloom noise becomes deafening, get yourself out there and party.

Select those good companies we've been talking about, apply a dash of patience, and let it happen. You'll know what to do when the music changes.

Is this easy or what?! Stock market volatility and Wall Street creativity will continue indefinitely, and I'm confident that the trading approach I have introduced you to here will continue to be a productive way to deal with our investment future. May The Force, and the investor's creed, be with you.

The Investor's Creed

"My intention is to be fully invested in accordance with my planned equity/fixed income asset allocation. On the other hand, every security I own is for sale, and every security I own generates some form of cash flow that cannot be reinvested immediately. I am happy when my cash position is nearly 0 percent because all of my money is then working as hard as it possibly can to meet my objectives. But, I am ecstatic when my cash position approaches 100 percent because that means I've sold everything at a profit, and that I am in a position to take advantage of any new investment opportunities, that fit my guidelines, as soon as I become aware of them."

Glossary

The purpose of the definitions, explanations, and descriptions provided below is to facilitate your use of the investment management methodology presented in this book. These definitions are the creation of the author—meaning they may not be in complete agreement with what you would find in *Webster's New World Dictionary* or from your personal financial professional.

A

Aging: The process of monitoring how long equity positions have been held in a portfolio. Since the objective is to trade quickly, stocks held more than a year should be looked at for sale at any profit, particularly when buying opportunities are plentiful.

American Depositary Receipts (ADR): American Depositary Receipts represent ownership in the shares of a foreign company trading on U.S. financial markets. Although ADRs are generally unrated by S&P, those that represent well known, profitable, dividend-paying companies are welcome in the selection universe.

Analysis Paralysis: A portfolio-threatening ailment developed by investors who tend to over-analyze things, impairing their ability to make timely decisions.

Annuity: A regularly recurring series of payments, typically guaranteed by some form of benefactor.

Annuity Contract: A contract where an insurance or annuity company guarantees a fixed and regularly recurring series of payments for the lifetime of the annuitant. It may have many actuarially sound variations, but stock market investments and variable benefits are not involved in any of them.

Asked Price: One of the three prices your broker should give you when you ask for a security price quotation. The asked price is the lowest price sellers are willing to accept for their positions. This is the price we will sell at, so long as it is at or above our planned selling price.

Asset Allocation: The planning process that determines the division of investment portfolio assets between equity and income securities, based on the personal financial situation, goals, and objectives of one individual or family. The cost basis of the securities held in the portfolio is used in all calculations. Asset allocation cannot be done properly with products.

ATH: All-time high.

ATH Decision: When a portfolio is at an ATH profit level, an examination of all positions should be made to identify the weakest issues—starting with S&P downgraded equities—and to consider them for loss taking. Downgraded issues must be sold eventually, but doing so all at once is unnecessary. Income securities with lower-than-normal payouts qualify for ATH loss taking. Fundamentally strong companies may be given years to produce a profit.

Averaging Down: The act of buying more of a security that has fallen in price since the original purchase. It facilitates profit taking at a lower level. Not to be confused with dollar cost averaging, which just buys more shares on a regular basis without regard to price.

Average Pricing: The buying strategy used within the working capital model results in multiple purchase lots at different prices. Sell decisions are based on the average price of the position, so avoid any accountant advice with regard to loss taking on portions of such positions, or at all, for that matter.

B

Base Income: The income derived from dividends and interest only, without including that received from capital gains. One of the key working capital model portfolio management objectives is to produce annual increases in base income, and at a rate that beats inflation.

Best Execution: Best execution is achieved with day-limit orders, assuring the best price for the security at the time the order is placed. But, price is only one factor in this vaguely defined concept. Advisors must consider the full range and quality of a broker's services, including research provided, execution capabilities, commission rates, financial responsibility, and responsiveness. To provide best execution, a professional must know what you are trying to accomplish and be supportive of the methodology you choose to use.

Bid Price: The low end of a security price quotation. The bid price is the price buyers are willing to pay for the security. This is the price we will normally buy at, so long as it is at or below our planned buying price.

Borrowing Power: The standard Wall Street euphemism for the amount of additional margin debt available to you, based on the market value of the securities in your portfolio. What happens when securities' prices fall? See margin call.

Breadth Statistics: See issue breadth.

Bull Pen: A mental folder where we place the names of our favorite trading stocks of the past, when we notice that their prices are approaching buying range. In deep dark corrections, I often leave space in the initial buy list, just in case.

Buy and Hold: An early 20th century investment strategy dinosaur, which held that, left alone, a diversified portfolio of high-quality companies would grow in value at a rate that would exceed the rate of inflation. All income would be reinvested in the same companies. It died many years ago, but Wall Street has created the core portfolio strategy, which is much easier to manipulate.

Buy More Target: This price is typically at least 25 percent or $14, if less than 25 percent, below the cost basis of an individual equity security now in the portfolio. There are several rules, but the most important is not to allow the new purchase to bring the total investment (cost basis) above 5 percent of the portfolio working capital.

Buy List: The two or three equity securities you will attempt to purchase today, but only if their prices fall to, or below, the pre-determined price. The more portfolios you are managing, the more stocks you will need to include in the daily buy list—but never more than twenty, once your portfolio exceeds, say, $100 million.

Buy Target: The price we are willing to pay for a security that makes it to our daily buy list. The calculation varies, but we never place an order at a price above this number. This price needs to be recalculated daily.

C

Calendar Year: The length of time for the Earth to orbit the sun. Interest and dividend rates are expressed as yields per year; working capital growth can be expressed as an annual rate; realized income and return on invested capital also lend themselves well to calendar-year analysis. The investment gods wanted you to you use peak-to-peak analysis for market value performance comparisons, but the wizards broke the DJIA.

Callable Securities: Many bond and preferred stock issues have call dates when the issuer can redeem the securities. Most are redeemed at face value, but some may involve a premium. Your best income producers will always be called first when interest rates fall.

Capital Gain Transaction: This occurs when a security or other asset is sold for a profit. The IRS inappropriately distinguishes between short- and long-term gains and taxes them differently. You should do all that you can to change this discriminatory confiscation of your assets.

Capital Loss Transaction: The IRS treats long-and short-term capital losses differently also, causing billions of wasted dollars annually as it encourages loss taking on perfectly good securities.

Capitalization: Corporations obtain investment capital by selling ownership shares (common stock) to the public and by borrowing money through the use of bonds and preferred stock. The value of stocks and bonds (theoretically) is a function of: 1) fundamental business and economic numbers and 2) the resultant credit rating of the company. Market capitalization is a whole 'nuther animal, used by Wall Street to create new classes of securities.

Certainty: This is something that really doesn't exist with regard to buy-sell-hold decision making in the securities markets.

Closed-End Fund (CEF): A managed mutual fund whose limited number of shares represent ownership in the investment company that owns and manages the fund. The shares trade on the stock exchanges like other equities, but the manager of the fund is insulated from the investment decisions and emotions of the shareholders. I use the term CEF in an effort to distinguish these working-capital-model-friendly managed funds from ETFs, which are generally unmanaged index funds.

Confirmation Notice: Brokerage firms are required to provide customers with written confirmation of all trades that take place in their accounts. Investors may check the accuracy of their brokerage account statements using the confirmations. All interested parties receive duplicates of confirmations and most save them for years, even though they duplicate information on the statements, which also have to be saved for many years by brokers and financial advisors.

Conventional Wisdom: The mythology of Wall Street, including: the sanctity of the DJIA, the safety of mutual funds, the buy and hold strategy, quarterly performance analysis, and nearly everything else that savvy investors think they know about the markets.

Core Portfolio: Stocks that you simply must own because they are the best or most popular companies and should be held indefinitely as your core portfolio. They will always perform well and keep your portfolio market value rising... until they don't. This is total nonsense, but it sure sounds sexier than buy 'n hold.

Correction: A period of generally falling prices in a market (stock, bond, real estate, etc.) identified by more securities moving lower in price than are moving higher, and by more securities striking new 52-week lows than 52-week highs. Wall Street doesn't care about such things.

Cost Basis: The total amount invested in a security, normally the purchase price plus commissions and fees, and the number used in determining the working capital model 10-percent sell target. Where a flat trading fee in lieu of commissions is paid, the cost basis is always slightly understated, and the 10-percent target is slightly overstated because the exact cost per trade is unknown.

Cycles: See market and interest rate cycles.

D

Day-Limit Order: The only method of submitting buy and sell orders to brokers using the working capital model trading strategy. It specifically limits the duration the order is valid and the price at which the trade may be executed. Better prices are acceptable but worse prices are not and must be busted at your broker's expense.

Day Trading: The practice of buying and selling financial instruments within the same trading day. All positions are usually closed before the market is. This is a highly speculative endeavor that should be avoided by working capital model users. A trade that is accomplished within one trading day using this methodolgy is rare but entirely possible, but more a function of luck than anything else.

Debt Securities: Negotiable securities issued by municipalities, corporations, government bodies, and other entities which represent contractual obligations (of varying durations) to pay periodic interest at a specific rate and to repay principal at the end of a specific, but varying, period of time. Wall Street loves to package these securities into various types of financial products.

Discount: Debt securities—all of them—will trade at a discount to par value when prevailing IRE are above par value, and at a premium when prevailing IRE are below par. A bond selling below $1,000 per bond or a preferred stock selling (most often) below $25 per share is selling at a discount. You will make a profit if you hold to maturity.

Diversification: One of the big three principles of investing, diversification is an investment management technique that controls the amount invested in any one security at a level below 5 percent of the total portfolio. It is not a market value performance smoothing technique. It is a risk minimization effort that will fail if not coupled with a seriously monitored commitment to high quality levels in all securities selected. It cannot be accomplished properly with products for myriad reasons. The 5-percent rule is not the only type of diversification you need to consider.

Dollar Cost Averaging: A robotic exercise designed to create poor diversification while it generates a constant flow of commissions. Don't do it. What dangerous emotion does it foster?

Dow Jones Industrial Average (DJIA): This was originally designed to be an indicator of the direction of the overall economy, but past more than future. When people refer to the performance of the market, most mean the DJIA, which is made up of just thirty companies. Until recently, only NYSE companies were considered for inclusion in this elite economic indicator. Since there are only thirty stocks in the average, it is susceptible to the artificial demand created by index funds, as are the other popular averages.

DRIPs: A form of Dollar Cost Averaging that has the added downside of impossible record keeping, and purchases made under conditions of artificial demand. Don't do this either.

E

Enhanced Index Funds: Unmanaged index funds that are enhanced with management, hedging strategies and higher internal fees. Hedging strategies of many varieties used to be reserved to hedge funds... how things do change.

Equity Securities: Equity securities, generally common and preferred corporate stock, represent ownership in the issuing company. Many executive suite occupants lose sight of the fact that their obscene salaries and perks come directly out of their shareholders' wallets.

Equity Bucket: See securities buckets

Exchange Traded Fund (ETF): Both unmanaged index funds and managed closed-end funds are exchange-traded mutual funds. I use ETF to describe the unmanaged and totally speculative index variety. What Wall Street knows, and what regulatory agencies ignore for some reason, is that these funds have a demand-pull impact on securities prices and the popular market averages. This adds additional risk and speculation to the investment environment.

F

Face Amount: The amount that is paid to the bond or preferred stock holder when the security either matures or is redeemed by the issuer. The call or redemption price of a preferred stock is usually the same as the issue price.

Fills: When large numbers of shares are traded, they may be filled in many different transactions and at many different prices, all at or below our limit on buys and at or above our limit on sells. Each is a partial fill until the final transaction, which "fills" the order. The fact that multiple fills are needed is evidence of the best execution efforts of your brokerage firm.

Financial Institutions: A catchall term that refers to all brokerage firms, banks, insurance companies, etc. who market securities and investment products and provide investment advice through various mediums.

Financial Risk: The risk of loss of the principal or capital that has been invested in some form of real property, such as securities and real estate, that is purchased with the primary objective of realizing a financial gain, or reward. The form of the gain is most often a combination of regular income and/or realized capital gains. In general, higher risk is associated with the prospect of higher reward, but the higher the risk, the less likely that any reward at all will be obtained.

Fixed Income Securities: Securities that pay a regular recurring, specific amount of income in the form of interest or dividends. Most bonds and preferred stocks are included in this sub-classification of income securities. See variable income securities.

Float: See liquidity.

Fools: Wall Street term meaning clients or customers.

Fundamental Analysis: This method of assessing the quality of a company and its securities uses revenues, earnings, return on equity, profit margins, and other data to determine a company's underlying value and potential for future growth. It focuses on the content of corporate financial statements. Two successful users of fundamental analysis are Warren Buffett and yours truly. One of us is a billionaire.

G

Gap Opening: A situation, usually the result of some form of corporate surprise, which causes a security to open well above or below the last trade of the prior session. Gaps may also occur during times of panic selling or buying in a security. You know what to do!

General Obligation Bonds: Bonds secured by the full faith and credit of the issuer, and generally considered to be the safest of all the debt of that issuer. GOs are generally less prone to default than are revenue bonds.

GOs: Common Wall Streetese for general obligation bonds.

Gold: A commodity that becomes particularly popular in stressful economic or political environments and in times of war. The logic is vague at best and the utility of ownership is non-existent. Gold is best owned in the form of jewelry or collectible coinage. I do not include gold in my managed portfolios, but qualifying companies whose business involves this and other commodities are welcome in the selection universe.

H

Hedge Funds: Studies show that very few hedge fund managers use the principles and practices discussed in this book.

High Yield Anything: High yield is a result of some form of higher risk, and is often used on The Street as a euphemism for junk bonds.

Hindsight: You must learn to ban hindsight from your investment efforts. Hindsight is evidenced by terms like: shoulda, woulda, and coulda, which are often used by accountants and salespeople who are trying to move you to the dark side.

Hydra: A mythical beast that could grow back two heads for every one a hero would chop off. Wall Street is no myth, and Joe DiMaggio has departed.

I

Income: One of The Big Three principles of investing; all securities owned by working capital model users must provide some form of income. With regard to equities, the ability to pay regular dividends, irrespective of size, is an indicator of fundamental strength.

Income Bucket: See securities buckets.

Index Fund: A mutual fund comprised of the stocks in a particular index, or more recently, a fund comprised of some of the stocks in an index, a market sector or industry group, or grocery store pet food aisle. Index funds create artificial demand for the stocks or groups of stocks involved, and are potentially, even more dangerous than variable annuities.

Inflation: A measure of changing purchasing power, but rarely downward because, in strictly economic terms, prices are sticky downward. (You can look that one up yourself.) Market value growth does nothing to increase purchasing power. Only rising income can keep pace with rising inflation.

Invasion of Principal: This is not a sci-fi flick title. When you withdraw more from your investment portfolio than the realized income that it generates, you are withdrawing part of the principle. The portfolio market value is likely to fall over time, but there is no one-to-one relationship. The working capital will fall on a one-to-one basis, absolutely.

Inverted Yield Curve: Simply put, this is a situation where short-term interest rates exceed long-term rates. Something you really need not be too concerned about.

Investment Account: An investment account is usually housed at a brokerage firm that acts as a custodian for the individual's cash and securities. The firms will provide one of a variety of non-standardized account formats that list, categorize, and often ineffectually analyze the assets in the account. An investment portfolio may include several accounts, but it is easier to manage the smallest number possible. Having accounts at many different firms is diversification gone mad.

Investment Gods: A figment of my imagination… they do not reside on Wall Street.

Investment Grade: Equities that are rated B+ or better by Standard & Poor's are considered to be investment grade, or less speculative, than those of lower ratings. The working capital methodology expands the definition to include a history of profitability, regular dividend payments, and (preferably) listing on the NYSE.

Investment Management: The planning, organizing, controlling, and decision making involved in implementing the investment plan.

Investment Opportunities: Securities that meet our price, income, quality, and diversification standards. No news, no we-thinks, no predictions.

Investment Portfolio: The total package of liquid assets, in the form of securities and cash, which we consider in our asset allocation formula and in our diversification decisions. Most non-security assets are illiquid.

Investment Products: Pre-packaged portfolios of various types of securities, commodities, derivatives, etc., managed or unmanaged by professionals, and designed to meet some specific or general consumer need in every possible area of investment or speculation. They include all mutual funds, closed or open end. We do not use open-end mutual funds, annuities, and most other products in our portfolios.

Investment Strategy: An approach to portfolio design and management that is applied consistently over an extended period of time. To be effective, it must be flexible enough to service a vast array of individual goals and objective combinations, and time tested for effectiveness under varying conditions in both equity and income investment markets. The working capital model is a construct of strategies applicable to all phases of portfolio design and management. The author developed the working capital approach between 1970 and 1975.

IPO: An Initial Public Offering of either an individual security or a mutual fund of either variety. Incredibly few become Microsofts or Googles—way up there on the list of speculations to avoid. Unfortunately, IPOs come with intentionally incomprehensible prospectuses that could easily be written in English, but that would eliminate the public market and put the things back to the venture capitalists, where they belong.

IRA: Acronym for individual retirement account and Irish Republican Army. There are too many forms of IRAs...and armies.

IRE: An acronym for interest rate expectations. You will learn that IRE are far more important than actual rate changes, especially with regard to the income securities in your portfolio. IREs are doubly sensitive to inflation expectations. Ironically, interest rates are a factor in calculating the rate of inflation and are raised in attempts to dampen it. Go figure.

Issue Breadth: One of the few statistics you really need to keep track of to get a feel for what has been going on in the stock market, particularly the NYSE. On a daily basis, track the number of stocks advancing vs. the number that are declining. Look at the names as well as the numbers to get a feel for the impact of IRE and other factors that affect market direction. Without this information, you won't know what to expect from the numbers on your monthly portfolio statements. The directional change in market value should never be a surprise.

K

KISS Principle: Keep it simple, stupid. Don't make things more complicated than they need to be, particularly with respect to research, statistics considered, analysis intervals used, and theories included in your strategies and selection techniques.

L

Laddered Maturities: A technique used by professionals to create an income portfolio with regularly maturing securities. Investment products are available that do the same thing. This is fine where disbursements are being funded at the same intervals as the maturities, and where an upward interest rate environment is expected to last for an extended period of time. It is ridiculous as a strategic effort to flatten the market value pain occasioned by rising interest rates, which are actually better for investors than lower rates.

Last Trade: One of the three prices your broker should give you when you ask for a security price quotation. The last trade price is normally between the bid and asked, but it doesn't have to be. This price should help you decide exactly what price to use for your day-limit order.

Leavenworth: A federal penitentiary where too few Wall Street con creators wind up.

Leverage: A strategy that involves borrowing money at X percent and investing it at X+ percent. This strategy is used regularly by CEF managers and by most business entities. Financial institutions will use it with both sides of the operational mouth: either euphemistically to refer to the excessive borrowing of companies whose securities they are marketing, or as a four-letter word when describing the drawbacks of investment products that are far better than the ones they prefer to sell.

Liquid Assets: These include cash and securities that can be converted to cash almost immediately, without any penalty other than the possibility of capital loss on the sale. Real estate, many open-end mutual funds, annuities, etc., are not liquid assets.

Liquidity: This is a measure of the ability to buy or sell positions in a security without impacting the price. It is also called float, and good liquidity is evidenced by high daily trading volume. Preferred stock and CEFs are likely to be less liquid than most investment-grade equities, and individual bonds are very illiquid. Larger positions of CEFs may have to be purchased or sold in multiple trades to attain the best prices. High liquidity is a positive factor in determining a security's quality.

M

Managed by the Mob: Open-end mutual fund managers, since the development of self-directed retirement plans, have been forced to make investment decisions merely to implement the wishes of unit-holding non-professionals. Thus, when panic strikes in either direction, managers cannot initiate any actions or decisions of their own. When the going gets tough, the manager gets fired. CEFs are not affected by shareholder emotions.

Margin Call: This is something you never want to experience. If the market value of your securities falls below a certain level you must: 1) sell securities to generate enough cash to satisfy the amount of the call, or 2) deposit additional cash or marginable securities. If you don't respond personally with instructions, the custodian is required to sell something to satisfy the call (see borrowing power).

Market and Interest Rate Cycles: Cycles are a fact of life in both markets and are measured in terms of the time from one significant peak to the next, but with at least a year in between. Wall Street has brainwashed nearly everyone to think in terms of calendar quarters and years instead, which is preposterous. Interest rate cycles are normally longer and flatter than stock market cycles. The stock market cycle is difficult to measure using any of the averages or indices that exist today because of the influence of index funds. Breadth and new 52-week high/low numbers are better, but there is no such thing as a pure stock market average or index.

Market Capitalization: Market capitalization is a mathematical concept that ignores the fundamentals of a company and focuses only on the value of its outstanding common stock. Many large-cap companies of the late nineties were small-cap just a few years earlier and cap-less just a few years later.

Market Order: A purchase or sell order that could not exist in any economic venue other than Wall Street. It is the act of buying or selling something at whatever price the next buyer is willing to pay or the next seller is willing to accept. If it's me, you'll pay more or get less than you deserve.

Market Statistics: Daily lists, available for all the major stock exchanges, which show the most active securities by share volume, those advancing by the most dollars and percentage points, and those declining by the same numbers. These are great tools to see what's going on daily and to spot both buying and selling opportunities. Years ago, they were broadcast regularly in the media. Hmmm.

Market Timing: Technical analysis gone mad.

Market Value: The amount that buyers would be willing to pay for the securities in your portfolio at any point in time if you were to choose to sell them. The transaction costs involved are not included. Non-security assets such as cars, boats, houses, non-public businesses, loans to relatives, etc., also have market values. Funny how differently people react to changes in the two types.

Masters of the Universe: The financial institutions of Wall Street.

Model Record Keeping: Performance statistics based on a hypothetical or model portfolio that does not change throughout the reporting period. Genuinely useless, and precisely what is done with the market averages and indices.

Money Streams: If you could color code strings of financial transactions, a money stream could be identified and analyzed. I've used this approach to describe the power of a series of trades with an average profit per trade of about 10 percent. It's certainly not something you should worry about while managing a portfolio. You'll know how you're doing.

N

NYSE Highs and Lows: In combination with issue breadth, the two most useful numbers for determining what is happening in the market now, and what has happened in the past.

Net/Net: Usually used to describe the terms of a lease or the results of a securities transaction. In a lease, it means that the tenant is responsible for all expenses except structural repairs. In a completed securities trade, it means that the reported gain is net, after all expenses and fees.

New York Stock Exchange (NYSE): Nicknamed "The Big Board", and based in New York City, the NYSE is the largest stock exchange in the world by dollar volume. It is where investors hang out.

NASDAQ Market: Although there are certainly some notable exceptions, the NASDAQ market is the refuge of most unrated and less profitable companies. This is the home turf of many more speculators than investors.

NYSE Index: A generally ignored market index, which is best positioned for use as a benchmark for portfolios designed and managed using the working capital model. But no index deals only with investment-grade securities. The NYSE includes most of the CEFs used in our model, but it also has index funds and preferred stocks in its numbers.

O

Odd Lot: Less than the normal trading amount of a stock or bond. Either $50,000 or $100,000 is considered a round lot for an individual bond compared with one hundred shares of a common or preferred stock, or a CEF. I strongly recommend trading only in round lots.

Open End Mutual Fund: A mutual fund whose unlimited number of shares represent ownership of an undeterminable fraction of the actual shares of stock held within the fund. The ownership shares do not trade on the stock exchanges like other equities, and the fund manager's decision making is influenced by the investment decisions of the shareholders. There is no place for open-end funds in the working capital model.

Open Order: An order that makes its home on the brokerage firm's computer until the price indicated on the order is reached, at which time it is filled at the indicated price or better.

Order Log: A worksheet, completed in pencil, and used to control the orders you plan to place each trading day if market prices cooperate. Buy-order prices must never be moved up during the trading day, and only bull pen items can be ordered instead of (or in addition to) the planned purchases. Sell orders are entered as soon as the noted price is achieved.

P

Par Value: The face amount of a bond or preferred stock, representing the amount that will be received by the holder at call or redemption. Some common stocks have par values, but little use is made of them in modern times.

Peak-to-Peak Analysis: A much more meaningful way of comparing your portfolio's market value performance with that of a stock market average or index over a relevant time period that normally exceeds twelve months. If from one peak to the next, your portfolio rises in value more than the index, you should know why. If not, there should be a clear explanation. The key issue is understanding the reasons for the differences. Working capital model portfolios differ in many ways from all market averages and indices.

Penny Stocks: You get what you pay for.

Portfolio Profit or Loss Level: Simply the difference between the net/net total of cash and securities deposited by the investor and the market value of the portfolio. An ATH profit level should cause a review of the portfolio for elimination of weak or nonproductive holdings.

Premium: Debt securities, all of them, will trade at a premium to par value when prevailing IRE are below par value and at a discount when prevailing IRE are above par. A bond selling above $1,000 per bond or a preferred stock selling (most often) above $25 per share is selling at a premium. You will take a loss if you hold to maturity.

Principal: The amount invested in a security or securities. Also the amount of the remaining debt owed to someone. It has nothing to do with market value, although investors often fail to make this distinction. See invasion of principal.

Q

QDI: An acronym for quality, diversification, and income.

Quality: Absolutely the single most important selection criteria of the big three. If you never violate the code of quality, you will rarely...

Quality and/or Value Stock: Stocks of historically profitable companies that are rated B+ or better by Standard & Poor's, dividend paying, and traded on the NYSE. Wall Street's definition is not nearly as conservative and is purely subjective and frequently based on guesswork about future market performance.

R

Rally: A period of generally rising prices in a market (stock, bond, real estate, etc.) identified by more securities moving higher in price than are moving lower.

Reasonable Expectations: Investment portfolios don't exist in a vacuum. But if you track issue breadth and new high and low statistics, you will learn how to develop reasonable expectations about the direction of your equity bucket market value. The income bucket market value is easy; it will move in the opposite direction of IRE.

Redemptions: Normally, income securities are redeemed on the stated security maturity date. Once the redemption is announced, you can expect the face value of the security to hit your account in a reasonable period of time.

REIT: A real estate investment trust is generally available in the form of a closed-end fund and purchased primarily as an income security. REITs that specialize in trading real estate could be looked at as equities if they meet all of the standard quality requirements. Private real estate investment trusts and REITs are fairly common, but also quite illiquid. Be very careful if you must, but I'd stay clear of these.

Revenue Bonds: Bonds secured by the revenue received from a particular project or system of a municipality, such as a bridge and tunnel authority, turnpike tolls, and hydroelectric plants. They are considered slightly more risky than GOs.

S

S&P: Abbreviation for Standard & Poor's Corporation.

S&P 500: One of the popular market averages, broader and more accurate now than the DJIA, but with no content similarity to a working capital model-influenced portfolio.

S&P Guide: A monthly publication used to select potential investment opportunities, keep up to date on rating changes, and to study company fundamentals. The guide also has listings of CEFs and preferred stocks.

Savvy Investor: What Wall Street wants you to think you are. A knowledgeable investor knows what he cannot know. A savvy investor is a speculator who thinks that he knows a lot about investing. There is no "know" in investing.

Securities Buckets: The asset allocation formula that we use with the working capital model has just two securities buckets: equity and income. Uninvested cash is destined for one or the other as soon as acceptable investment opportunities can be found.

Selection Universe: The hundreds of stocks that meet all of the working capital model equity selection criteria: (1) rated B+ or better by S&P, (2) dividend paying, (3) profitable, and (4) traded on the NYSE.

Sell Target: A price that would produce a net/net profit of 10 percent. This is a target, not a set-in-concrete rule, and a smaller profit is always acceptable. Holding out for a larger profit is unacceptable, ever.

Smart Cash: Cash accumulated in an investment portfolio from dividends, interest, and profit-taking activities. It is held awaiting the identification of new opportunities for investment based on asset allocation considerations only. It is absolutely not an attempt at market timing.

Socially Conscious Investing: Don't play politics with your investment dollars. Corporations are generally much better citizens than the media allows us to believe—probably the biggest philanthropists on the planet. Similarly, most corporations insist that executives, even at lower levels in the organization, participate in their communities. You'll make more money if you invest with QDI in mind and vote for the right politicians, if there is such a thing.

Spin Off: When a company spins off a subsidiary or unit of its organization, shares of stock in the new entity are given to existing shareholders to demonstrate their interest in the new company. It is not uncommon for: 1) the new company to offer to buy up the odd lot holdings of its shareholders, or 2) for the spun-off entity to be all or a portion of an earlier acquisition by the larger company. The value of the spun-off stock becomes its cost basis, and the same amount is deducted from the cost basis of the original shares. Spin off price adjustments are sometimes not immediately reflected in market quotation systems.

Spread: Many factors of supply and demand are involved in determining the spread between the bid and the asked price of a security. Less liquid securities generally have bigger spreads than the most widely held issues. The tighter the spread, the more likely it is that an order placed outside the limits will be executed.

Squeezes: Wall Street term meaning clients or customers.

Standard & Poor's Corporation: See S&P.

Stock Dividend: See stock split.

Stock of the Week: Salespersons of brokerage firms, particularly new recruits, are given new issue securities or products to sell to their few existing clients and to people they cold call. Every week or so, they will be instructed to push a new name.

Stock Quotation: A complete equity quotation will include: the bid price, asked price, last trade, and an indication of the difference between the last trade and the prior day's closing price. You should know that you need all of this information. Most brokers will ask if you are buying or selling before they provide a quote. Don't fall for it; tell them you want what you're paying them for.

Stock Split: A decision by a company's management to increase the number of its outstanding shares by some multiple or ratio such as two for one, or 40 percent. The stock price is reduced proportionately. A falling stock price and a new buying opportunity often follows such actions. You should always take your profits normally if a split candidate is kind enough to go up in price before the split. A stock dividend is a stock split on a much smaller level, typically 5 percent or so.

Stock Watch List: The collection of all stocks in the selection universe that are either at or within striking distance of our buy target.

Stock Worksheet: A listing used to track both securities owned and a reasonable number of others that are in the selection universe. It is used to identify both purchase and sale opportunities and must be updated daily.

Stop-Loss Order: An order that is unnecessary in a working capital model portfolio because we are only buying the highest quality securities. We expect continued downward movement and save room for additional purchases of the security at a later date.

Suckers: Wall Street term meaning clients or customers.

T

Tax-Exempt Securities: Interest on municipal securities is exempt from federal income taxes but may be taxed by other states. Tax-exempt income is absolutely the best kind of income, including all forms of deferred income.

Tax Lots: The IRC allows taxpayers to track their security purchase dates and to specify which ones are being sold when a sale is made. Some brokerage statements keep track of this information for you. This is the AICPA lobby at work, helping increase the billing hours of its members. To run a portfolio wisely, you have to use average pricing—find yourself a CPA who agrees.

Technical Analysis: Technical Analysis refers to the study of past financial data in a hopeless effort to predict the future movement of general and specific security prices. This is investment fantasy in its purest form, but it has become more popular than fundamental analysis.

The Beast: The financial institutions of Wall Street.

The Fair Tax: Some pretty good tax reform ideas that you should familiarize yourself with. Its congressional backers could use your support.

The Investor's Creed: You need to know this by heart (can be found at the end of chapter 8).

The Street: The financial institutions of Wall Street.

The Working Capital Model: A complete methodology for the design and management of investment portfolios created by Steve Selengut, author of this book, between 1970 and 1975. It includes techniques, rules, and guidelines for security selection, trading, and performance analysis.

Tick: Wall Street terminology for a change in price of a security during the trading day; there are upticks, downticks, and deer ticks. Avoid the latter, and look at the tick indicator stats occasionally. Interday changes in direction could be interesting.

Total Return Analysis: Total return on an investment is the total realized income in your pocket. Wall Street tries to brainwash you into thinking that changes in market value are of equal importance. Funny, they won't let you pay them with a change in market value.

Trough-to-Trough Analysis: Similar to peak-to-peak analysis, but it examines performance between market low points.

U

Uncertainty: The normal environment for investment and management decision making. The more variables (economics, politics, meteorology, astrology, etc.) that are active in media reports, the more uncertain the future becomes. Wow.

Unit Trusts: An investment product that is generally suitable for fixed income investing within the working capital model framework. Trustees hold a portfolio of income-producing securities and distribute interest and principal returns to unit holders until all the securities within the trust mature. They assure diversification and a steady cash flow, but are expensive in small quantities. Investors must avoid spending the principal portion.

Unsuitable: Investment salespersons are required to "know their clients" to the extent that they do not recommend (or allow them to purchase) securities and/or products that don't suit client circumstances. A zero coupon security for a person who needs income would be a good example.

V

Variable Annuity: An oxymoron.

Variable Income Securities: Some securities, such as royalty trusts, REITs, unit trusts, and GNMAs will produce slightly different amounts of income from month to month. This may be caused by the economics of an industry or the diminishing principal on which interest is being paid.

Verbal Confirmation: Most brokerage firms train their representatives to verbally confirm that a trade has been executed. I find it annoying when a broker doesn't provide this kind of simple service—just not the sign of a dedicated professional.

W

Window Dressing: A fraudulent but legal activity undertaken by institutional investment managers every quarter, in anticipation of preparing reports of their securities holdings. They will systematically unload weaker and unpopular issues and accumulate stronger ones to present the appearance of brilliance in their quarterly and annual reports. In August 2007 the SEC began investigating this practice in the industry.

Wire House: A brokerage firm. This outdated term comes from the use of an employee called a wire operator, whose job was to send orders to the floor of the stock exchange over the wire.

Wizards of Wall Street: The financial institutions of Wall Street.

Working Capital: The total cost basis of the securities and cash in an investment portfolio. Working capital is increased by all forms of income and deposits and decreased by capital losses and any form of withdrawal.

Wrap Account Programs: A sham program offered by most Wall Street Institutions that pretends to provide personal investment management when, in fact, every portfolio is identical. One fee is charged that pays for brokerage charges and investment management—yet another of the fraudulent product ideas now coming under SEC scrutiny.

Index